Suicide and Christian Beliefs

What's next, mercy or punishment?

By

Dahk Knox, Ph.D., Ed.D., Psy.D., D.Sc.

Published in the United States By The Tennessee Publishing House 496 Mountain View Drive Mosheim, Tennessee

September, 2011 First Printing, First Edition

Suicide and Christian Beliefs

What's next, mercy or punishment?

By

Dahk Knox, Ph.D., Ed.D., Psy.D., D.Sc.

The Tennessee Publishing House
496 Mountain View Drive
Mosheim, Tennessee
37818-3524

Suicide and Christian Beliefs

"Suicide doesn't necessarily equate to a person desiring death, but it could more simply mean they've lost the will, personal endurance and inner strength to go on living as they have been living."

"Surely you know that you are God's temple and that God's Spirit lives in you! God will destroy anyone who destroys God's temple. For God's temple is holy, and you yourselves are His temple." 1 Corinthians 3: 16-17 (GN)

"If you forgive others the wrongs they have done to you, your Father in heaven will also forgive you. But if you do not forgive others, then your Father will not forgive the wrongs you have done." Matthew 6: 14-15 (GN)

"If you have no belief in Jesus Christ, or room in your heart for God and His Word, then my advice to you is, don't buy this book. You won't believe or use one thing that is mentioned, discussed, or offered in it. That is your personal loss! This advice is sound, and better yet, it works! I personally guarantee it."

Dr. Dahk Knox

Permission

Suicide and Christian Beliefs

Cover Design: Kellie Warren-Underwood

Disclaimer

To achieve Harmonious Wealth:
Feed all 5 everyday:
(Relational-Spiritual-Physical-Financial-Intellectual)

How? FIRE UP ALL THREE:

MIND + BODY + SPIRIT

Positive   Positive   Positive
Thoughts + Actions + Feelings

Printed in the United States of American
Library of Congress
Cataloging-in-Publication
ISBN: 978-1-58275-257-0
Copyright © September, 2011 by Dr. Dahk Knox

ii

Dedication and Acknowledgements

This book is dedicated to all Christians who care for and give their time to those who suffer and desire to die, rather than live. May your efforts be fruitful and compassionate and ultimately, successful. May the Lord bless and reward your efforts and private sacrifices of which nobody knows except God.

Thank you to David Fry, a dear and knowledgeable Christian friend of over thirty years, who has provided much valuable information concerning his theories on death disposition, i.e., the status of the soul and the spirit after physical death, and demonic oppression. This is somewhat different from what I believe.

I thank my numerous Christian clinical colleagues from over the past four decades, some living but most now gone, who though our dealings with potentially pre-suicide patients, and their personal understanding of the subject of suicide, dissociative behaviors, and how we've been able to diagnose the majority of such mental disorders which may have led to suicide, have been an inspiration and considerable help. When lives are saved the Lord is always pleased. I don't like having suicides to ever occur, and especially not on my watch! But take heart, this does happen and sometimes when the prognosis actually looks good and should be treatable.

Table of Contents

Suicide and Christian Beliefs

"REITERATION IS A GREAT LEARNING TOOL/TECHNIQUE AND I WILL REITERATE/REPEAT MUCH THROUGHOUT THIS BOOK SO YOU WILL GET IT SOLIDLY INTO YOUR MIND, REMEMBER WHAT I'VE SAID AND LEARN ALL OF THE ESSENTIALS I PRESENT TO YOU – ALL OF THEM."

Suicide and Christian Beliefs

Introduction

There were several good reasons for writing this short book about suicide, I was moved to do research, compile information, and then analyze suicide, as best as possible, in order to create a work of Christian worth and value. This is my third book of suicide and Scripture.

At first, I examined my own beliefs concerning suicide; I came from the school of thought that when a person commits suicide, he or she would suffer eternal damnation. Or, is there room for merciful thinking by God due to mental illness or drug overdoses and such similar types of accidental deaths? The *Holy Bible* leaves room for speculation on these particular beliefs because there are only a few places which give reasonable reference to suicide. I have listed those cases in the Addendum.

Although what I have written will cast doubt upon what suicide victims will discover after death, is not just pure personal conjecture, but it is formed by what I have turned up and shared in the text and content of the body of this work. Look at this material with open eyes, not prejudiced feelings, and not with expectations which may be shattered because of any personal preconceived beliefs. Read this book looking for answers which may satisfy you and give you greater insight into suicide. Don't condemn this writer for what I report, but support my writings for what I have learned.

Let's talk about what this book is or is not. It is the author's viewpoint and educated opinion upon which I have based on personal research plus available findings of secular data (which were very scant and not very valuable or applicable to this book). I also included some information of a clinical nature which had little or no relative correlation to my work, especially with the "Jesus factor" being left out and scriptural evidence which was the most profound for building my case and it should have been, after all, this is a Christian opinion. As far as clinical concepts, thinking and evaluation of suicides is concerned, they will not assist in this religious Christian viewpoint. Such a diagnosis of suicide will not make any difference in how God feels about such sudden, and unplanned for death. Although the potential for suicidal behavior may be accurately diagnosed upfront during clinical treatment, it has nothing to do with what may or may not be explained in the *Holy Bible*. All final interpretations were made by me, the author.

Suicide and Christian Beliefs

What I have reported and written about is not the end all to the subject of suicide, but it is a good beginning. This text does not provide the final solutions or resolutions to all questions about suicide. This book is not an authoritative text which disputes any or all other similar types of work and effort, it is a book which provides answers, of a religious nature, which relate to suicide where few other books provide anything substantial to think about, learn from or digest. This book discusses my expressed opinions which deliver a message more of doom than of hope. If the reader is looking for hope, you'll find more hope in accepting Christ as your personal Savior, reading God's Word and walking obediently in His ways, than you will find any measure of hope among the pages which follow.

The subject of God having mercy, for one reason or another, will also be discussed and you'll have to

Suicide and Christian Beliefs

draw your own conclusions about that possibility. The closer the suicide is to home, the more family members and friends believe God will show mercy. So look at that possibility with realistic discernment and not prejudiced eyes. Be sensible in your thinking and not prone to jump into any non-fact-based conclusions. You will get past the pain which you suffer, but it will take time. It is okay to grieve and ache inside, but God will provide you comfort if you turn to Him and allow him to take over. He will heal and mend you. Just let Him do His job. He loves you and His process will be a healthy one. Don't try to grieve by yourself. There are suicide grieving groups that could help you immensely to get past your sorrow.

I had a neighbor couple which lost their adult daughter to an over doze of drugs. It was an untimely death, as all deaths are, but because it was by drugs, and because the lady who died was a user with not much speculation for a return to a productive and clean-living side of life, it became questionable; leastwise, to myself, if her death was an escape on her part, not so much to die, but to leave the situations and conditions under and within which she lived. The mother, after about six years now, has never recuperated totally from that death and still remains entrenched in grief. Like I said, that are grief groups which one can turn to, or

Suicide and Christian Beliefs

Christian clinical counselors who can help a depressed person get healthy again. That choice is yours, if the shoe fits. Please don't try to do this grieving by yourself.

This book will not purport the position of suicide as being acceptable to God. I will not say that people who commit suicide will be forgiven and eventually end up with Jesus. I will not direct you down the gracist path of "once saved, always saved", but I will point out the biblical warnings of going against God's commandments and directions. It would be ludicrous for me to tell you suicide is okay with God. It is not! I am not serving up any free tickets to Heaven. There will be no direct speedy linkages between suicide and Heaven found in this text. I do suggest that you purchase and read my book, *Eternal Security: Fact or Fiction?* This text discusses whether a person can lose their salvation, or whether they will not! Trust me! They can!

NO SUICIDE TICKETS GIVEN OUT HERE!

Suicide and Christian Beliefs

Back to this book! When you read this book and possibly deduce that suicide victims will go to Heaven (which I will not support), don't make a decision to take your own life because things overwhelm you too much, don't expect a fast one-way track through the Pearly Gates, but rather a complete cutting off from the divine presence of the Lord. If I said that suicide was okay with God, which is what everyone that is overly sensitive would like to believe, then you will not like what you are going to read. No free tickets from me!

This book is not for the super sensitive; I will not be putting up any façades for those who need extra stroking and compassion. Although I have much compassion for the loved ones who are left behind, I will not be providing a thoughtful, compassionate, sensitive, nor comforting book for you to read. If this is a portrait of you, then close this book now and forget reading the remainder of the text. You may bury your head in the sand, as an ostrich, and hope the scary truth passes you by. I guarantee that you will not only dislike what you read, you will find fault in its interpretations because of personal ignorance, or from a myopic gracist view, or perhaps from fearful personal images of death and dying, or from any number of other reasons which seem more suitable and convenient to you. As the

Suicide and Christian Beliefs

popular statement goes, "You'll have to build a bridge and get over it." Won't you? Or not!

You get to choose! When you form your own opinion, if you already have, then let's hope you did so with as much effort and study as I have. Get involved and dig into the nitty-gritty of the subject matter available material before you determine what your own viewpoint will be. Accept only what you personally are willing to verify and prove to yourself; do not form an opinion based on emotion or shallow beliefs. **Look at the facts! Think with a very conceptual outlook, and not a narrow one.** God's chosen were sanctified before they were born, as stated in *Jeremiah 1:5 (NKJV)* Sanctified chosen believers do not and will not commit suicide, except for Sampson who sacrificed himself to blot out evil – his actions were for a much greater good by executing the idol worshipping and blasphemous Philistines. God took His vengeance through Sampson's actions, as he gave his life for others.

SAMPSON GAVE HIS LIFE BY PUSHING DOWN THE TEMPLE OF DRAGON AND KILLING MORE PHILISTINES AS HE DIED THAN WHEN HE LIVED.

Suicide and Christian Beliefs

Your opinion is one hundred percent okay. . .but ask yourself the question, "Have I done my own home work, in detail, before I refute the facts presented, or have I just felt so strongly about my own opinion that I am being blinded by personal inhibitions, long held deceptions, and/or obtuse and imperceptive thinking? The standpoint of "once saved, always saved" is much too simple. It simply doesn't work and is not biblically correct. Please don't forget that. Maybe you should get angry enough to do your own scriptural casework and present a more clear understanding of what God hasn't told us about suicide. If these statements rile you and strike a sour chord inside your heart, then perhaps you need to do something which will significantly contribute to a better comprehension of self-destruction and what can be done to prevent it from occurring.

When an individual commits suicide, he or she falls outside of grace by sinning as such. As a sinner, doing such a deliberate act is obviously without the powerful protection of God's Holy Spirit in his or her heart. It is an act of transgression against God and His commandments. *"For if we sin willfully after we have received the knowledge of the truth, there no longer remains sacrifice (Christ' death for the forgiveness of all sins) for sins, but a certain fearful expectation of judgment, and fiery indignation which will devour the adversaries."* Hebrews 10:26-27 (NKJV)

Suicide smacks of insult to God, rejection of God's gift of life and His grace. Punishment in death follows this act of selfishness. *"Of how much worse punishment, do you suppose, will he be thought worthy who has trampled the Son of God underfoot, counted the blood of the covenant by which He was sanctified a common thing, and insulted the Spirit of grace?"* Hebrews 10:29 (NKJV) One must do the will of God to receive His promise. *"Therefore do not cast away your confidence, which has great reward. For you have need of endurance, so that after you have done (His will) the will of God, you may receive the promise."* Hebrews 10:35-36 (NJKV)

Ephesians 2:8 (NJKV) says, *"For by grace you have been saved through faith; and that not of yourselves, it is (grace) the gift of God."* This gift of grace, as the scripture says comes through faith that one is saved. Through faith, through faith, through faith! Let me really hammer that home to you. . .through faith! Suicide victims had no faith and showed no faith by their selfish voluntary act of self-murder hoping to escape this life, and speed up receiving the Lord's gift of grace and be saved. No faith, no grace, no saving! Gractists go spastic when confronted with such statements. Why? Because their answer is grace covers all sin, subject closed, eyes closed, heart closed, mind closed – closed, closed, closed!!! Sorry, this grace thing is easy and it is a "God-thing" and it is good, but you can lose salvation.

As one rejects any decent gift (from another person or from God), it is an individual choice to spurn or not accept that offered gift, with or without conditions. **Grace, for the most part, has no**

Suicide and Christian Beliefs

conditions: it's a simple act of repentance, belief and acceptance which render one totally saved. But is this platform substantiated in biblical truth, or is such belief and practice just a manner of "grace space," you can decide. If any of us contrive not to walk in obedience with God's Will, do we still inherit His Kingdom as an active rebel, being fully recalcitrant to His Word, while claiming to be a saved Christian? I believe if I fully keep my bargain with God, He will keep His bargain with me. There is no cheating, nor are there any short cuts or "grace space" to cover 100% of everything understood or not understood.

Through my faith, I am saved by grace. Many gracists sadly lack real faith, they simply say, "All I need is grace." Well, the Beatles said, "all they needed was love." It is so much more than needing, wanting, and accepting God's blanket coverage of grace for our sins; it is living His grace. A Christian friend said to me that if Jeffery Dahlmer had been a saved Christian (and I always thought all people who called themselves Christian "were" saved) then it didn't matter if he killed all those men, because he was forgiven due to grace. Get real! I could go on with numerous statements made by many "made men" (the inflexible gracists) who claim to be men of God, our pastors and lay ministers, who purport outlandish claims without merit or substance. I heard one reverend say concerning a suicide, "Well, so and so is up in Heaven today with God." Where in the good book does that statement hide? I cannot find it anywhere! I believe and will show reasons why suicide victims will not be part of God's Heaven, now or ever. Read on and envision and reflect about what is said.

This book is not a suicide prevention manual or self-help book. You will not find any lists of who to call, and so forth. I have purposely not gone into the instruction and counseling business in this book. I have only examined the subject of suicide and made some educated statements based on my substantiated findings. You do not have to agree with those findings. Although you will read about my random survey of folks who were questioned as to their beliefs concerning what happens to a soul after committing suicide, you may or may not agree with those findings either. I don't care; it is not up for debate. The findings are fact. You may wish to dispute the answers I received and once again, I don't care. Surveys do not make my work authoritative in any way or by any means. But what this survey did was to provide me with information about what various random samplings of people think and say about the death state of a suicide victim. When speaking with gracists, they all believe the suicide victim's spirit goes to be with God. Hmmmm?

It has been said, in Scripture, that (saints) worshipers once purified will have no more consciousness of sins/s. Read *Hebrews 10:2 (ESV)* *"For since the law has but a shadow of the good things to come instead of the true form of these realities, it can never, by the same sacrifices that are continually offered every year, make perfect those who draw near. Otherwise, would they not have ceased to be offered, since the worshipers, having once been cleansed, would no longer have any consciousness of sins? But in these sacrifices there is a reminder of sins every year. For it is impossible for the blood of bulls and goats to take away sins. Consequently, when Christ[a] came into the world, he said, "Sacrifices and offerings you have not desired, but a body have you prepared for me; in burnt offerings and sin offerings you have taken no pleasure. Then I said, 'Behold, I have come to do your will, O God, as it is written of me in the scroll of the book.' "When he said above, "You have neither desired nor taken pleasure in sacrifices and offerings and burnt offerings and sin offerings" (these are offered according to the law), then he added, "Behold, I have come to do your will." He does away with the first in order to establish the second. And by that will we have been sanctified through the offering of the body of Jesus Christ once for all."*

If we accept Christ as Savior and strive for the righteousness we are commanded to seek, then God's supernatural power of the Holy Spirit will become part of us, as we have been purified and sanctified; the spiritual power and supernatural extension of God, the Holy Spirit will prevent us from sinning. This includes and self-murder by suicide. And if we consciously choose to sin, going against the wishes of God and the power of His Holy Spirit, our obedience toward the Lord is of a sinful nature. This happens when we experience a lack of faith which produces a lack of hope and no trust in the God's Holy Spirit to protect us from others or ourselves. Suicide victims have abandoned hope, if they ever truly had it; thus, they sinned. *Hebrews 10:10* says we have, by God's Will, been sanctified through the offering of Christ's body. This was done once – for everyone.

Suicide and Christian Beliefs

God knows who has been or will be sanctified before they were born. These folks are His saved elect, as was Jeremiah. *Jeremiah 1:5 ". . .before you were born I sanctified you; . . ." (NKJV)* God ordains all saved and chosen Christians in this manner. *"For by one offering He has perfected forever those who are being sanctified." Hebrews 10:14 (NKJV) Christians* who have truly dedicated their lives to God, do have their sins forgiven and they, with the strength of the indwelling presence of God's Holy Spirit, experience, *". . .having our hearts sprinkled from an evil conscience and our bodies washed with pure water." Hebrews 10:22 (NKJV)*

This book is not for folks clinging to their pity-pots. Although grieving is normally automatic and may last for very long periods of time, life goes on and no solace is going to ever be found, for any individual that is not ready to go forth with his or her life and get beyond the death of their loved one or friend. This too will pass! If you feel that I am a hard-hearted Christian, so be it, but I am not. I have a tremendous amount of love in my heart, but I am also a realist who recognizes that being dynamic is much healthier and better than remaining static and stagnant. Maybe this is common sense love.

You will not find any practical encouragement in this book unless it is by accident, got past the editors, or unless I purposely provided such. My encouragement to you is to get to know Jesus and take Him into your heart and life. Read my book, *Gypsy Heart, Restless Spirit* if you want peace, comfort, solace and harmony by seeking and obtaining a close lasting relationship with God's Holy Spirit, so get the Spirit in your life today! **Learn how to gain a shepherd's heart and a consoling spirit.**

THE SHEPHERD'S HEART!

This book is meant to be tough and not for the faint-of-heart, touchy-feelie, fuzzy-tingly, or bleeding hearts of the world. The *Holy Bible* is not a book about sensitivity. It is about God's Perfect Will for humanity, it is about relationships, it is about simple blueprints which God has given us to live our lives by in peace and harmony with His Divine Will. It is a book of love, hope, promise, comfort, faith, mercy and so forth; it is also a book about God's wrath, expectations of man, and commandments for living, punishments for evil, judgment and death. It is about resurrection and life everlasting, and the *Holy Bible* is about fulfilling God's purposes. It is His plan for mankind. It you want to read about pleasant topics, consider the books, *God's Greatest Gifts, Delighting In God's Work* (published by Segen books and Black Forest Press) or *The Jericho Syndrome* (published by Vital Issues Press) also written by the author. And, consider buying and reading *The Plan*, (The Tennessee Publishing House) also written by me.

This book has not been written to shock you, but to wake you up. Life is not all cherries and gum drops. We live in a rough world and terrible things do happen. Satan has his way more often than not. So get tough back! Become more prepared for the unexpected by educating yourself about important issues. Suicide is an important issue. Like the common saying, **"It is a permanent solution to a temporary problem."** Yes, it is! As Christians, we need to do our very best to stop others from prematurely ending their own lives. If you know someone in danger of committing suicide, it is your Christian duty to seek help for them. Start with your minister and professional clinical counseling, or an appropriate psychotherapy treatment. Start now if the shoe fits!

Many authors claim to have written their work/s with divine intervention from God. Some authors say God told them and directed them to write their work, it was not their own. Fortunately, I look askance at such claims, as the bulk of those were obviously not written by the hand or voice of God, let alone commissioned or even directed by Him. This is not to belittle such claims of well-meaning authors, but to make sure that their claims are considered to be God-driven, induced, inspired and so-forth. Is so, prove it! They can't! They'll say I have to believe and have faith, well; I do, in God's Word but not theirs. If God was behind this book, it's news to me. If He was, "Thank you, God!" Be very careful of those authors and their books who claim to have received their message directly from God because they can NEVER prove that it is.

Death is a tragedy in itself; giving up the ghost and passing into another time-space continuum has to be either a time of shear excitement, depending upon how one dies, or it must be one of the scariest things and the last event taking place in a human's life, or we simply die, lay in our grave until resurrected and whether ten years or centuries pass by, or ten minutes, we'll never know because we have been conscious of nothing at all! That is scriptural and will be dealt with later in this book.

For some interesting possibilities, read *The Illusion of Time (Seeing Scripture through Science)* by Dr. William R. Nesbitt Jr. People who say they know, feel, and walk very closely with God, tell me that being so close to the Lord, their feelings of fear melt away. I suppose that is true because I have felt the presence of God as well, and I have written about such. Consider reading *Recognizing His Presence And Knowing His Perspective*, another of my books. But the thought of leaving this life and going into the unknown, or into nothingness is still a frightening feeling for many people. I trust in God, and I believe He will be waiting there to greet me, but the apprehension making the transition is still with each of us individually. This time comes at the Resurrection during Christ's Return, and not before.

Knowing Jesus takes away the fear and gives us peace of mind. There is nothing to fear if you have Christ as your Savior. I do not believe people supposedly die and see "great white lights" at the end of tunnels, and that Jesus or some angel was or is there to greet them. It is unscriptural and not good sound thinking for a Christian believer. Yet, for some unknown reason, these "great white light" folks, get sent back to the world of the living. Hmmmm? This is also unscriptural. Maybe there are medical explanations. Such would make much better sense than God playing tug-a-war with our souls. Satan would like you to accept this notion, because it works to his benefit and increases charlatans chances of taking your money, or try to change your thinking by talking to spirits (demons) in séances. If you take the time to read this book, you can't but help believe that God has a plan for us and that dying and retuning after seeing "great white lights" is not part of His plan; unless you are named Elijah or Enoch, or even Moses. Now those names

Suicide and Christian Beliefs

have some possibilities, but without the trip through the tunnel or the "great white lights."

If you are a Christian or perhaps a minister, pastor or missionary, don't think I am taking this attitude about life so lightly that I overstep the bounds of good Christian taste. Even Calvin had his moments. Let's face it, if we were made in God's image and if we have His best attributes, then humor is one of them. So is the ability to be able to discern and deduce what I consider to be taken with care and concern, and what I consider to be dealt with in a much lighter vain. Stuffiness is not one of my personality traits, and I hope it isn't one of yours. I do not have a "holier than thou" perspective in my life, and I never will. If your head is filled with personal perspectives and beliefs which only you alone can discern, then get a grip!

Nobody has all the answers, especially people who have exalted themselves rather than having humbled themselves before God and others. A humble person finds comfort and wisdom in the Lord, and He will impart special insight into the minds of those that believe and trust in Him. If you want answers that give you comfort, then go directly to the Lord in prayer. In His time frame and manner He will give you the responses you need, but quite possibly not what you were expecting. So learn to live with those answers, if you asked for them.

I have found the content of this book to be within the expectations and limitations of those that are seeking educational counsel, solid answers, and knowledge concerning suicide. If I have failed to do this, shame on me, but you have been given my best efforts in supplying information and scriptural-based data which provides answers and further interest in researching the topic of suicide. If you feel the urge to criticize, or not believe what you read, for whatever reasons, don't prejudice yourself by contending that things just can't be that way, because they can. If you find error or fault, good for you. When you write your rebuttal, I am sure you'll have something concrete to offer, just make sure it is biblically-based, properly applicable, and easy to find in Scripture.

Some people may not want to believe or accept what I have written because it hits too close to home. Step back and look into the reality of a situation and the circumstances that surround a suicide; make judgments based on scriptural guidance and reference. That which lies in God's Holy Word is the final authority. If what I say about forgiveness and the various scriptures concerning warnings bother you. . .well, let it be another form of a wake- up call for you. Start studying your *Holy Bible* and see what it says for yourself. If you feel that I have distorted, twisted or written what I have to suit my personal opinions, that is your prerogative and right to do so. However, I challenge you, the reader, to open your mind and let reason and common sense take hold; that is, as long as it is coated with God's inspiration and blessings. In this way, I believe that spiritual truth is more easily discerned. If you are studying for your doctorate degree, then here is an interesting project for your dissertation. Go for it!

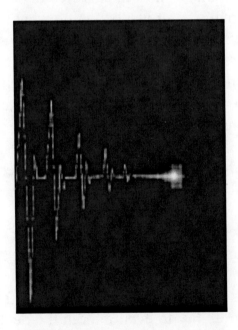

SOMEBODY JUST FLAT-LINED!

Prologue

My favorite verse of Scripture is and always will be the words of Jesus Christ which spoke of everlasting life. *"For God so loved the world that He have His only begotten Son that whosoever believeth in Him shall not perish but have everlasting life." John 3:16 (KJV) That* verse is so powerful and so well recognized that you do not have to think twice about the impact it has on people's lives. It's all about accepting Christ's ransom sacrifice and gaining the gift of eternal life for just believing what He did was so. Salvation is a gift for just believing. Through Christ's grace we gain salvation. I may add this is undeserved grace. This verse is all about life and not just life here on planet Earth, but afterwards, in the heavenly realms where Jesus has gone ahead of us to prepare a separate place for each of us. Just the thought of that possibility sends shivers up my spine. So, if Christ's gift is so powerful and awesome, why do some people turn their back on His wonderful offer? Why do some people turn away from Christ as their personal source of protection, comfort, forgiveness (from sin) and resolution? Why? What the Lord offers is far beyond our ability to even fathom the depths of His gift. So, why do people turn down such a beautiful present from God? Why do they end their own lives far short of God's plan? Why do people interfere with the Lord's time table by issuing their own self-proclamation of when their life should end and when the next step of their journey should begin?

There are many answers for these questions, and each question has a different answer, because each question is in direct response to the individual that made their own personal "faithless statement of finality." There is only one answer which will always be acceptable: only God has the power and authority to choose the termination time of one's life. Only God has the right to make decisions concerning all life and death. We read His commandments, but those commandments are really directed at how we live our lives, treat others and respect God's wishes. The commandments are not about dying. When we do this, we prosper, when we fail to meet God's expectations, we fall short in many aspects of life. If we find favor with God, as did Jabez, we prosper even more. Read what the *Holy Bible* says *in 1 Chronicles 4: 9-10.* God smiles on us when we please Him and He becomes irritated, angry, upset, sad, full of sorrow and tears and alarmed when we go against His sacred plans. The Holy Scriptures are full of terribly explicit examples of the Lord's dark side. The Lord is also tender, merciful and forgiving. *"The Lord is gracious and compassionate, slow to anger and rich in love. The Lord is good to all; He has compassion on all He has made." Psalm 145:8-9 (NIV)* and he tells us what He simply asks of us to do, *". . .what does the Lord require of you but to do justice, and to love kindness and to walk humbly with your God?" Micah 6:8 ((ESV)*

Even when we fail in the eyes of the Lord and have angered Him, He still has the compassion to forgive us the things we do and have done which bring Him sorrow and disappointment. Scripture says, *". . .if you have burdened me with your sins and wearied me with your offenses. I, even I, am He who blots out your transgressions, for my own sake, and remembers your sins no more."" Isaiah 43:24-25 (NIV)* During those trying times of suicide, or even death in general, everyone again seeks reasons for just and unjust finality. We all search for the answers of self-destruction and termination in our prayers offered to God, hoping, just this once, that He will provide us a clear answer for our request. But if you stop and listen, the only voice you will hear is your own, the only tear you will feel is the one running down your cheek, and the only comfort you'll be aware of comes from those that surround you with their love, understanding and affection. This is the nature of life. God transcends our knowledge and understanding, but through His powerful Holy Spirit we reap benefits that we cannot see. God is our voice, He is the essence of our tears, He is our comfort and He sends us friends that know the score of life. Vicariously God will be there for those that are left behind trying to put together the broken and missing pieces of the vacuum created by the suicide victim.

The Lord gives us all we need, He provides for all of His children when they suffer and hurt. God mends our souls, our minds, and our bodies. When we tremble, He calms us and we ask Our Father Almighty in Heaven to give us peace and rest. The spirit of the suicide victim must be in a place of rest and finality as well. As you read through the pages of this book, read slowly, taking in the thoughts I have provided for your consideration. You must make the call as to your own belief, and you must captain your own thoughts as to the dwelling place of the departed soul. I give you an interpretation of what perhaps, God has made known to me through His Scriptures, or perhaps He hasn't. You know my feelings on that issue. I am nobody special in such regards or considerations. The conclusions you will draw are totally up to you. Don't kill the messenger or condemn what you cannot accept because it doesn't agree with your beliefs, but carefully digest this information presented to you, look at it from all angles, and without bias or prejudice, and then determine your own images from having an open mind and an open heart.

If you are floating in a bubble of grace – pop it and take a hard look at what grace is really all about. Martin Luther said:

> *"Grace can be lost by unbelief, undoing the act of faith and rejecting Christ."*

Without exhortations to Godly living, we tend to flounder and flail with the grace issue. Read *Titus 3:5-7 (ESV)* "*. . .he saved us, not because of woks done by us in righteousness, but according to his own mercy, by the washing of regeneration and renewal of the Holy Spirit, whom he poured out on us richly through Jesus Christ our Savior, so that being justified by his grace we might become heirs according to the hope of eternal life.*"

PRAISE AND THANKFULNESS
CONDEMNATION AND HOPELESSNESS
REPENTANCE AND CONFESSION
TRUST AND BELIEF
FORGIVENESS AND MERCY
COMPASSION AND LOVE
JUSTIFICATION AND GRACE
RECONCILIATION AND SALVATION
PEACE OF MIND AND SANCTIFICATION
ETERNITY EVERLASTING AND HOLINESS
GOD'S HOLY PRESENCE AND GLORIFICATION

Chapter One
Examining the Facts

The Permanent Solution to a Temporary Problem

For eons of time, suicide was always looked at as being something akin to not having all of one's faculties in tow. It was also seen as being a way out of this life when things really got too much to handle. It seemed an honorable way to depart the world, a place the victim could no longer tolerate or in which he or she wanted to live. At other times, suicide has been known as "the coward's way out". Except in cultures that see this act as the pinnacle of escaping this world in some state of honor and respect; the act of suicide is seen for what it truly is, a "dissociative behavior that fatalistically culminates in self-destruction". Such a selfish nihilistic act, oftentimes, allows the memory of the victim to carry a legacy that seems to be more acceptable to those that are living and are left behind. For the survivors, this may seem more acceptable then the victim having continued to live in the manner in which he or she had existed. This legacy, in some cases, enshrines the victim, whether it is deserved or not. Sickness takes many forms and this is one of those forms not based in healthy thinking.

Nowhere in the Holy Scriptures has anyone who committed suicide been immortalized, put on a pedestal, memorialized or honored for taking his or her life. God is not happy when one of His children decides to check out early and change His scheme of things and plan of life He had for that person. God, being all merciful, would probably shed tears, as would His angels, over such a death.

If only the suicide victim had known the power of God and how He moves in our lives. Without Him we are lost, afraid and alone with nowhere to turn for help when pressures mount up. We must call on the name of the Lord to know His ways. *"The Lord is kind and merciful, slow to get angry, full of unfailing love. The Lord is good to everyone. He showers compassion on all His creation." Psalm 145:8-9 (NLT) and "The Lord is close to all who call on Him, yes, to all who call on Him sincerely." Psalm 145:18 (NLT)*

Suicide usually affects those left behind; those people that were either close to the victim or related to the victim; or. in many other ways. Survivors feel pain, often to the point of agony, turmoil, and depression. They seem to be engulfed by a huge

Suicide and Christian Beliefs

black cloud, or trapped inside of some terrifically big void; an abyss of detachment and loneliness, helplessness and personal failure. Survivors and loved one may seem to exist in a vacuum of total loss, and/or blaming themselves for not doing more. This is the ultimate guilt trip because the victim probably did not consider such feelings before he or she took his or her own life. Normally, if the victim really wanted help, he or she would have asked or shown some abnormal behavior which would have been indicative of him or her taking the next step toward suicide. There are times when those individuals that are thinking about suicide don't allow anything to happen that would tip another person off. I even have experience with one individual that talked about suicide and how he would never do it, and then went home and killed himself with a gunshot to his right temple.

WELL, THIS IS THE QUICKEST WAY I KNOW!

Suicide and Christian Beliefs

Several times during my lifetime, I've been part of a group of people that have lost loved ones to self-destruction. Let's call it what it is. Each time there has been an initial sense of unrestrained awe and sudden disbelief, only to be followed by the first onset of shock, then anger or disappointment, and then finally a certain significant amount of reconciliation with the reality of the suicide. This does not mean the surviving victims get over the death, but hopefully and God-willing they are eventually able to come to grips with the tragedy. This usually takes longer when the victim is a child or a young adult, someone that had so much to learn with so much time to live and enjoy the life, life with which God so richly blessed the victim. Each such soul had been singled out for a future in God's Kingdom; the Lord had a plan for him or her to live and mature within His decreed framework, not to expire before his or her time and learning was fulfilled. Such termination is never good.

God does not create us without a reason and a purpose. We know our lives are meant to oblige God, as His friend, *"This is my commandment, that you love one another as I have loved you. Greater love has no one than this, that someone lay down his life for his friends. You are my friends if you do what I command you. No longer do I call you servants, for the servant does not know what his*

Suicide and Christian Beliefs

master is doing; but I have called you friends, for all that I have heard from my Father I have made known to you. You did not choose me, but I chose you and appointed you that you should go and bear fruit and that your fruit should abide, so that whatever you ask the Father in my name, he may give it to you. These things I command you, so that you will love one another." John 15:12-17 (ESV), and to do His Perfect Will and not our imperfect will. However, the relationship He wants for each of us is to mature in His grace and abounding love.

God wants us to grow into the being that He intended us to grow into; we will have work to do for God when we meet Him fact-to-face. The Psalmist said, *"The Lord looks down from heaven and sees the whole human race. From His throne He observes all who live on the earth. He made their hearts, so He understands everything they do." Psalms 33:13-15 (NLT)* and *"But the Lord watches over those who fear Him, those who rely on His unfailing love. He rescues them from death and keeps them alive. . .We depend on the Lord alone to save us. Only He can help us, protecting us like a shield. In Him our hearts rejoice, for we are trusting in His holy name. Let your unfailing love surround us, Lord, for our hope is in you alone." Psalms 38:18-22 (NLT)*

Suicide and Christian Beliefs

Read below how King Solomon told us, in his infinite wisdom supplied by God, who made him the wisest man in all of the earth, in his time and in ours. So move over Nietzsche and all you self-acclaimed geniuses in the world today, those of you nihilists that have continually purported how "our lives are meaningless". Are we here without understanding God's loving purpose for us, and His intent to produce fruit which will ripen immensely in the life to come with Christ? What do you think? *"In this meaningless life, I have seen everything, including the fact that some good people die young and some wicked people live on and on. So don't be too good or too wise! Why destroy yourself? On the other hand, don't be too wicked either, don't be a fool! Why should you die before your time? So try to walk a middle course, but those who fear God will succeed either way."* *Ecclesiastes 7: 15-18 (NLT)*

In terms of our Christianity, God expects us to allow Him to accept our burdens. He guarantees us that He will lighten our loads. The Psalmist also said to us, *". . . the Lord lifts the burdens of those bent beneath their loads."* *Psalm 146:8 (NLT)* Many victims of suicide have never known the Lord and what He can do for us. If they had known the Lord, they would have known His power is almighty and healing; that He and He alone can change our

34

thoughts and ideas of self-destruction. He gave us His powerful Holy Spirit to be with us through any such crisis where one's thinking and planning has a goal of self-fatality. God embraces all those who suffer and need Him, but too many professed Christians say they have accepted Jesus Christ into their hearts and inside God lives. . .then they kill themselves. If Jesus lived in their temple, He would have shielded any self-imposed attack against that human temple. Why? Because where Jesus dwells no evil can manifest itself; no demon can enter into the thoughts of the righteous and claim victory over their thoughts and actions, because Christ and the prevailing Holy Spirit are their Holy Protectors.

When Christ lives inside of us we are free to think clearly with a cheerful heart. When He has not been invited into our hearts and minds, for all eternity, then we live without His comfort and protection. We must humble ourselves for Him to care and show us mercy and protection. *"The Lord supports the humble, but He brings the wicked down into the dust." Psalms 147:6 (NLT)* He is the Guardian of our soul; through supernatural intervention the Holy Spirit has become the Guardian of our temple; God is the Holy Landlord or the "Super" of our temple; He collects the rent. Only God can approve the lease given to us at conception, and only God can revoke it and determine when it is no longer valid. Satan will not evict me from my temple, only God has that authority.

Suicide is the final act in the victim's life. It is an act which gives very little closure (as most of us clinicians have used and still use, but I feel it is the wrong term – "acceptance" is much better, as there is never total closure) and oftentimes, suicide leaves many questions about the victim unanswered. I feel the word closure is incorrect. I believe the appropriate word here is acceptance and I use that word in place of closure when I counsel. Why? It is because you can never completely close your mind to a plethora of issues and unfinished business which almost always exists and is directly attributed to the suicide. There is always a crack left in some mental window, somewhere in your mind. You can forgive, but it is truly very hard to forget. Even God doesn't forget, He remembers, but He does forgive. There is a huge difference. I'm just saying!

HER CHOICE WAS PILLS!

Suicide and Christian Beliefs

Suicide happens so suddenly, either through impulse, short-term thinking, or in many cases, it is planned. Assisted suicide is one type of planning, but putting together a personal plan for self-destruction is quite another. When the victim's spirit is restless, ridden with guilt over some foolish or trivial matter, antagonized by either his or her troubled thoughts, demonically persuaded to commit killing oneself, or even pushed against the wall by his or her own making (as in committing some crimes which will demand and receive punishment for when caught, the traits of a troubled sociopath), and/or having feelings of anguish which could lead to hurting another person, or lastly, rejected by love, friends or family, the spirit itself implodes inside of itself and the victim takes the next step and destroys himself or herself.

This behavior is not an act of God-induced thinking or divine approval. God loves us and wants us to meet Him on His own terms and at His appointed time. When a victim of suicide tries to speed things along, he or she has lost all hope and all trust in God, in his or her life, and in family and friends. This is true of most suicides, but it is less true of professing Christians who spontaneously lose control and without thinking things through, kill themselves. If a person was given one extra minute to think about suicide and its repercussions on themselves, their family, and with how they would be going to deal with God, I believe many suicides would not occur. And, this is why if you ever feel you are talking with a person close to doing the big bad deed, and killing themselves, then I think you should be responsible enough to take he or she by the hand and get help for them – do it together, making sure they get there. Being with them insures they will seek counsel. Start your interaction with them, about what you have noticed in their speech and behavior. Then take them by the hand and go into prayer together, seeking God's help, as they may not do so themselves out of shear embarrassment or shame. Your caring and praying with this individual may be the turnaround point in changing their mind and their overall outlook about suicide as an answer. You could be their life key.

When I was on active military service in the Air Force and stationed at the National Security Agency, I experienced my first taste of someone committing suicide. He was a person who I knew and respected rather well. His name was Woody; he was a Staff Sergeant and quite a good Russian linguist. We were taking security classes together with several other colleagues and learning about new equipment we would be using in the field as Voice Intercept Processing Specialists. I was young and the world was still very new to me. To have someone I knew commit suicide was devastating and unbelievable. I can't begin to tell you the shock and helplessness I felt - I was numbed and jolted.

When Woody did not show up for class in the morning, we all wondered where he was; we knew he would be in big trouble, having a Top Secret Crypto Security clearance and knowing that he could receive military punishment for his absence. We all worried. Class had begun at 0730 hours and no Woody! Around 1000 hours a senior enlisted instructor interrupted our class when he entered with his boss, a Captain, our Program Director. This was unusual, and we had all on edge. After apologizing for the interruption, the Captain told us that on the preceding evening, Woody had argued with his wife. I don't recall what the problem had been, but Woody had taken his revolver and placed it to his head, positioning it behind his ear. In a fit of anger and despair, he pulled the trigger. Apparently the single shot did not instantly kill him, and, as he lay on the bed, he said to his wife, "I don't want to die. Why did I do this? Forgive me, I'm sorry." That was the account we were told. Those words have echoed in my mind for ages and still those thoughts sadden me today, I can't easily and won't forget. I've personally never had any closure, but I have been able to accept and I do try to forget. Try is a very negative word, it means I probably won't.

Suicide and Christian Beliefs

I never found out if he said anything else, but Woody regretted his instantaneous decision to take his own life. One more minute of lucid thought could have made the difference between him living and dying. He died about 20 minutes later on the way to the hospital. Our class was so shocked that we sat there lost in our own thoughts for at least 15 minutes before anyone was brave enough to speak. Even the instructor, that didn't know Woody as well as we did, was quiet and respectful. Nobody could muster up the courage to talk. Our camaraderie in the Air Force was always a behavior of mutual concern and respect for each other. This moment in our lives not only gave us time to reflect but to be there for each other.

What was really strange was that the day before, during our lunch together, (we all ate in the classroom) Woody was engaged in a conversation about suicide. People distinctly remember him saying how he would never do such a thing, that it was stupid and that there was always another solution or option to be considered. Yet, without clearly thinking things through and allowing himself to feel hurt beyond caring about his own precious life, Woody made a decision to end his own life, not adhering to or recalling his words during lunch that day. Yes, suicide can happen that fast, though it is often a premeditated, carefully planned act of a

Suicide and Christian Beliefs

desperate and hurting individual. It was my first of other similar suicides, lives that ended foolishly.

When such tragedy occurs in our lives, we must find comfort in the Lord. He will give us peace and takes away the sorrow that we feel, if only we allow Him to enter into our heart and mind to soothe our aching spirit. Only God can provide the healing we need so desperately, and He will come through and show us the kind compassion we need to cope with the death of the victim. God always grants us respite and gives us the strength we require to be refreshed, as we struggle to sustain ourselves through the difficulty of our loss. The lord will fully mitigate our circumstances and restore order where chaos has flourished. If we are truly saved by Christ's grace then the serenity we should experience will tone down our pain and clear our visions. *"Therefore, since we have been justified through faith, we have peace with God through our Lord Jesus Christ, through whom we have gained access by faith into this grace in which we now stand." Romans 5:1 (NIV)*

WE ARE FULLY JUSTIFIED THROUGH OUR FAITH WHICH GAINS US ACCESS INTO THE STATE OF GRACE THAT GOD FREELY GIVES US, UNDESERVED AND SINFUL AS WE ARE.

41

Suicide and Christian Beliefs

HIS SACRIFICE WAS FOR EVERYONE, YET SOME HAVE REFUSED TO ACCEPT HIS GIFT OF ETERNAL LIFE!

Many people fully believe that saved Christians will go to Heaven to be with God, and that the last choice of a suicide victim may not necessarily determine where he or she will go after his or her death (suicide). This school of thought thinks that only the Lord can accept and understand the state of mind of the victim, that awful mind-set that he or she was locked into prior to killing themselves. Five individuals in the *Holy Bible* were revealed to have committed suicide. Three of those people were Saul, Sampson and Judas. About Saul, the *Holy Bible* says in *2 Samuel 1:23, "How beloved and gracious were Saul and Jonathan! They were together in life and in death." (NLT)* Saul was a special case: he committed suicide to avoid a

Suicide and Christian Beliefs

horrible torture by his enemies. He also had been anointed by God years before, but he'd become a different person in the eyes of God, This type of behavior is not and has not been unusual in battle. Look at all of the Japanese soldiers who committed suicide during World War II, in the Pacific Theater of Battle. They were afraid to surrender to our forces, for many reasons and stories of how we'd treat them. So to them suicide was the better choice, and it was considered to be quite honorable.

As a matter of fact, there have been individuals that have fallen on grenades or exposed themselves to fatal gunfire or cannon fire simply to save their comrades lives, knowing they would sacrifice their own life in one final act of unselfishness and absolute protection. Sampson pulled down the pillars of the Philistine temple of Dagon in order to kill about 3,000 of his enemies and all of their rulers. *". . .Oh Sovereign Lord, remember me. O God, please strengthen me just once more, and let me with one blow get revenge on the Philistines for my two eyes. Then Sampson reached toward the two central pillars on which the temple stood. Bracing himself against them. . .he pushed with all his might and down came the temple of the rulers and all the people in it." Judges 16:28-30 (NIV)* Was this a God-sanctioned act of suicide? Was it for the purposes of Sampson, or for the purposes of

God? Did God allow this act of suicide to exact His own revenge upon the Philistines, and was Sampson his instrument to do so. Was Sampson forgiven? This is open to speculation on whose purpose was actually fulfilled: God's or Sampson's. I think the purposes of Sampson and God were both fulfilled, and therefore, he was granted mercy even before he destroyed the wicked Philistines.

Don't ever forget that it was Jesus Christ who gave us His example of laying down His life for us, for our salvation and He did this out of His tremendous love for us all. Christ was God in the flesh. So, did God allow Himself (His Son) to die when He could have saved Himself? Is this some sort of a suicide, because His sacrifice could have been stopped and not offered? Did He forgive Himself, or was His sacrifice so necessary that He had to sanction it? Therefore demonstrating that suicide is alright if it is for the correct purpose/s. . .usually the saving of many. If our Lord could give up His life, and it agonized Him to do so, perhaps there are forgivable instances when an individual relinquishes his or her life for the better of another, or maybe for a whole group of deserving people. *"Greater love has no one than this, that one lay down his life for his friends." John 15: 13 (NIV)* Courage and honor are displayed in many ways; as long as the motive is not selfish, aggrandizing or martyring, God will probably honor that death, allowing His precious soul to enter into His eternal kingdom at the appropriate God-planned time. Why would God reject such an act, especially when this person was a saved and committed follower of the Lord?

FORGIVENESS, FORGIVNESS, FORGIVNESS
MERCY, MERCY, MERCY
HOPE, HOPE, HOPE

Forgiveness seems to be the way of our God we love and cherish, our God who grants us unlimited mercy no matter what we do or how we sin. He forgives us, even though we make His heart ache and stab His Heavenly soul. He is quick to forgive us. So, why not forgive suicide? *"Oh, what joy for those whose disobedience is forgiven, whose sins are put out of sight. Yes, what joy for those whose sin is no longer counted against them by the Lord."* Romans 4:7-8 (NTL) There are many scriptures which give us hope for those who have taken their own life. Another scripture of hope is *". . .and anyone who has committed sins will be forgiven."* James 5:15 (NLT) Of course, this promise was particularly for those who were sick and needed healing. Through a prayer of faith, it was promised that they would be healed and forgiven. I believe those who contemplate or commit suicide are sick and need healing; if not physically, for sure mentally and spiritually. Through faith they must put their trust in God and request healing through fasting, confession, repentance, and prayer. *"While they were worshiping the Lord and fasting, the Holy Spirit said, 'Set apart for me Barnabas and Saul for the work to which I have called them.' Then after fasting and praying they laid their hands on them and sent them off."* *Acts 13:2-3 (ESV)* When anyone fails to communicate with their Heavenly Father, it is their act of remission and not God's failure. When a person feels guilt or shame and has a special need to ask God for forgiveness even though they already have it, but it somehow seems to elude them, then there is nothing wrong with going to God to specifically ask Him to fulfill your needs concerning your personal understanding of forgiveness. Part of those forgiveness requirements are: fasting, confession, repentance, and prayer. Then believe, trust and have faith in the Lord when you ask for your forgiveness; besides, you already have it – Jesus did it for you on the cross. If this makes you feel better, then fine, but you don't have to cover the same ground twice!

On the bleaker side of things, except for the gracists, general Christian attitudes do not support the soul of a suicide victim going to Heaven. Why? This thinking is also worthy of consideration because there is great feeling for the damnation of those individuals who commit suicide. Again, why? It is because they have rejected and had no faith in the saving power and grace offered to them, through Christ's own personal sacrifice, for them. This is a slap in Christ's face and a denial that God is all powerful and forgiving, being able to not allow us to suffer more than we can handle. All we have to do is turn to Christ and ask for His help. If we do not fear the Lord, then we shouldn't take the risk of ending our own life. Fear of the Lord should prevent suicide. But how can you fear God, when you don't trust Him or show that you believe in Him? Fearing God is the beginning of receiving wisdom, and wisdom should keep anyone from committing suicide if they apply that gift from God. *"The fear of the LORD is the beginning of knowledge, but fools despise wisdom and discipline." Proverbs 1:7 (NIV)*

TRUSTING THE LORD IS MUCH BETTER, DENYING HIS ABILITY TO BRING ONE OUT OF MENTAL AGONY AND MISERY, OR OFF OF DRUG ADDICTION, IS MAKING A MAJOR MISTAKE. THERE IS NO BIBLICAL GUARANTEE THAT A SUICIDE VICTIM WILL RESIDE WITH JESUS IN HEAVEN. BUT A GRACIST WILL TELL YOU IMMEDIATELY THAT THE VICTIM IS RIGHT THERE RUBBING ELBOWS WITH GOD, WHILE THE REST OF US STRUGGLE ONWARDS TO PLEASE GOD AND BE THERE WHERE THE SUICIDE

Suicide and Christian Beliefs

VICTIM ALREADY IS. WELL, I'LL BE! HE BEAT ME THERE BY NOT PLAYING BY THE RULES. SUICIDE IS THE ULTIMATE STATEMENT OF DISBELIEF THAT A PERSON CAN PURPOSEFULLY MAKE. SUICIDE SAYS THAT THERE IS NO HOPE AND FAITH IN CHRIST TO RENDER ASSISTANCE TO THEM AND LEAD THEM OUT OF THEIR MISERY. IF THE SUICIDE VICTIM SIMPLY BELIEVED ENOUGH IN GOD, THEN THEY WOULD TRUST THE LORD TO CLEANSE THEIR THOUGHTS AND ACTIONS. MAKES SENSE TO ME!

Therefore, by simply showing faith in God and accepting Christ's salvation, and receiving the Lord's untainted and undeserved grace, God would not deny such a suicide victim His merciful and loving help. If there is not belief in one's petitions to God, then nothing will happen. God should not be expected to perform for an unbelieving audience, nor should He be expected to honor and receive a soul who has given up the hope of Christ's salvation. That is part of why Jesus died for us, to give us hope. If a suicide victim has no faith in God to cure their affliction, then why should they expect God to greet them cheerfully into His glorious kingdom? God does not play charades, nor does He hide behind a mask about His Perfect Will being done, nor does He masquerade as a charlatan who will be happy with any soul that has turned away from His saving grace. This may seem hard and cruel especially to those that are still living and associated (or who lived) with a victim of a suicide. But the fact of the matter is that the general consensus of Christian belief says a suicide victim will not be residing in Heaven with the Lord.

THIS IS A SAMPLE OF SATAN'S COLD AND DARK CEMETERY AT NIGHT. IS THIS WHAT YOU THINK ABOUT? IS THIS WHERE YOU SEE YOURSELF PLANTED FOR ALL ETERNITY? JUST BEING SURROUNDED BY BLACK, ICY EMPTINESS AND NOTHINGNESS? LIFELESS YET SUFFERING FROM GOD'S SEPARATION WHILE ENDURING UNSPEAKABLE PAIN AND AGONY. IT'S YOUR CHOICE! I REALLY DISLIKE BATS!

A Final Statement of Disbelief

Let's take a look at the facts, the causes, risk factors, incidences and reasons for one taking their own precious life, that wonderful gift from a loving God. A prime reason for a suicide victim to end his or her life is from various emotional disturbances. Behaviors such as psychotic maladies, various forms of schizophrenia, depression and excessive anxiety, feeling things are overwhelming and uncontrollable; such as, a serious illness which will most likely be terminal or continue in unbearable pain and suffering (with little or no hope of a cure or any relief from the pain), financial difficulties and employment problems, wherein a person cannot find suitable employment or any employment at all due to any number of reasons. Because these behaviors are or can become psychological emotional problems or psychiatric illnesses, suicide looks like an acceptable way out to those who see no other option or alternative. The attitude of "let's just get this over" will permeate the victim's thoughts and lead them to no good conclusion. . .thus, suicide.

Suicide victims also find that social isolation and rejection can send them into a state of mind saying, suicide is an okay way out. So may such emotions like feeling badly about getting older, or being elderly and wanting the Lord to speed up the dying process, so the suicide victim has had enough and has grown impatient with God's time table. The loss of a spouse, a child, or a love-mate (there are many teenage suicides from boyfriend girlfriend break-ups), or a close family member can trigger the taking of one's own life, as can deep-rooted feelings of guilt, or a tremendous bout with an emotional trauma. And children who get constantly harassed, made fun of, or bullied at school. Homosexuality causes considerable suicide, as do similar maladjusted thoughts and behaviors of perverse sexual identity; so do such relationships which have gone wrong leaving a person doubting themselves and who they should be – a man or a woman. And there is substance abuse and/or an ongoing, seemingly never ending battle of winning over one's chemical dependency habit and this includes alcoholism.

I THINK HE DRANK ALL HE COULD WHILE TRYING TO KILL HIMSELF OVER A PERIOD OF TIME.

Recent and overnight fame can also cause a person to lose control of his or her life. He or she may turn first to drink or drugs, and then to suicide because they cannot cope with their new life of being a well-known celebrity. They've achieved a status uncomfortable to them which they cannot maintain with a healthy and accepting attitude, so they pack life in without much consideration or thought.

Suicide and Christian Beliefs

Some of them want to make a statement of sorts, for whatever their reasons may be, and they are never the right ones. They have received their rewards here on earth, as Scripture says, but will not receive any rewards in their afterlife.

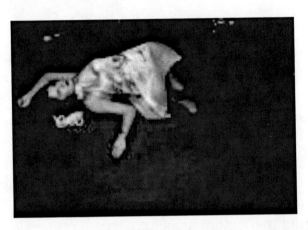

THERE IS NO REWARD IN THE AFTERLIFE WHERE SHE IS GOING. NO! NONE AT ALL!

There are so many ways to blot out one's life. It is not necessary to discuss those ways or means, because the outcome is the same. Any road of fatal destiny will get you there – that choice is individually yours. But hopefully, you will decline the trip. The suicide victim has exercised their own free will to employ a permanent solution to a temporary problem; how common a statement, but how utterly true. No one can deny that so many suicides must end with their last split second of knowing there is no way back. Nor will the suicide victim be able to escape once on the other side and change their decision. What is done is done! It is what it is!

One must consider what the alternative is to suicide. It is seeking help, either for yourself, if you are considering suicide, or if you suspect someone else is being capable of suicide. Those individuals who may be considering taking the final step can oftentimes be noticed by what they do, or don't do. They will show symptoms of nervousness, insomnia, expressing evil thoughts or being bothered by demons which they cannot get rid of, or having control issues, impulsiveness, and an inability to deal with an unacceptable or perceived health problem, and/or a soul wrenching need to be overly compulsive (which has probably become obsessive) to the degree that they begin to drive themselves off the deep end.

Also showing a loss of appetite or weight, an increase in dealing with stress, pressure from some external source which has infiltrated into their own internal thinking and polluted it. There are guilty feelings, highly emotional views of life and various expectations which they cannot handle, and certain general or unusual instances of personal grief from tension, anxiety and the beginnings of a loss of reality, or even an escape from justice or legal action. Many sociopathic personality disorder individuals choose this last reason for checking out.

Detrimental and critical observations would be: (1) any direct attempt to commit suicide which falls short of actually allowing it to happen, or leaving a way out – this is a huge cry for help. **(2)** Any quick unexpected change in behavior like going from a highly agitated and aggressive behavior, or being very angry, to being very serene and calm. **(3)** Suddenly and inexplicably freaking out after being very settled and at peace with oneself, as though suddenly attacked by some unseen entity. **(4)** And indirect and direct threats or statements, showing the individual is obviously considering suicide. These are other great cries for help.

ANOTHER SUICIDE SUCCESSFULLY COMPLETED!

Suicide and Christian Beliefs

When a person begins to put their possessions in order, by giving things away, especially valuable items they have cherished and are very dear to them, or are in the process of selecting specific people that will receive their personal gifts or treasures, and without apparent motive or reason, this is very indicative of a person that has not only considered suicide but will carry through with the act itself. Most likely they will not tell anyone of their intentions, and they may not give away their valuables until after they have committed suicide. A note or a letter will be left stating who will get what while mentioning what services or functions will be necessary to find closure (I still like acceptance better) in their ultimate act of death. If you suspect a person is considering suicide, you must talk with them. If they reveal what you thought was true, then you MUST lead them to medical/clinical care and/or clinical Christian counseling, and pray with them immediately. Their life is in danger and you may be the only one they tell; therefore, you are the only one who can urgently get them help. Don't neglect that responsibility or you'll regret it later.

Get this troubled person to focus their mind on the Lord Jesus Christ and start reading God's Holy Word so that the Lord may comfort them and show them direction. Sometimes the laying of hands and an oil anointing can be a great start. *"Surely, He took up our infirmities and carried our sorrows, yet we considered Him stricken by god, smitten by the God His Father, and afflicted. But He was pierced for our transgressions, He was crushed for our iniquities; the punishment that brought us peace was upon Him, and by His wounds we are healed." Isaiah 53:4-5 (NIV)*

Emmanual Kant and Feodr Dostoevsky both viewed life without moral obligation and as life without meaning. Suicide victims must see their life the same way. That is perhaps why many individuals commit suicide – they do not have any purpose left or never saw their purpose. Worse than that is how they never felt obligated to another human being, and that is so pitiful, having lived the bulk of their life inside of a vacuum of utter emptiness. If they did feel that way, or do feel that way prior to committing suicide, then, if you have the chance to prevent it, remind them that their feelings of emptiness will only be traded for unresolved issues on the other side where more emptiness will exist for them. This is just a thought, perhaps a ploy, but if it works and gets them thinking, they just may change their mind due to your intervention and explanation for the emptiness and unknowns of the other side – the dark side. The very dark side!

Chapter Two
Personal Dealings with Suicide

Some Solutions to Feelings and Thoughts of Committing Suicide

An unbeliever who struggles with suicidal temptation or a non-Christian loved one dealing with the effects of a suicide, does not have the grace of God, the comfort of Scripture, or the support and nurturing of fellow believers. If suicide was a good thing, then everybody would want to do it. It's the same with homosexuality. Do you see the dumb animals of the world, of the same sex, having sexual relations or obviously preferring them to their opposite sex – the natural order for propagation? No! Why? Because even the dumb animals of the world are smart enough to know what sex they should be having sexual relationships with. And that is a good thing. So it is with committing suicide, it clearly just doesn't feel right. Like homosexuality, it is a travesty and an affront to God, and engenders feelings of guilt and awkwardness. Non-believers have a path that is vastly more difficult to follow. They have started out on the wrong track and it keeps leading them farther into perdition. How blessed we are as believers to have these avenues of help. When things begin getting out of hand and it seems there is no way out and life has become one big impossible mountain to climb, then think of what our Lord and Savior Jesus Christ has said to us, *". . .what is impossible with men is possible with God." Luke 18:22 (NIV)*

There is nothing a person cannot accomplish, change or get rid of, including a self-destructive attitude, if only a person would listen to God. All things are possible with God because He will show you the way to heal through His grace, mercy and understanding love. When life becomes so tiring and fatiguing, so exhaustible that searching for a cure in death seems to be the only answer, then remember what Jesus offered to us, *"Come to me, all you who are weary and burdened, and I will give you rest. Take my yoke upon you and learn from me, for I am gentle and humble in heart, and you will find rest for your souls. For my yoke is easy and my burden is light." Matthew 11:28-30 (NIV)* God gives us perfect peace and rest; His tranquil covering will be a blessing which can take away the curse of suicide. Do not doubt this!

When guilt is overwhelming and it is no longer an option to see oneself free of that agony and constant annoyance, then recall what is said in Holy

Suicide and Christian Beliefs

Scripture, *". . .God is light; in Him there is no darkness at all. If we claim to have fellowship with Him yet walk in the darkness, we lie and do not live by the truth. But if we walk in the light, as He is in the light, we have fellowship with one another, and the blood of Jesus, His Son, purifies us from all sin. If we claim to be without sin, we deceive ourselves and the truth is not is us. If we confess our sins, He is faithful and just and will forgive us our sins and purify us from all unrighteousness."* 1 John 1:5-9 (NIV)

HOW CAN I EVER FORGIVE MYSELF? I JUST CAN'T – I JUST CAN'T!

The problem herein is that many folks cannot forgive themselves and sink into a black hole, an abyss, or fade away into an endless void of misery and eventual oblivion. Such people just cannot free themselves from guilt and they do not ask for God's assistance which He would give them. As the scripture says, Christ has forgiven everyone that has confessed their sins to Him before they ever approached Him as such. What great assurance we have when we bend to God's ways and find real solutions to our problems that seem unsolvable. God is always right there to heal us, our bodies and our minds. He wants our soul to be His and He gives us everything we need to be part of His team, that group of Christian followers that love and honor Him without reservation.

TOO MUCH FEAR – WAY TOO MUCH FEAR! AND FEAR CAN KILL. IT CAN MAKE YOU KILL YOURSELF JUST TO GET RELIEF!

Suicide and Christian Beliefs

Another obstacle is fear. When someone is afraid, God will once again come to the rescue. He is always willing to provide comfort, peace and courage; He will strengthen and help you. *". . .lift up your voice with a shout, lift it up, do not be afraid; . . .'Here is your God!' See, the Sovereign Lord comes with power, and His arm rules for Him. See, His reward is with Him, and His recompense accompanies Him."* Isaiah 40:9-10 (NIV) and also the verses which say, *". . .I have chosen you and not rejected you. . .do not be dismayed, for I am your God. I will strengthen you and help you; I will uphold you, with my righteous right hand."* Isaiah: 41:9-10 (NIV) God is our refuge and our Savior, He unconditionally gives us the support and direction we require. All we have to do is to trust in Him and ask for His Will to be done in us. All we need to do is ask the Lord for His help and intervention in our life. It is that simple. God's Perfect Will should be yours too.

Without examining the Scriptures, a suicide victim can easily lose his or her perspective on life and throw in the towel on their own continued existence. Quitting without taking the time to examine Holy Scripture, is like telling God we don't have time to read about His love for us, or to find His many solutions and support. A wise person will read and study the Scriptures of the Lord daily, as did the

Suicide and Christian Beliefs

people of Berea in ancient Macedonia. See *Acts 17: 10, 13.* Quitting too soon without even considering conferring with God does not honor His plan and purpose for us. When we don't take the time to communicate with God, we sever our personal relationship with the Lord and finish our act of self-destruction which falls outside of our original covenant with the Lord. That is, if we have accepted Christ as our Savior but have not developed the type of relationship with Him that shows we were truly serious about that acceptance, and it also says that we didn't take the time to learn about His Father's grace and forgiveness for our sins. When we purposely shun God, our Father and Creator, what do you think He feels for us? Probably sadness and disappointment for starters.

If you were the father or mother of a suicide victim, how would you feel knowing you were not given the chance or opportunity to save your child? Or were you so self-absorbed that you failed miserably to hear the child's cry for your love or help? Were you the cause of it? I have met and known people like that, that had the means to help their child grow and flourish, but spent nothing in time or resources to make that happen due to their own greed, self-absorbsion, and selfishness. Suicide causes God great hurt and pain. That is how God must feel; only more so, because He is Our Creator, the

Creator of all mankind and each heart and soul is vitally precious to Him.

YES, EVEN THE ANGELS CRY WHEN SOMEONE IS LOST TO SATAN AND HAS GIVEN UP A CHANGE OF LIFE EVERLASTING IN HEAVEN WITH CHRIST.

He hurts badly and the angels of Heaven drop their heads in sadness and tears and without the understanding of why a person chooses to suicide when they are so special to God; being well beyond the specialty of angels themselves that were created to serve God, while we were created to be His friend and communicate with Him in love and purpose. We have yet to learn our final destiny and mission for eternity, but that will come for those of us that walk in obedience to His Word and remain faithful to the Lord in righteousness and commitment.

When you become worried and anxious about your life and depression starts to take hold of your inner soul, then it is time to turn to God once again. God has that special cure for the tension and pressure we experience. Jesus wants to take our problems and cares unto Himself. He has the power and authority over evil to do so, He is the Sovereign Lord of the universe and as such, He holds the remedies for our troubles in His divine healing hands. All we have to do is humble ourselves and call on His name and He will be right there for us. Let Christ anchor your spirit in Heavenly cement, the type of concrete which secures itself to that which is good and right. Humble yourself before the Lord and pray for His help. He will come, he always does. *"Humble yourselves, therefore, under God's mighty hand, that He may lift you up in due time. Cast all your anxiety on Him because He cares for you."* 1 *Peter 5:6-7 (NIV)*

For those sad and troubled individuals that feel alone, like an outcast, simply because there is no one in their life that seems to care about them, the world takes a harsh toll. Nobody wants to lack love and affection; nobody wants to go through life by themselves; nobody wants to be left incomplete or even in partial isolation from a normal, warm relationship with others. But this happens, and when it does, it creates feelings of terrible loneliness, which are every bit as painful as other feelings that debase your self-worth mentioned above. Christian fellowship can ease or remove one's feelings of loneliness by letting others that care for you into your private world.

When someone feels alone in the world they need to be reminded that God did not intend for such to happen to them. The situation individuals find themselves in has usually been self-induced, self-created for one reason or another, or perhaps others have pushed them into the box in which they find themselves. Christ Jesus has said something comforting about those feelings and those situations, He said, *". . .God has said, 'Never will I leave you; never will I forsake you.'"* Hebrews 13:5 (NIV) Forsaking is not done by God.

Consider this statement: *"Unhealthy thoughts precede unhealthy manifestations."* Most secular thinkers and proponents of medical or other clinical professional help, usually scoff when Christians offer up reasons for why suicide victims will allow themselves to reach rock bottom and seek a way out through self-destruction. I know this, because I work within a clinical environment. The possession of anyone's mind may very well be the actual manifestation of a hurtful demon controlling and convincing a person to end his or her life. This is a victory for Satan and not God. Suicide gives the Devil his claimed success by putting an end to another of God's plans and keeping a soul from its proper rest and peace. It is not God who brings about the problems of suicide victims; the victims themselves cause those problems. Only they can choose to follow the order of the world set by the Lord, or they can rebel against God's beautiful plan for themselves and reject it by committing suicide.

DON'T LISTEN TO THOSE SPIRITS AND DON'T PLAY ANY GAMES THAT WILL LEAD YOU INTO THE GRASPS OF HUNGRY DEMONS AND EVIL PEOPLE! YOUR DEATH IS THEIR VICTORY!

Suicide and Christian Beliefs

Christian thought is entrenched in the belief that demons are the cause of most suicides. Horrible stories exist about people witnessing demons attacking human beings and driving them crazy. This is not some far-fetched fable. It is not a stupid notion or ancient myth, this is reality; today, we are caught up in any number of ways which can lead directly to demonic possession. You can laugh, but a time may come when you will be embarrassed, by mocking the Holy Word of God and the warnings and lessons it imparts to you. Be aware of what forces surround you and seek to gain control over you. Evil manifestations exist, so open your eyes!

YES! DO BEWARE OF THOSE EVIL FORCES THAT MAY SURROUND YOU, WANTING TO GET TOTAL CONTROL OVER YOU WHILE YOU HAVE NO HEDGE OF HEAVENLY PROTECTION AROUND YOUR BODY AND SPIRIT. KEEP YOUR MIND CLEANSED! THINK HOLY! THINK JESUS!

Suicide and Christian Beliefs

The battle of most suicide victims has been with entities which have found a suitable resting place in an unassuming body of an unsuspecting soul. The demons have found a weakness in which they can use to enter the mind and body of a person that will eventually succumb to the will of evil and blot out their own life. *". . .be strong in the Lord and in His mighty power. Put on the full armor of God so that you can take your stand against the Devil's schemes. For our struggle is not against flesh and blood, but against the rulers, against the authorities, against the powers of this dark world and against the spiritual forces of evil in the heavenly realms. Therefore, put on the full armor of God, so that when the day of evil comes, you may be able to stand your ground, and after you have done everything, to stand, stand firm then, with the belt of truth buckled around your waist, with the breastplate of righteousness that comes from the gospel of peace. In addition to all this, take up the shield of faith, with which you can extinguish all the flaming arrows of the evil one." Ephesians 6:10-16 (NIV)*

Knowing and being able to discern the evil around us is a benefit we receive from having a close relationship with Jesus Christ, our Savior and Redeemer. Jesus is protection and safety; it is the Lord alone Who gives us the insight, knowledge and understanding that is necessary to be aware of the forces which surround us and are simply looking for a chance to influence us or possess us with their filth and misery. There exists today many ways that demonic influence and possession can take place. Secular thinking denounces what I will purport to you in the information and Christian opinion which follows. *". . .in the last times, there will be scoffers who will follow their own ungodly desires. These are the men who divide you, who follow mere natural instincts and do not have the Spirit." Jude 18-19 (NIV)*

It is the position of any God-reading Christian to put aside the various secular ideas which espouse other avenues of cause instead of the obvious nature of the infliction. Our clinical side would say, and has said and adequately stated that any number of dissociative behaviors were the cause of the potential suicide victim's mental instability. Therefore, there are several types of psychological modalities and therapies which we might want to put the potential suicide victim through, or engage in by convincing him or her to admit themselves into a clinical setting for observation and clinical assessment. This is a worthy consideration and there is nothing wrong with using clinical help. It can be much easier with such help than without it.

Suicide and Christian Beliefs

A clinical intake would be done and a program would be set up for the benefit of that individual. Let me clear, conventional treatment programs do work, in many instances they have helped cure multitudes of people. Many sick Christian individuals have been successfully released from and cured of their suicidal intentions. There are alternatives to a cure or a suicidal release: treatment, education, and significant changes in the person's environment, and life style are just some of those changes. Having and experiencing the proper choice of psychotherapy which is "mind healing". Making changes in: one's acquaintances; so-called friends; everyday peer pressure, misunderstandings about life and death; fantasizing about death; being or feeling unaccepted by others; general past bad influences and activities; and unrecognized demon harassment can be problems which lead to or instigate suicidal intentions. I just cannot say these things too much. I want this point to be made very clearly. . .very clearly. Don't deny what you don't know or understand, that which actually works!

Suicide and Christian Beliefs

ONE MORE FOOLISH GAME WHICH COULD LEAD TO
DEATH! IT'S YOUR DESTRUCTION YOU'RE MESSIN' WITH!

Various activities which influence a potential suicide victim and open them up to a hungry demonic appetite are: **(1)** Satanic or cult music; such rap music whose lyrics are usually perverted, twisted and aggressive in nature. (The beat is on the wrong measure for pleasure. Instead it is on the abnormal beat, it actually induces anger and hostility in a person.) When was the last time you heard rap music with its lyrics which were a glory to God? **(2)** An infatuation with bands or rock stars who support behaviors and beliefs which run counter to God's teachings and normal Christian living, can lead to demonic oppression, and **(3)** so can possessing books which are Satanic, or studying from texts which are obviously foreign to Christian concepts and beliefs and have a spiritual influence which is definitely not from our God of the *Holy*

Suicide and Christian Beliefs

Bible. "*. . .do not let your people practice fortune-telling or sorcery, or allow them to interpret omens, or engage in witchcraft, or cast spells or function as mediums or psychics, or call forth the spirits of the dead. Anyone who does these things is an object of horror and disgust to the Lord.*" *Deuteronomy 18:10 (NLT)*

IS THIS YOU? I HOPE NOT!

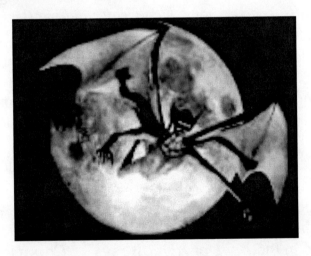

IS BLACK MAGIC IN YOUR LIFE? DO YOU CONSULT
WITH MEDIUMS? ARE YOU EASILY TAKEN IN BY THE
OCCULT? IF SO, YOU MUST LIKE THIS PICTURE
ABOVE?

Such behavior was so detestable to the Lord that He commanded such practitioners of black magic be put to death. *"Men and women among you who act as mediums or psychics must be put to death by stoning. They are guilty of a capital offense."* *Leviticus 20:27 (NLT)* This is serious stuff with God. So beware and back off, Jack! Don't even experiment with such for the shear interest of it, you will tick God off and open yourself up to demonic involvement at the same time.

God loves you and He wants you to be safe and clean of Satan's sick intentions and perverted goals. *"I will destroy your witchcraft and you will no longer cast spells."* **Micah 5:12 (NIV)** Yes, God says He is going to put an end to all witchcraft and there will not be any more fortune-tellers with whom to consult. God is going to pour out His vengeance on those who refuse to obey Him. Folks, this is not an idle threat, this is God's plan for those who are guilty of disobeying Him. We are told that turning to Christ will allow Him to expel any demons bothering or possessing us, and His Word will heal all of those so inflicted. Proof of that is found in the *Book of Acts*. It says, *"Crowds came in from the villages around Jerusalem, bringing their sick and those possessed by evil spirits, and they were all healed."* *Acts 5:16 (NLT)*

Suicide and Christian Beliefs

When people are innocently influenced by external forces which purposefully seek an opportunity to captivate, intimidate or control their thinking, then your knowledge and awareness of such possibilities is one way of stopping Satan's attempts of seduction. Substance abuse is another opening for ominous entities to enter into one's mind and body and take over their whole being, because a person's shields are down and they are not coherent enough to stop such from happening. It's like taking your gas mask off during a poison gas attack. Hypnotism may very easily allow a demon to enter into one's body when his or her shield is down. This creates an opportunity for the Devil to spin his horrible magic and command a demon to take over one's thoughts and actions. You're being "out-of-it" on drugs, is simply an open door invitation to such demonic influences and spirits; it is a gateway or portal into their world and territory. This entrance might be yours or whoever their victim is. Stay sober, life has too many grand offerings to entice you into the real joys of the world, and not the vices which conjure up evil.

OUIJA ANYONE?

Suicide and Christian Beliefs

BELIEVE IT OR NOT, PROPER MEDITATION TECHNIQUES ARE USEFUL, JUST DON'T LET GO OF YOUR MEDITATIVE GRIP OR FALL INTO SOME EVIL INDUCED TRANCE. WHEN YOU DO – YOU LOSE AND GIVE UP YOUR MENTAL CONTROL!!!

Meditation is something that is very good for relaxation. We do this ourselves to release any built up pressure, stress or tension. But, we do this in an environment which is totally uninhibited, without any profane influences around, and through music which is suitable to achieving the intended purpose and not meant to put us into a trance or mesmerize us. Don't go into any Buddhist traces and begin chanting mantras and such – this is not Christian and it is not what is intended during Christian meditation. It might be acceptable to Tina Turner or the Dalai Lama, but not any Christian; there are no compromises with God. It's all or nothing.

DON'T START DOING THIS NONSENSE OR BEGIN CHANTING! DO YOU WANT TO SUMMON THE EVILS SPIRITS OF THE WORLD? DO YOU SEE HOW THESE CLONES LIVE? IS THAT WHAT YOU WANT OUT OF LIFE? I CERTAINLY HOPE NOT!!!

One must use his or her head when specifically choosing their modality of mental relaxation. I find that while I write, I oftentimes enjoy some soft and mellow background music playing. Various tracks from Green Hill Music® out of Nashville, Tennessee are perfect for my subliminal listening while gently soothing my artistic soul. Also, the music of Kitaro® is a great relaxing way to soften the tension from my computer keyboard and CPU. Some people say this is New Age Music and normally all New Age music is considered taboo. I would not put John Tesh® or Kitaro® in a class of music that is anti-Christian. You either like the music or you don't. It either works for you or it doesn't. Please don't attach some silly and unreasonable label to good music that only does one's spirit good. You have to use your head when specifically choosing your modality of mental relaxation. I've heard it said that Ozzie Osborne® claims to be a Christian, but you won't ever find me listening to the garbage he calls music. Like Black Sabbath® and AC/DC®, his genre of musical entertainment is beyond the scope of my personal Christian acceptability. Who's knows, maybe it's just my age; however, I do think that Sharon is a kick! Besides, envision yourself at God's throne or in the New Jerusalem. Now, what kind of music do you hear or feel in your hear? Uh, huh! Just as I thought it's not weird stuff, rap, or heavy metal.

The studying of false religions and theocratic notions and concepts, running counter to Christian teaching can also influence someone to consider various thoughts which may lead to committing suicide. One example is: the Islamic tradition of terrorist suicide for the good of their faith. I understand that it says in the *Qur'an*, fourth chapter, surah 29, that no Moslem should kill himself. Well, that is a good thing much like our Christian belief. But do most Moslems live up to that commandment

Suicide and Christian Beliefs

of Allah? Where and when does the God of the *Holy Bible* ask someone to sacrifice their life for such a terrible purpose, especially for the killing of innocent people? You won't find such a statement in Holy Scripture. It would be directly contrary to what God is all about. The Christian god is a god of mercy and love, not a bloody vengeance seeker. Nowhere in the *Qur'an* or the *Hadiths* will you find a statement that says the Muslim God loves his subjects, or that he is love. Nowhere! Hmmmm!

HE'S JUST ANOTHER MUSLIM SUICIDE BOMBER. BOMBING FOR SOME ASININE CAUSE AND KILLING YOURSELF IS NOT ACCEPTABLE FOR ANY RELIGION. IT IS NOT THE DESIRES OF A LOVING GOD, BUT THE CRAVINGS OF A DEVIL-GOD WHO DOESN'T HAVE YOUR BACK, BUT THAT DOES GET YOUR SOUL. SO MAYBE THAT ENTITY YOU ARE SERVING, LIKE THIS MAN ABOVE, WITH THE TOWEL ON HIS HEAD, IS YOUR GOD! IF SO, YOU NEED TO RETHINK YOUR BELIEFS. DO IT TODAY!

Suicide and Christian Beliefs

Our Christian God Jehovah can accomplish His purposes with gentleness, patience, and forgiveness; He does not need to order people to destroy themselves for His needs or desires and in the name of His Holiness. That kind of warped thinking should have gone out with the Crusades, for Catholics and Moslems both. Only fanatical satanic religions demand an ultimate sacrifice of one's precious God-given life. The early Christian Church demanded blood be spilled; if you were a non-believer, you would have been persecuted. Not for having a close relationship with Jesus Christ, but for not having a close relationship with the Holy Roman Catholic Church. That relationship exists today but without the obvious blood-letting. It's too bad Islam cannot claim the same thing. What is it they say? If it looks like a duck, waddles like a duck and quacks like a duck, then it must be a duck!!! False religion! Quack! Quack! Quack! To think how many people are committing suicide for this utter stupidity and deception, God must be so hurt and angry. I just don't believe all those brown-eyed female virgins will be handed out by the Lord to such suicide victims, or brown-eyed virgin boys, if you happened to be a male Muslim homosexual.

Only real satanic beliefs and sickness can lead such folks into taking their own lives. So, they train them young, filling them with hate and animosity. Geez! What do kids know anyway? God tells us that those who take the lives of children are in deep trouble with him, or as we use to say in the Air Force, "deep *kimchi*." *Kimchi* is a Korean delicacy of eggs that have been buried in the ground for a very long time, then dug up and eaten. I tried a bite once. . .not my cup of tea! *"But if anyone causes one of these little ones who believe in me to sin, it would be better for him to have a large millstone hung around his neck and to be drowned in the depths of the sea." Matthew 18:6 (NIV)* Also read *"And if anyone causes one of these little ones who believe in me to sin, it would be better for him to be thrown into the sea with a large millstone tied around his neck." Mark 9:42 (NIV)* And once again in, *"It would be better for him to be thrown into the sea with a millstone tied around his neck than for him to cause one of these little ones to sin. So watch yourselves." Luke 17:2 (NIV)*

BRAINWASHED TO DEATH!

Suicide and Christian Beliefs

REACH OUT TO THE LORD ALMIGHTY IN PRAYER AND HE WILL MAKE YOUR BURDEN LIGHT, OR REMOVE IT ENTIRELY!

Christians consider the power of prayer to be an answer or at least an intervention with God. It is a way of communicating with the Lord. We may not get a verbal answer, but some form of direction and counsel will be offered to us through the power of the Holy Spirit which, once again, is God's presence and supernatural intervention into our lives. The Holy Spirit is here not only to comfort and protect us against the evil forces of the world but to also be our personal intercessor with God. The closer our personal relationship with God Almighty becomes, the more we are able to discern His Will for us and live up to His purposes. I hope you have noticed how very many times I keep saying "plan" and "purposes" as concerns our life in conjunction with the Lord. The meaning of life for a Christian is to honor God by doing His Perfect Will, not our imperfect will. We live to help God achieve His purposes, not ours. When we become too involved in the things of this world, the Earth becomes our chief downfall especially if that is where our life is centered and our love is cemented. Materialism and self-growth become words and ways of life that detract from the humility the Lord would like to see in us. If we are too much into this world, then the desires that God has intended for us to perform become mute to us and useless to God. This facility is more like a partnership of mutual assistance, sharing and gain for the benefit of all God's creations.

Using Prayer as Our Chief Communication Tool

Prayer is the recognition of the Lord's sovereign power; prayer is a personal acknowledgment of our dependency upon a Higher Architect and Power; and prayer is fairly universal. Not all cultures pray to the same god. Many cultures pray to entities that are of a pantheistic nature, or made of earthly materials or believed to be living the heavens or in the bowels of the earth. Some people are so confused that they pray to many gods, and/or to gods that demand the blood of their enemies, or that represent something totally foreign to any semblance of normalcy. Others have chosen the pathway to destruction and give their total reverence to Satan and his nefarious forces of evil. They think that communicating with the Prince of Darkness will provide them with special powers here and now, or they'll receive a head's up on any other competition with which they may be dealing. But they are deceived. Such spiritual affiliation only creates openings that the demons of Hell need to improperly introduce themselves more efficiently.

Stay away from spiritual powers that demand prayers to their unknown god. It is not worth the trouble it will begin. God Jehovah of the *Holy Bible* wants to hear your troubles, as David called to God. Don't give your troubles to the Devil, he'll simply want a pact for your soul. God wants your soul unconditionally because He has a spiritual plan for you that is heavenly and not hellish. David said, *"O Lord, God of my salvation, I have cried out to you day and night. Now hear my prayer; listen to my cry. For my life is full of troubles. . ." Psalm 88:1-2 (NLT)*

Suicide and Christian Beliefs

SATAN CRIES OUT FOR YOUR SOUL. HE WANTS
YOU TO JOIN HIS TEAM AND HE WILL ENTICE
YOU WITH MANY LYING PROMISES MADE BY HIS
HELLISH COHORTS, FAMILIARS, OR DEMONS.

YES, THE LORD WILL HEAR YOUR PRAYERS
WHEN YOU COME TO HIM IN TRUTH AND FAITH.
BELIEVING THAT HE WILL BE THERE FOR YOU
IS WHAT YOU MUST DO, AND HE WILL BE AT
YOUR SIDE.

God hears our prayers. Heaven hears our prayers.
The Lord will let us know what we have to know to
sustain ourselves. My wife, Jan, always says,
"God's delay is not necessarily God's denial."
Don't ever forget that! God sent a messenger to
Daniel, the message he delivered went just like this,
"*. . .Since the first day you began to pray for
understanding and to humble yourself before your*

Suicide and Christian Beliefs

God, your request has been heard in Heaven. I have come in answer to your prayer." Daniel 10:12 (NLT)

God does not fail us, but we can fail Him. All the Lord asks of us is to call on His name. When we have a close relationship with Jesus and walk in obedience to God's Will, we should not be troubled by the Wicked One, but this does happen and we must be ready to do battle with the Lord of Evil and his nefarious Unseen Forces. Satan is still the god of this system of things and the world. The Lord Almighty has never changed his commission, plight, or position. He can come at us with anger and fury. Be ready! We have God's assurance of that.

"The Devil attacks those who threaten his Kingdom and plans, as well as the person living in total deception and darkness. In order to not be defeated, we have to take authority over him, bind him, plead the blood of Jesus, and offer God praise."
Elizabeth Farrell

Suicide and Christian Beliefs

MY SAVIOR, JESUS CHRIST. HE MAY BE YOUR REDEEMER TOO, IF YOU WILL LET HIM.

We must pray to communicate, how else will God know? He may read our thoughts but unless we petition Him to answer us, He will not. Prayer is our communication method which works. *"Keep on asking, and you will be given what you ask for. Keep on looking, and you will find. Keep on knocking, and the door will be opened. For everyone who asks, receives. Everyone who seeks, finds. And the door is opened to everyone who knocks." Matthew 7:7-8 (NLT)*

Our prayers must be in harmony with God's purposes. God does not want our advice, nor does He want us to suggest ideas to help Him better take care of His own affairs. God's divine plan sees us praying for thanksgiving for the blessings He has bestowed upon us, and usually very abundantly. When our faith is strong and we give God our full cooperation and believe in His ability to answer our prayers, we see the majesty in His answer. When we pray in adoration we acknowledge the wonderful attributes of the Lord and how He alone is all powerful throughout the universe. However, we must pray to glorify God, more than to petition Him for our needs. God knows our needs before we begin to pray to Him.

We may pray for blessings, like the resolution of personal concerns for the perilous situations of others, or for health, peace and prosperity, and we must go to God as a sincerely believing Christian. When God answers prayers, it is because it is keeping within His Will to do just that. God's plan is fulfilled in God's time; our prayers must mainly lie in the fulfillment of God's Will and the purposes of His plan for us. If suicide is our intention, then it is not part of God's plan and He intends for His plan to be completed. But if we mess up that plan, it means we have acted contrary to God's Will and objectives for us, and have not truly given our committed and so-called saved life to the Lord, which we once professed. Therefore, we have not honored our promise to God. He will not be a very pleased or happy camper! God wants us to come to Him on His terms and within His framework of time and structure. We don't define His parameters!

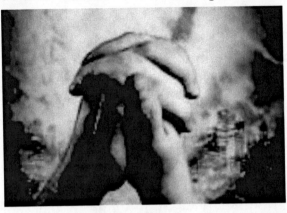

LEARN TO BE COMMITTED TO GOD AND STAY IN DAILY COMMUNICATION WITH HIM. HE LOVES YOU AND THAT IS WHAT HE ALSO WANTS – TO TALK WITH YOU.

It is important to stay in communication with God if we really meant what we agreed to when we gave Jesus Christ our life. When we renege on that promise, we have lied to God and not trusted Him to do His Will with us. We have botched up His plan and He is upset about it. Jesus told His disciples, *"But if you stay joined to me and my words remain in you, you may ask any request you like, and it will be granted. My true disciples produce much fruit. This brings great glory to my Father." John 15:7-8 (NLT)* Do the words and thoughts of a suicide victim reside in Christ, and what words resided in Him? The answer is no, or they would not have committed self-destruction.

When we are walking correctly with God, His thoughts become our thoughts and our thoughts become His thoughts and His plans become our plans. The message is clear, the *Holy Bible* says we must surrender our personal will to God, through Jesus, and we will have no will of our own, as such, but we then reside in God doing His Will. And, what kind of a will does God have? Yes, a Perfect Will. So where is the problem? This is in harmony with Scripture. If we pray while in such harmony, then we can be assured of the possibility of receiving more favorable answers from God. It is this favorable position for which we should clamor; we need God's favor for our own protection and salvation. Without the Lord commanding our soul, we can easily fall away and let the lord of this earth take over in our heart and mind. Can we get back to where we were before we lost God and started thinking in an unacceptable and unclean manner, exhibiting a behavior foreign to God which greatly saddens Him? Quite possibly not, but God may remind us of gift of forgiveness and show His mercy for our proper change of heart. It's just that so few individuals do seek a positive change, a return to the Lord; therefore, this unsettling behavior takes on a very negative perspective and outlook. Scripture says, *"For it is impossible to restore to repentance those who were once enlightened, those who have experienced the good things of Heaven and shared in the Holy Spirit, who have tasted the goodness of the word of god and the power of the age to come and who then turn away from God. It is impossible to bring such people to repentance again because they are nailing the Son of God to the cross again by rejecting Him, holding Him up to public shame."* *Hebrews 6:4-6 (NLT)*

WE FIND PEACE IN GOD!

In prayer, God gives us rest. We need that rest to be healthy in mind, body (soul) and of spirit. God tells us, *"So God's rest is there for people to enter. But those who formerly heard the Good News failed to enter because they disobeyed God. So God set another time for entering His place of rest, and that time is today. . .So there is a special rest still waiting for the people of God. For all who enter into God's rest will find rest from their labors, just as God rested after creating the world. Let us do our best to enter that place of rest. For anyone who disobeys God. . .will fall. For the word of God is full of living power. It is sharper than the sharpest knife, cutting deep into our innermost thoughts and desires. It exposes us for what we really are. Nothing in all creation can hide from Him. Everything is naked and exposed before His eyes. This is the God to whom we must explain all that we have done." Hebrews 4:6-7 & 9-13 (NLT)*

Can you possibly imagine having to confront God after committing suicide? This God of creation and love, the One who never destroys anyone or anything unless it is detestable to Him because of practiced beliefs or behavior, is the One Who will judge the soul who has short changed itself and rejected His plan for salvation. The words of the Holy Scriptures are clear. They may be painful but they are God's truth and they are flawless and unmistakable. Only the spiritually blind find misunderstanding, fault, and error with God's words. The fool perishes in his or her own folly.

Serving in the military was quite an experience. To be an officer meant enlisted personnel were to behave accordingly and respect my higher rank just as I had done when I was an enlisted man prior to me being commissioned. When a subordinate stepped out of line and did not do the will (following orders properly) of the officer commanding or leading a task or an exercise, that person was always held accountable and responsible for their behavior. Such was called insubordination. The person who committed the infraction, purposefully or in negligence, was punished. There was never an acceptable excuse for not doing what was expected. Serving God and doing His Will is very similar. Whether we are totally innocent of knowing His Will for us, or if we wholeheartedly went against His Will, doesn't really matter to God. Although He is much quicker to forgive than is the military, His command/s will always prevail one hundred percent of the time. If we go against His Will, we can count on receiving His punishment and deservedly so. Scripture again mentions to us, *"Anyone who wants to do the will of God will know whether my teaching is from God or is merely My own. Those who present their own ideas are looking for praise for themselves, but those who seek to honor the One who sent them are good and genuine." John 7: 17-18 (NLT)*

God is seeking those who want to and have done His Will. God will judge those who have failed to keep His Will. This is a tragedy, but no matter how you slice the bread, God's butter will only be found on one side. We cannot have our cake and eat it too unless we walk in righteousness and obedience with God's Word and Will for us. When we think our prayers have gone unanswered, they have only been held for a better purpose and a better result for more than any of us could have ever hoped. *"'Then you will call upon me and come and pray to me and I will listen to you. You seek me and find me when you seek me with all your heart. I will be found by you,' declares the Lord."* Jeremiah 23:12 (NIV)

STUDY THE SCRIPTURES DAILY FOR ANSWERS.

The Suffering of Christ: Scourged and Crucified

Why do I bring this topic up in a book about suicide? This is not just some information after the fact, but a section of consideration for anyone who may be contemplating suicide. If one knows what Jesus Christ suffered for them, so that they may be free of sin to live a life for the purposes of God, by accomplishing His sovereign Will, then perhaps this section may open a few eyes and save a few lives. The happiness we garner from Christ's crucifixion and resurrection should be apparent to everyone who knows Christ, but there are those who don't have a clue about Him. That is why we must discuss the ultimate penalty Jesus Christ suffered unto death for all mankind. Suicide is unnecessary, Christ's sacrifice will heal us and that alone should be more than enough. Yes, Christ could have easily prevented His life being taken, but it was a necessary act of love for the forgiveness of our sins. He gave His life for men and women who have lived, are living, and will live before He returns, so that we may be cleansed wholly of sin and all of our filthy transgressions which we all have had.

Any act of suicide then becomes selfish, cowardly, irresponsible, salvation-ignorant, and immature, no matter what the age of the victim may be. It is a selfish act for "self" only and a horrible committed crime against God and His love and mercy. How is it possible to know and live for Christ and be saved, yet take your own life and expect God not to be offended and insulted by cravenly sneaking out the back door? Sorry, but my feelings and beliefs, especially gleaned from my findings and research, tell me that suicide victims will not inherit anything but total blackness and nothingness. As sad as it may make us, it is reality and truth has a horrific tendency to hurt. But Christ's love provides comfort, tender mercy and forgiveness without exception for anyone that believes, trusts, and has faith in Him. We can find peace and happiness in His presence, and He is here with us!!! Let's look at his unbelievable sacrifice and how it can affect our lives for the ultimate better. I suggest reading my book, *Recognizing His Presence and Knowing His Perspective.*

YOU'LL FIND COMFORT, MERCY AND PEACE, IN GOD'S TENDER LOVING HANDS.

The agony and painful suffering that Christ endured for our salvation, was beyond description. Crucifixion is one of the worst and most degrading deaths one can experience. Although it originated in Phoenicia (ancient Canaan and Sidon), the Romans used it to meet their own cruel ends; so much so, that crucifixion is usually thought to be a despicable Roman invention for torture and death.

Suicide and Christian Beliefs

There are other deaths which are perhaps worse, but such deaths are not a concern when considering Christ's sacrifice. With any other form of death, the things that transpired during the time that Jesus hung on the cross, would not have been manifested while being eaten by a lion, or burnt on a stake, or slowly drowned in a pool of boiling water, or swallowed whole by a Great White shark. Christ's death had to come slowly and go through the wickets which God had set up for the totality of this sacrificial scenario. The holiness of this entire ordeal had to be played out so the impact of what Jesus had volunteered for could be totally understood by those that knew Him and would know Him. A better explanation I have not yet heard. . .but give Satan time!

So what happened? What is this crucifixion all about? Let's put a picture together without having to cover every little detail, yet including as much as should clarify what Christ suffered in His last days on this earth. First, I believe that Christ paid for our sins, all of them, by His Atonement, a propitious ransom sacrifice which further added to His physically painful crucifixion by taking on the Wrath of His Father God (His fury toward man's sin), His intense hatred of our sins and His vengeance for all sin since the world's creation. We are talking "heavy duty" sin. Christ undertook to do this for us, all of us who have ever lived and will yet live. Jesus faced this awful agonizing pain alone, abandoned by God, His Father, and rejected by man. He stood up to the full brunt of the absolute evil of all sin.

CHRIST'S CROWN OF THORNS THAT HE WORE FOR YOU AND ME.

God considered Jesus to be the bearer of complete guilt for all of humanity's sin; therefore, Christ was seen as liable for punishment: His crucifixion. **Remember:** Jesus, (the Son of the God Family) alone offered Himself for this mission, to knowingly suffer and atone for our horrible sins, and that is exactly what Jesus did. He paid one hundred percent plus. *"Surely He took up our infirmities and carried our sorrows, yet we considered Him stricken by God, smitten by Him, and afflicted.*

Suicide and Christian Beliefs

But He was pierced for our transgressions, He was crushed for our iniquities; the punishment that brought us peace was upon Him, and by His wounds we are healed." Isaiah 53: 4-5 (NIV)

Can you possibly imagine the Lord Jesus after a night of mental agony in the Garden of Gethsemane, totally tired and fatigued, needing nourishment, rest and thirsting for a cool drink, and then He is accosted by those who were to take Him and make Him suffer. *"During the days of Jesus' life on earth, He offered up prayers and petitions with loud cries and tears to the One who could save Him from death, and He was heard because of His reverent submission. Although He was a son, He learned obedience from what He suffered and, once made perfect, He became the source of eternal salvation for all who obey Him. . ."* *Hebrews 5: 7-9 (NIV)*

THE GARDEN OF GETHSEMANE.

Suicide and Christian Beliefs

CHRIST BEARING HIS CROSS WHILE BEING ESCORTED TO CALVARY BY A SMILING ROMAN SOLDIER.

Being led to the Romans was a time of terrible reality for Christ, He knew His time had come and God His Father would be watching to see Him deliver the promised goods. Christ was undressed and made to look foolish before those that jeered at Him, mocking Him with ignorant laughter and jest. He was pallid of face with crimson blotches and lines on His forehead where beads of blood ran down from the gashes made from the thorns of the quickly fashioned crown that was forced down over His head. His garments became blood-stained and dirty with perspiration, and the soldiers made Him further unclean from their harsh treatment and undoubtedly profane accusations and insults. Yet Jesus stood the test and did not run from His demons, the stabbings of mental torture and humiliation and obscene physical abuse.

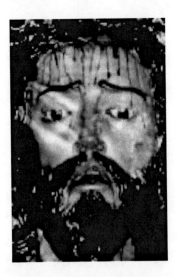

HOW CHRIST MUST HAVE LOOKED AFTER BEING TORTURED AND BEATEN.

These uncivilized and cruel men, supposed protectors of the Roman citizens and gods, tied Christ to a stake and tried to make Him recant. How? By slashing Jesus with leather thongs loaded with lead and armed with spikes and bits of sharp broken bones. They whipped Jesus and lacerated His back, chest and face; they kept it up until the flesh on His face was torn away. You don't see that in the movies, no director has gone that far to show the truth of Christ's barbaric flailing, but the film, *The Passion of the Christ* probably came the closest – so close that many people cannot watch it!

FOR A WHILE ROMAN SOLDIERS GUARDED CHRIST ON THE CROSS AND LATER STOOD GUARD AT HIS TOMB.

Then the soldiers made the Lord drag His cross through the streets to a hill called Golgotha (which means skull; the hill was a skull-shaped place). It was an unholy and melancholy procession which proved to be overwhelming for Jesus. The weight of His cross became overbearing and He was unable to carry it any longer. He fell with the weight of the wooden cross coming down on His back, crashing Him to the ground His hands were swollen and bloody. Our Lord was beyond recognition and those who knew Him wailed and cried; He could hear them but He did nothing. He was refused water, and He was spit upon while others pulled whiskers from His beard. *"I offered my back to those who beat me, my cheeks to those who pulled out my beard; I did not hide my face from mocking and spitting."* Isaiah 50:6 (NIV)

When Jesus finally arrived at the spot where He would be crucified, He was roughly situated onto the cross lying on the ground. As the soldiers shoved Him upon the splintery wood, His head and neck were most likely fastened within the patribulum section of the cross (the area where the two pieces of plank which make up the cross, meet horizontally) this was where He was initially bound, holding Him in place for the cold iron nails. The cross was probably like the traditional *"crux immissa"* (✝). At this point, there are two theories about where the spikes were driven: into His wrists or into His hands. Which is it? It depends upon which medical and anatomical information you read and accept. For the purposes of this book, I choose to accept the belief that the iron spikes were driven into His wrists and not His hands. There is no absolute evidence for either, although the Catholic Church rests its beliefs upon the *stigmata*, a claimed appearance of nail marks and blood stains appearing in the hands of one so afflicted. This *stigmata* has only been seen on others, not Christ; as is the theory of the nails in the wrists, so it is with the hands, there is no solid proof where the nails pierced Christ's hands. The *Holy Bible* also calls the cross a tree, so the choice is yours with hands or wrists.

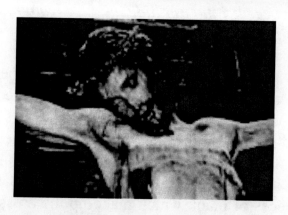

OUR SAVIOR JESUS CHRIST ON THE ROMAN CROSS.

So, it is my belief that iron spikes were driven into His wrists, not His hands. If the spikes has been driven into His hands, the weight of His body would have pulled through His palms and torn the flesh in His hands apart, forcing Christ to fall forward from being improperly fastened and nailed to the cross; so they drive the spikes through His writs where the weight of Jesus body would be less of a factor and remain in an upright position held by the iron nails.

Thus, His arms supported His weight somewhat better. His tarsals produced searing pain with each jerk or twitch He made in order to breathe. His flexed elbows made His wrists rotate about the spikes and send blistering pain like stinging fiery darts up His damaged median nerves. This torture would have caused muscle cramping and paresthesias (a sensation of pricking) of the Lord's outstretched arms, and it would have caused extreme respiratory effort so agonizing and fatiguing that the result would have been eventual asphyxia.

As Jesus painfully lifted His weight upward, it meant putting His feet in such a position that He had to put all of His body weight on top of the nails holding His feet in place. The pain would have also been unbearable. When he bent His elbows and pulled upward on the spikes that held His wrists against the wood of the cross, it produced more aggravated and severe pain and torment. His already overly flogged body wreathed in insufferable pain from every simple movement and twist of His bleeding body while His back constantly rubbed against the splintery wood of the cross. Jesus could actually prolong suffocation when He pushed His body weight up with His feet, which produced a more natural support for His own weight.

Suicide and Christian Beliefs

A slow death by suffocation is what crucifixion is all about. As our Lord would pull His chest cavity upward and outward, it made it very hard for Him to breathe, while either inhaling or exhaling. When Jesus needed more air, He probably shoved Himself upward, striving unbearably to get a breath of fresh air. As the Lord asked for water, a sip of some refreshment to cool and moist His parched lips, soldier soak a sponge in vinegar and attached it to a short stalk of hyssop and offered it as a disgusting and unacceptable substitute for water. Satan and His demons must have been cheering in glee and dancing in a drunken stupor, satisfied with their false victory. Their squeals of joy must have been insidious and sickening to God. Their delight in Christ's suffering must have delighted them beyond our comprehension, as most all suffering inflicted on a person delights them. It is demonic nature to find joy in suffering and agony. But their day will come and it will be far worse, and it will be eternal.

NEED I SAY MORE?

Suicide and Christian Beliefs

While hanging on the cross, a soldier pierced Christ's side with his spear, shoving it into His right lung. This action produced a double stream of blood and water that flowed from the deep wound. The lance cut into the lung, filling it with blood, possibly from a partial rupture of Christ's heart; then the pericardium filled with fluid (water). As all of these horrible sufferings mounted, asphyxia took over and the Lord suffocated, while dying of a broken heart. God had sent Jesus to cleanse us of sin and He loved us so much that His heart must have melted from what He went through. Scripture tells us, *"This is how God showed His love among us: He sent His one and only Son into the world that we might live through Him. This is love; not that we loved God, but that He loved us and sent His Son as an atoning sacrifice for our sins." 1 John 4: 9-10 (NIV)*

Through this horrendous pain and sacrifice, Jesus was able to vanquish death and corruption; with His ultimate resurrection, He claimed victory over death and the grave and over His chief adversary, Satan the Devil. It is Satan that produces scenarios which lead many unwary minds to commit suicide. . .if only these victims of Satan had known Christ, really known Christ, not just having gone through the motions and words of promise, but had lived their lives for Jesus. However, those souls are gone, but other people suffer the mental torment of wanting to take their own life. . .let's stop them!

When the time is announced, or you are able to discern great inner suffering and need coming from another person, see what you can do to save them from personal self-imposed destruction. Learn, then listen, then go into action when and if that time comes for you to step out and stretch your hand out, and lend your heart to one in fear and pain. Christ is the answer. He is our only salvation from death and Hades. *"You are going to have the light just a little while longer. Walk while you have the light, before darkness overtakes you. The man who walks in the dark does not know where he is going. Put your trust in the light while you have it, so that you may become sons of lights." John 12: 35-36 (NIV)*

THE ASCENSION OF JESUS CHRIST.

Chapter Three
After Life Analyses

The Dispensation of the Soul
After Death

Jesus Christ gave us another message about what happens to His children when they depart from His ways. He is very clear and His example permeates the heart of the matter of suicide. Any potential suicide victim considering taking his or her own life should read these verses and try to understand what Christ is saying. If you have had the veil of blindness lifted from your eyes you will see this vivid message immediately. If you are bothered and harassed by demons or have been mired in your own depression, then you may need a clear-thinking Christian to explain this simple analogy to you. If you do not believe in the sacrifice of Christ and God's Holy Scriptures, then these verses won't make any difference to you at all. This is what Jesus said, *"Remain in me, and I will remain in you. For a branch cannot produce fruit if it is severed from the vine, and you cannot be fruitful apart from me. Yes, I am the vine; you are the branches. Those who remain in me, and I in them, will produce much fruit. For apart from me you can do nothing. Anyone who parts from me is thrown away like a useless branch and withers. Such branches are gathered into a pile to be burned." John 15: 4-6 (NLT)*

I started out in my research quest to find answers that would purport the possibility of a suicide soul going to be with the Lord. I was eager to turn up biblical evidence which would corroborate my hopes for such a result. Remaining are people who have loved the individual that had chosen to depart this life and give up the gift of such existence which God so lovingly gave him or her. Suicide victims have no future in the heavenly realms, no matter how much you want this to be true, it just doesn't seem to be so. What we then have to do is to cherish the memories of our loved one that is gone, and remember all the good things about that person.

When Jesus Himself says that He is the vine, an illustration of Him being the answer to life and the way for salvation, and then says that if a branch, you or me, choose to denounce His authority and love and therefore depart from His blessings, mercy and saving grace, then we will amount to nothing. Christ says that such unbelievers or believers, that have had little faith and not trusted in His ability to comfort and save them, will be thrown away like a useless branch that withers. He further says that such branches are gathered up into a pile and burned. This is an everlasting cutting off from the presence of God, and perhaps a suffering of eternal punishment. We can only assume, by what Christ has said, that suicide victims will experience a void of existence without a chance of recompense or rest. If we destroy our temple (our body) God will destroy us. See *1 Corinthians 3: 16-17 (GN)*

IS YOUR GOD, THE FIRE GOD?

Much secular speculation has been shared about the residence of the soul after death. One of the common beliefs is that there is no soul. That this life is all there is. This is a fatalistic and nihilistic belief. It is a depressing process of thinking existentially: a philosophy of life that is nothing but hopelessness and despair. Agnostics don't know or are not sure what occurs after death; habitually they haven't a clue, nor are they truly interested in what is correct, what is speculation, or what is just not Hoyle. Atheists just naturally assume there is no god of any kind, thus there is no other life beyond this one. The possibility of there being a god is all superstition to them. For them to think there is life after death is like admitting there is some greater power that does have a plan for us and that controls our state of being (whereabouts) after death. Others think that the soul transmigrates to some other parallel universe, or to a mystical plane where one's life begins again in a new body and comes back to the earth as a reincarnated new life. A great deal of this thinking is shrouded in secular and religious controversy. Each cult has its own viewpoint and beliefs where the soul goes, or if a soul exists.

The spirit of a living person is oftentimes seen as an entity that will live in limbo, or in some place called purgatory where souls are considered to be locked up in a hellish abyss that reeks of punishment and spiritual torment. This is not the Christian belief of how a soul is handled after death. Scripture is full of references about God's love for us and the wonders He will give us in our new heavenly home; this is where Jesus has gone on ahead of us to prepare a place for us to be with Him. God has His plans. *"'For I know the plans I have for you,' declares the Lord, 'plans to prosper you and not to*

harm you, plans to give you hope and a future.'"
Jeremiah 29: 11 (NIV)

Death has always captivated the imagination of thinkers, people who intelligently consider thoughts and ideas about an afterlife and what it could mean. Many theories have been espoused, and many notions have proven to be interesting enough that millions of individuals with hunger for knowledge become enamored with the concept of death. *James Hunt Cook* wrote the following words concerning death.

> *"Across a cradle where sunk in satin pillows, lay a still, pale form as droops a rose from some fierce heat, the evening shadows fell aslant, and spoke of peace. The twilight calm enclosed the world in silence deep as Truth, and on the little face the wondering look had given place to one of sweet repose. It was the mystery of Death."*

John J. Ingalls further stated in his eloquent writing about the mystery of death. He wrote that,

> *"In the democracy of the dead all men at last are equal. There is neither rank nor station, nor prerogative in the republic of*

the grace. At this fatal threshold the philosopher ceases to be wise, and the song of the poet is silent. The rich man relinquishes his millions and Lazarus his rags. The poor man is as rich as the richest, and the rich man is as poor as the pauper. The creditor loses his usury, and the debtor is acquitted of his obligation. There the proud man surrenders his dignities, the politician his honors, the worldling his pleasures; the invalid needs no physician, and the laborer rests from unrequited toil. Here at last is Nature's final decree in equity. The wrongs of time are redressed. Injustice is expiated, the irony of Fate is refuted; the unequal, distribution of wealth, honor, capacity, pleasure and opportunity, which makes life such a cruel and inexplicable tragedy, cease in the realm of death. The strongest there has no supremacy, and weakest needs no defense. The mightiest captain succumbs to that invincible adversary, who disarms alike the victor and the vanquished."

We all have our thoughts and our beliefs, some are the same as others, and some of our personal feelings and attitudes toward death are quite different what another may wholeheartedly believe and accept as the truth about death. One individual, *Benjamin Franklin*, had something to say about the aspect of death and that of his friend, which most likely spurred him on towards writing what he did.

"We are spirits. That bodies should be lent us, while they can afford us pleasure, assist us in acquiring knowledge, or in doing good to our fellow creatures, is a kind and benevolent act of God. When they become unfit for these purposes, and afford us pain instead of pleasure, instead of an aid become as encumbrance, and answer none of the intentions for which they were given, it is equally kind and benevolent, that a way is provided by which we may get rid of them. Death is that way. Our friend and we were invited abroad on a party of pleasure, which is to last forever. His chair was ready first and he has gone before us. We could not all conveniently start together; and why should you and I be grieved at this, since we are soon to follow, and know where to find him."

Recorded in the **Book of Ecclesiastes**, written by King Solomon, the wisest man to ever live, are his thoughts about death, the finality of all finalities. In Scripture that is usually considered to be a real "downer". For me, I see this as a passage of hopelessness for anyone who dies. Thank God for the sacrifice of Christ which allows us to fall under His grace and be saved from such an existence. This is a sanctifying grace, a real transformation of our spirit infused with God's grace through the power of His Holy Spirit. Sanctification is the process of being made holy; it is a state of which saved saints are considered being free from sin. Solomon unfortunately did not know Christ. He did know of the wonderful preparations that Jesus would speak about, which secured for all saints the magnificent home built for us in His heavenly realm. King Solomon wrote about those things as he knew them to be, or believed them to be. He wrote with conviction, *"For the living know that they will die, but the dead know nothing; they have no further reward, and even the memory of them is forgotten. Their love, their hate and their jealousy have long since vanished; never again will they have a part in anything that happens under the sun." Ecclesiastes 9: 5-6 (NIV)* This thinking was also Old Covenant and not New Covenant. The reality of hope for life after death was much different. There was nothing concrete prior to the promises of Christ. If Solomon was the wisest man in the world and if the Lord Jesus Christ has permitted Solomon's words to stay in place in the *Holy Bible*, after thousands of years, my guess is that what he wrote and recorded in the Scriptures is true, accurate and valid; however, with Christ we've added hope for life eternal with Him and the Father.

SOLOMON IN HIS COURT.

It is believed by millions that what Solomon wrote is still true today. So by believing such, is the glory taken out of God's Son's sacrifice on the cross? No! It is His blood that provides us with the redemption God wants us to have and experience. Granted, when we die it is too late for some to realize this wonderful gift that has been offered to all who have accepted Jesus Christ and God's Word. His Holy Spirit was given to us to interceed for us before God. That powerful force was not part of the Hebrew times nor noted in Hebrew Scriptures. This comfort was unavailable during the times of Solomon. However, God, on several occasions sent one or more of His holy angels to bring peace and understanding to one of His elect.

Suicide and Christian Beliefs

ONE OF THE LORD'S HOLY ANGELS THAT BRINGS PEACE AND UNDERSTANDING TO HIS ELECT.

The lost that die may not experience anything at all; they will be cut off from God forever, He has promised this and God never lies. There is no reward or way out for the lost souls who have not chosen the Lord's way and have turned their back on His salvation. There will be no further memory of them as time passes because the *Holy Bible* says even that too will be forgotten; finally, there is no part for them in anything else because they are conscious of nothing at all. Their spirit has been given up and only God truly knows what happens to it after death. That is God's business and not ours.

As He created souls from the beginning, so He alone knows what the lost soul's real condition is. Where has the spirit of a once living man or woman gone when they chose to speed up their process of life and seek the cold world of death? What lies on the other side? Through pure conjecture and subjective thought we can only imagine and fabricate in our mind what we conceive to be the truth of a death we have accepted. If we live a righteous life in tune with God's Will, we will be sanctified and glorified when we see God. If we have failed by not abiding by His Will and not living in righteousness, having not trusted the Lord with our life and eternal soul, then we will suffer consequences which we do not know, but God alone does know. Again, our trust in the Lord, walking in obedience to His Will and commands and being righteous in His eyes, will be our keys toward preparing for eternal life. Rejecting His Will and trust, and Christ's Holy sacrifice on the cross is an insult to His loving gift of grace and to our Master Himself. People doing God's live and living as holy living sacrifices for God don't commit suicide and certainly never contemplate it. *"The wicked are crushed by their sins. But the godly righteous have a refuge when they die."* *Proverbs 14:32 (NLT)* *"Whoever abandons the right path will be severely punished; whoever hates correction will die. Even the depths of Death and Destruction are known by the Lord. How much more does He know the human heart!"* *Proverbs 15:10-11 (NLT)* But with a note of hope,

Suicide and Christian Beliefs

"Death is the opening of a more subtle life. In the flower, it sets free the perfume; in the chrysalis, the butterfly; in man, the soul."
Juliette Adam

Scripture tells us that people that lack wisdom and die without it are most likely destined to an uncomfortable and painful death. For those that do not have the insight to call on the name of the Lord for answers to their personal dilemmas, or to find resolution to problems that have them dismayed, lack essential wisdom. Such people are usually the spiritually lost, the very young, or the innocent who lack knowledge of life and how to live it. They may be the ignorant, rebellious, and weak in spirit; criminals escaping worldly punishment that opt for a greater penalty which lasts forever; those trying to avoid shame; those that are depressed and consider themselves without hope; those overwhelmed by the physical or mental harassment of demons; those that are seekers of the mystical and paranormal; and/or those involved with cults that require strange and dangerous rituals such as Satanism, demonic Spiritualism, black witchcraft, and ancient religious covens. Perhaps they are those who are influenced by the trappings of impure music found in verses which advocate suicide, death, criminal activity, irreverence towards God and the Lord Jesus Christ, and that which promotes the use of illegal drugs.

Suicide and Christian Beliefs

There are numerous others who are spiritually lost, especially those making the news for their desires for assisted suicide by the late "Jack the Dripper" and other doctors who favor euthanasia as an alternative to living in pain with a life-threatening disease.

GUESS WHO? JACK THE DRIPPER!

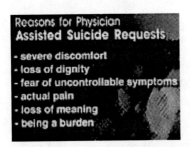

Reasons for Physician
Assisted Suicide Requests

- severe discomfort
- loss of dignity
- fear of uncontrollable symptoms
- actual pain
- loss of meaning
- being a burden

SURELY YOU'VE HEARD ABOUT SUCH INSIDIOUS METHODS OF HELPING OTHERS DIE? IS THAT A SICKNESS OR WHAT? HEY! MANY FOLKS DON'T THINK SO. IN FACT, THEY BELIEVE IT IS MERCIFUL. MAYBE IT IS, BUT IS IT OF GOD? IT'S YOUR CALL! BUT I SERIOUSLY DOUBT IT.

Suicide and Christian Beliefs

Patients in hospitals, rest homes, sanitariums, private medical facilities and private homes that suffer intolerably with an agonizing and constant pain coming from their infliction, will oftentimes seek a way out by committing or attempting to commit suicide. No matter how it is done, this manner of chosen death is not acceptable to the Lord. *"Only God has the right to take back a life."* There is more to that sentence than it just being an empty statement. What does it mean that only God has the right? The saying, *"only God has the right to take back a life,"* is not without recourse. That saying did not just come about. It means what it says; *"only God has the right. . ."*

Therefore, if someone commits suicide, they have infringed upon God's right; they stole from God His right to take back their life at His predestined hour. Obviously we are penalized for sinning directly against God (and His rights). Who are we to usurp God's power and rights? The last God-created living creature that did so was Satan, and we know what kind of trouble he has caused himself. **If you do this, then expect to be punished by God's wrath, not coddled in His love and mercy.** Break a rule and you pay the delicate price of being an outlaw who has defiled a Godly creation, by destroying it when "only" God had/has the right.

Suicide and Christian Beliefs

Unless your thinking is clouded in "grace space", it will be abundantly clear to you that the Lord does not sanction having His "right" usurped. Grace provides comfort and forgiveness to sinners, those that believe in and have faith in His loving grace and His word, but not to transgressors that have not exercised genuine truth in His gift or salvation in Christ, or have fallen away. There are many warnings verses in the *Holy Bible* you should become aware of and learn. You can lose your salvation by transgressing against your free gift of grace. How many times should I say this? How many times must I warn you? Read my book, *Eternal Security: Fact or Fiction?* And you'll find over 90 verses to prove such a loss is possible.

A PERSONAL CONCEPTION OF PARADISE.

Suicide and Christian Beliefs

Those that are considered righteous in the eyes of God will be with Him in paradise. It should be an easy passage for such souls, as opposed to the souls of the lost that will not have a safe harbor or an easy passage in the afterlife. *"The righteous perish, and no one ponders it in his heart; devout men are taken away, and no one understands that the righteous are taken away to be spared from evil. Those who walk uprightly enter into peace; they find rest as they lie in death." Isaiah 57: 1-2 (NIV)* To lie in a state of death is to sleep until awakened by the voice of the Lord. Go figure! Where's the difficulty in understanding this verse?

For eons, mortal men have pondered over the dispensation of the body's soul when it dies. There are no clear cut answers apart from what our Holy Scriptures record. As concerns suicide, there are words of comfort which are spoken to those left behind trying to sort out all the reasons and causes for the self-destruction of the suicide victim, but such words only go so far. What people want to know is beyond and well outside the confines of their minds. We can guess and attempt to put together the pieces of suicide, trying to figure out just what suicide is all about, or we can lay this enigmatic problem in the hands of our Creator and let Him deal with the death of a loved soul. We keep thinking that God is merciful and maybe that gives us comfort. If it does, then God's loving and flowing mercy is what we want to hear.

WHO WOULD WANT TO LISTEN TO SOMETHING CLAIMING THAT THE SOUL OF THE SUICIDE VICTIM IS ON A ONE-WAY TRACK TO HELL, ONLY TO BE GREETED BY THE SAME DEMONS THAT INFLUENCED HIM OR HER TO BUY THEIR DEATH TICKET, SUCCUMBING TO THEIR DEVILISH PERSUASIONS? WOUD YOU?

The salesmanship of Satan and his dark angels is very powerful and persuasive; it is also very persistent and potent. Oftentimes, the truth hurts and fills us with anguish, making it very hard to see and understand the real truth of the Lord. We each have to deal with suicide in our own way and with our own beliefs.

THIS IS NOT WHAT YOU WANT TO THINK ABOUT IF YOU'RE SERIOUSLY CONTEMPLATING SUICIDE; HOWEVER, THIS JUST MAY BE WHAT IS WAITING FOR YOU. YOU BETTER THINK TWICE!

Suicide and Christian Beliefs

We petition the Lord to send His loving Spirit to guide those of misfortune and to counsel those that may consider a quick way out of this life. We do not want to see, hear of, or experience anyone exiting God's world before his or her time.

"This life we have been given is a gift to us from God; our gift to God is what we do with our life, and we will be judged on how we used that gift of life."

We ask our Almighty Father to be merciful and understanding for those who have not fully trusted in His protection and healing ability and have gone on their own, without His consultation or permission. We ask God to be kind to the lost spirits who have committed suicide, seeking an escape from their personal trials, ills and problems. We remind those who are left behind, or are themselves considering the taking of their own life, that suicide is, **"A permanent solution to a temporary problem."**

The Death State

There are a couple of theories about what happens to a person after death; theories which most Christians accept and consider to be set in cement. Personally, I do not own or possess a crystal ball that tells me what I may want to hear, nor do I have a direct link with God Who is giving me the information about which I write. However, I will discuss the best evidence or understanding that I have based on *Holy Bible* scripture. Also read my book, *The Plan*, especially *Chapter Eight: Death, Body, Soul and Spirit*. Please take your time and digest what I am about to present, it is not difficult, but going slowly will help clarify what I say. In this manner, everything should make excellent sense to you. This is not my thinking alone, but others that after careful study and examination of Scripture, also believe the way I do. Let's give this a shot!

Assuming that we are all made up of the body or (the soul/physical body) and the spirit, then the rest of this chapter will consider this state or condition as being fundamental. I see the body as being our physical make-up, tissue, blood, bone, hair and so forth. The spirit is the breath of life or intelligence of each person; it will leave the body at death and return to God. *"They kept on stoning Stephen as he called out to the Lord, 'Lord Jesus, receive my spirit!' He knelt down and cried out in a loud voice, 'Lord! Do not remember this sin against them!' He said this and died."* Act 7: 59-60 (GN)

All spirits do this, no matter if they are good or evil. The spirit goes back to God. *"Then the dust will return to the earth as it was, and the spirit will return to God who gave it."* Ecclesiastes 12:7 (NKJV)

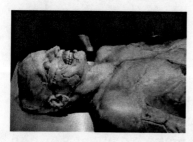

A DECAYING CORPSE.

Although the body (the physical body) lies dead in the grave, and rests, the spirit, or our intelligence, which is like a memory back for us humans, returns to the Lord. When we die God stores our spirit some place in His memory bank. I believe this is where and how all spirits securely rest. The system for this must be considerably more difficult, detailed and sophisticated than we can possibly imagine, but you can easily see the illustration. Death is having no consciousness for the body/the soul; but the spirit ascents to God. *"Who knows the spirit of the sons of men, which goes upward, and the spirit of the animals, which goes down to the earth?" Ecclesiastes 3:21 (NKJV)* Perhaps this means we will not find out pets in Heaven. However, a book by *Dr. William Nesbitt, Jr.*, titled, *The Illusion of Time – Seeing Scripture Through Science*, gives a new account of how we may see our pets in Heaven.

Suicide and Christian Beliefs

Dr. Nesbitt has many other interesting theories which will make any thinking Christian open his or her mind and consider various possibilities they never before contemplated. These are simply new ways of understanding how God may exercise His various plans and put them into motion.

The soul, which is our body (understand that Scripture tells us that the soul lives, breathes, eats, sleeps and dies; it is our physical body) and our spirit, is composed of our thoughts, habits and actions, the seed of our mental, spiritual, and physiological body which goes to Heaven to be transformed into immortality (as there is no such thing as conditional immortality), will all be somewhere in the God-realm. I believe this is more or less for safe keeping until our body and spirit are reunited at the resurrection and with Christ's Second Advent. The soul seed may contain programming for a new glorified body which will have our physical recognition and it will die; it will become unconscious and rest in the security of God, in the grave, but it will not be forgotten. However, it will die. *"Behold, all souls are Mine; the soul of the father as well as the soul of the son is Mine; the soul who sins shall die." Ezekiel 18:4 (NKJV)*

This particular reference is to the second death mentioned in the New Testament, for unrepentant sinners, which is an eternal death. The first death is only a temporary death. Unlike the spirit, the soul lays in the grave waiting for its resurrection after the first death; it simply remains in the grave, it is the physical body. King David said, *For You will not leave my soul in Sheol, nor will You allow Your Holy One to see corruption.*" *Psalm 16: 10 (NKJV) Sheol* means the grave, and the verse means that our soul will not be left in the grave by God, as He did not allow Jesus to remain in the grave, but resurrected Him to glory.

All souls will be resurrected. Where will your soul be resurrected to, Heaven or to an infernal place of final destruction? This verse is stated truth, God would not allow David to write such and have it in His own Holy Word, if were not truthful and accurate. Think about it! If we know the second half of the verse is correct, and Christ was resurrected, then why should be deny or doubt the first half of the verse. I trust God and His Word, and I have no doubt when I die, what will happen to my soul/body and spirit. So why should you doubt or deny this concept? Is His written Word, the *Holy Bible* not good enough for you? **Remember:** you were originally created to live in purity forever with God. You were created perfectly with divine designs and godly attributes incorporated into you both mentally and physically in the image of God

Himself. You were to be spiritually, if not also physically, connected to God for direct communicate with Him in person. You are and were to be His friend, not His servant. Unlike the angels in Heaven, you were made to be like God. He has divine plans and purposes for you – His comrade.

IS THIS OUR SPIRITUAL LIVING FORCE?

Jesus Christ further tells us that the body can be destroyed, but not the soul (the spiritual living force of the body). *"And do not fear those who kill the body but cannot kill the soul. But rather fear Him who is able to destroy both soul and body in hell."* *Matthew 10:28 (NKJV)* And just for the record, there is no biblical reference to us having an immortal soul. Look all you want to, but you will not find such a reference. The soul part of the body does die; it sleeps in the grave while the body perishes and decays. *"As indeed he says in another passage, 'You will not allow your faithful servant to rot in the grave* (our soul: emphasis mine).' *For David served God's purposes in his own time, and then he died, was buried with his ancestors, and his body rotted in the grave." Acts 13: 35-36 (GN)* Yes, you will find immortality mentioned in the *Holy Bible*, but not in such a context of us having an immortal soul.

God allows all those that die to have rest, to be unconscious until He alone is ready to raise them, to awaken them to His voice, and His voice only. **I do hope you understand this: as the physical body/soul decays in the grave, the spiritual essence of the body is sleeping and waiting for resurrection.** This spiritual part of the soul is our link directly to God, Who is our eventual life line for our future state of life with Him. No evil monster like Satan or any of his demons, can do that accept perhaps vicariously and deceptively through mediums that actually speak with demons. To my knowledge this was only done once and is an example for us, so we understand the power that Satan still has to interrupt a sleeping soul while waiting for Christ to return and bind Satan. Satan has no ability to create or restore Godlike life. I am sure he'd like to, but sorry Mr. Devil, you do know your limitations and boundaries now don't you? Life has nothing to do with you accept that you like to antagonize, torment and destroy it.

This is what happened: King Saul, in *1 Samuel, chapter twenty-eight*, consulted a medium to raise the dead prophet Samuel. Saul was in big trouble with the Philistines; in fact, they were about ready to kill him. Saul needed advice, so he had his servants find him a medium to perform a séance. The witch of Endor was brought to Saul and he told her what to do. The witch brought forth a spirit out of the ground which spoke to Saul and pronounced his destiny. It was not a future for which Saul had been hoping. The spirit claimed to be Samuel. Was this spirit really Samuel's spirit, or was it the voice of a demon?

THE WITCH OF ENDOR DISTURBING SAMUEL'S SLEEPING SOUL. OR DID SHE DISTURB SOMETHING ELSE?

Suicide and Christian Beliefs

Remember: our "spirits, at death, go to be with God, but our bodies/souls are at rest in the grave, not our spirits. The spirit told Saul he would die, and Saul would be with his sons and Samuel the next day. Saul was wicked but his sons had not been evil. Samuel was a prophet of God, yet all of these men, good and bad, and ugly too I assume, would be together in the grave. But in what manner? Although their bodies would corrupt and decay, their spirits, both those wicked and those that were good would be at rest until some future time when God would awaken them for resurrection and judgment. I believe this is a time when we receive our celestial bodies which are joined with our spirits, which God has safely kept somewhere.

Was this speaking spirit, actually Samuel's spirit or some demon, because he spoke directly to Saul and not to the medium? Mediums always do the talking to the spirits they conjure up. Why? Because those spirits are actually demons posing as the departed spirits of deceased human beings. They can do that, and they do. Besides, I don't think God would allow a witch with a familiar spirit, more in tune with Satan than with Himself, to raise His dead prophet Samuel. No, not on that day or any day. No way!!! This scripture also does not say that Saul was deceived by a demon; it says he spoke to Samuel. If Samuel's spirit was with God, and his body was rotting in the grave, then the entity raised by the witch of Endor was either the essence of Samuel's spiritual soul (but probably not), or a satanic demon. This further proves that our souls are simply resting, unconsciously in the grave – aware of nothing at all. I believe a demon could have spoken to the witch of Endor, OR Satan himself. BUT if this apparition of Samuel was a demon, it would not have delivered a true prophecy, it couldn't and it would not have been a part of the make-up of a real demon, nor would a demon have the prophetic ability to appear and communicate as what was witnessed. The witch sensed something other than what she had ever sensed before and it frightened her. She realized this was not a normal spirit she was used to speaking with – something was wrong. Did God allow this to happen, and was it really Samuel's spirit speaking to Saul, because what the spirit said came true! Necromancy was a terrible sin to the Lord, so would He allow such to happen in His or out of His presence? I just don't think so. God will not say one thing and do another.

Our Lord Jesus Christ has told us that death is as rest or a sleep. *"Jesus said this and then asked, 'Our friend Lazarus has fallen asleep, but I will go and wake him up.' The disciples answered, 'If he is asleep, Lord, he will get will.' Jesus meant that Lazarus had died, but they thought he meant natural sleep. So Jesus told them plainly, 'Lazarus is dead, but for your sake I am glad that I was not with him, so that you will believe. . ." John 11: 11-14 (GN)*

So, did the witch from Endor disturb Samuel's rest? I don't think so For more clarity on this matter, see *The Complete Works of Flavius Josephus*, (Section One) *The Antiquities of the Jews*, chapter six, verse two.

Consulting mediums is forbidden by God. It is detestable to Him when someone consults a medium to conjure up the dead. God knows that such a medium is simply contacting satanic beings, his despicable demons, by using familiar spirits which may somehow deceptively convince someone ignorant that they really can disturb the resting souls (the body's spiritual essence) of the human dead. This is very tricky, sticky stuff to understand.

"There shall not be found among you anyone who makes his son or daughter pass through the fire, or one who practices witchcraft, or a soothsayer, or one who interprets omens, or a sorcerer. Or one who conjures spells, or a medium, or a spiritist, or one who calls up the dead. For all these things are an abomination to the Lord, and because of these abominations the Lord your God

drives them out from before you." Deuteronomy 128: 10-12 (NKJV)

IS THIS YOUR FORTUNE TELLER?

This story of Samuel also proves that when we die, our bodies/souls go to the grave and not to Heaven of Hell. If Jesus, Who we know died, was buried, and then resurrected had gone directly to Heaven, there would have been no need of a period of time spent in the grave, or that of a resurrection from the death state. *Christ had to conquer death.* Christ would have gone directly to Heaven, because He did and still does have that ability, He was and is God. Instead we have a different set of circumstances: He died, we die; He was buried, we will be buried; He rose, we will be raised. Praise the Lord for that comfort. Scripture says, ***"'Do not hold on to me,' Jesus told her, 'because I have not yet gone back*** *up to the Father. But go to my brothers and tell them that I am returning to Him who is my Father and their Father, my God and their God." John 20:17 (GN) and "I am telling you the truth: those who hear my words and believe in Him who sent me have eternal life. They will not be judged, but have already passed from death to life. I am telling you the truth; the time is coming – when the dead will hear the voice of the Son of God, and those who hear it will come to life. Just as the Father is Himself the source of life, in the same way He has made His Son to be the source of life. And he has given the Son the right to judge, because He is the Son of Man. Do not be surprised at this; the time is coming when all the dead will hear His voice and come out of their graves; those who done good will rise and live, and those who have done evil will rise and be condemned. John 5: 24-29 (GN)*

Therefore, was it truly Samuel's soul that ascended from the ground, which we call the grave, or Earth? He did not descent from Heaven or any other celestial place. If Christ couldn't go to Heaven directly after death, Samuel certainly didn't go before Him. **Remember:** familiar spirits are lying spirits who impersonate dead souls; mediums converse not with dead souls but with demons. Samuel was not a lying familiar spirit, but he could have been a disturbed soul that was resting in God's peace if The Lord had permitted such. But I don't believe He did. As I said, it's so contrary to what God is all about and wants us to believe is His truth. Deception is not part of God's truth. If God allowed this, it was not in Satan's ability to promote it or permit it – he didn't have that kind of power then, and he doesn't have it now.

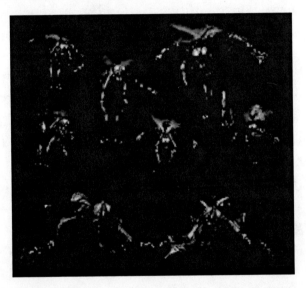

A HOST OF MERRY DEMONS!!! ARE THEY LURKING OVER YOU? ARE YOU SURE? VERY SURE?

If Samuel was actually disturbed and rose to the wishes of Saul, it would also prove that his soul was not dead, but only sleeping, as Scripture says it should have been. It had not been destroyed by death, but it had been simply resting. It was alive in an unconscious state of being; a state from which only God could allow a sleeping body/soul to be disturbed or awoken. This state of death is called the first death.

God does speak to dead souls. Consider the case of the dead souls under the altar, and consider the fact they were conscientious of God's presence. Was this because they will become conscientious of their death state the closer we get to the resurrection hour? Or was this because they had only been slain a short while before and perhaps, this is only a picture of what will happen just prior to Christ's return? *"When He opened the fifth seal, I saw under the altar the souls of those who had been slain for the word of God and for the testimony which they held. And they cried with a loud voice, saying, 'How long O Lord, holy and true, until You judge and avenge our blood on those who dwell on the earth?' Then a white robe was given to each of them; and it was said to them that they should rest a little while longer. . ." Revelation 6: 9-11 (NKJV)*

Had Samuel been a demon, then Saul would have had to join him in Hell, but Samuel returned to his rest in the grave. And had Samuel been a demon, God would not have allowed the medium to conjure up Samuel nor permit Saul to speak to an imposter-demon. These things are abominations to God. Next time you decide to visit a psychic, or have Tarot cards or your palm read, think about how God feels about such behaviors and those who support and participate in them. These are not good things! Why put your spirit and life at risk? There is absolutely nothing for you or anyone to gain and you'll be the eventual loser. You may get some information which proves to be true and entices you to seek more, but that will be your final downfall. This behavior only opens the doors and windows of your soul to invite Satan and his demons into your body.

ANYBODY FOR A GAME OF TAROT? AHH, COME ON! WHAT CAN IT POSSBILY HURT?

Suicide and Christian Beliefs

"For the living know that they will die; but the dead know nothing. And they have no more reward, for the memory of them is forgotten. Also their love, their hatred, and their envy have now perished; nevermore will they have a share in anything done under the sun." **Ecclesiastes 9: 5 (NKJV)** Therefore, the body/soul lays quietly in its grave until finally resurrected. The soul has no consciousness or mental activity unless disturbed by God, or someone or something He allows to make such communication happen. These souls are sleeping in their graves. *"Do not put your trust in princes, nor in a son of man, in whom there is no help. His spirit departs, he returns to his earth; in that very day his plans perish."* **Psalm 146: 3-4 (NKJV)** and *"Whatever your hand finds to do, do it with all of your might; for there is no work or device or knowledge or wisdom in the grave where you are going."* **Ecclesiastes 9:10 (NKJV)** I think this verse says it pretty clearly.

After the resurrection of our Lord Jesus Christ, a huge change in the condition of the dead took place.

Suicide and Christian Beliefs

The Blood of the Lamb paid the price for man's original sin and man is now responsible for his own sin and not Adam's sin. The prophet Jeremiah wrote of God establishing a New Covenant with mankind, one where every man and woman will be forgiven their iniquities. This is the umbrella of grace we live under today. This protection is provided by our Lord Jesus Christ, by His sacrifice on the cross. The shedding of His precious blood has cleansed us from all of our sins. All we have to do is accept Him as our personal Savior. He gives us that salvation. He has that power, and He has the keys to the Kingdom and all power over the grave.

Jesus had the power to awaken Lazarus who had died, but was only sleeping in a state of soul rest. He returned Lazarus to life. His soul had been unconscious, but became mentally active with the sound of Christ's voice and command to come forth. His soul had been dead, as we understand death, but not as God understands death; to God, Lazarus' soul was alive, it only slept till it was revived. This powerful stuff, amigo! Further proof of Lazarus being dead, was that he and his grave smelled from the stench of death. That doesn't happen to someone only sleeping and still alive. Just think, we can have a relationship with a Creator who won't let us perish in the grave; He will not let us die. We are embedded in His memory and forever we can share in His Kingdom. That's got to make you feel awful special. No matter what we've done, we're reconciled to Christ and forgiven our transgressions.

Humanity, *per se*, was totally doomed before the resurrection of Jesus Christ. That victory of Christ over death and sin is good news for all dead saints. Saints are believers in Jesus, those who have accepted Him as their Redeemer, Lord and Savior. Saints, in the Protestant sense, are not persons who have died and been canonized by a body of mortal men with a limited and fallible ability to relate to God on His level of intelligence. At the Second Coming of Jesus Christ, all these righteous saints will be summoned from their graves and their bodies/souls will be united with their spirits; both being awakened by the Lord and transformed into a new glorious celestial body, so they eventually will be judged according to their deeds, attitudes, beliefs and actions. We will all be held accountable before

God. *"They will give an account to Him who is ready to judge the living and the dead. For this reason the gospel was preached also to those who are dead, that they might be judged according to men in the flesh, but live according to God the spirit."* **1 Peter 4: 5-6 (NKJV)**

The bottom line is, if Christ had not won victory over Satan's claim to rule this world, then the body and spirit would have remained in their respective graves until the Great White Throne Judgment. Therefore, the body and spirit will be raised and not decay forever in the grave. **Remember:** the spirit is already alive to God. Had Christ not won this victory over death, then Satan surely would have kept all dead bodies/souls in the grave forever, unconscious and unaware of any flicker of life. Praise God, the devil lost!

Suicide and Christian Beliefs

Also, there were graves opened and the sleeping dead saints of Christ's time, were actually raised when the Lord Jesus was resurrected. They came out of their graves and went to be with the Lord. Notice how amazing was the time that Jesus came forth from His grave and how it just have totally mesmerized those who witnessed what the Holy Scriptures claim to have happened. *"Then, behold, the veil of the temple was torn in two from top to bottom; and the earth quaked, and the rocks were split, and the graves were opened; and many bodies of the saints who had fallen asleep were raised; and coming out of the grave after His resurrection, they went into the holy city and appeared to many. So when the centurion and those with him, who were guarding Jesus, saw the earthquake and the things that had happened, they feared greatly,, saying. 'Truly this was the Son of God!'" Matthew 27: 51-54 (NKJV)*

JESUS CHRIST AT THE ENTRANCE OF HIS TOMB.

Suicide and Christian Beliefs

You can see, once again, how these dead souls had been sleeping. You can also see that the righteous were resurrected to be with God, and it is apparent that they were seen by many after they had been resurrected. However, the wicked were not raised, but only those who were considered to be saints in God's eyes and holy estimation. God's opinion and/or viewpoint is the only one that matters! What a glorious position to be in. Wow!!! Glory be to the Lord for the wonderful works He performs!

What I have learned is that Jesus Christ died as a man, flesh and blood, with a body/soul and spirit. He commended His spirit to be with God while He expired on the cross and His spirit went back to God, but His body/soul went into the grave just as that of any other man. Christ had to totally fulfill His mission. He had to go through all of the physical steps of life and death as that of any other mortal man. *"And Jesus cried out again with loud voice, and yielded up His spirit."* *Matthew 27: 5* and *"And when Jesus cried out with a loud voice, He said, 'Father, into Your hands I commit My spirit.' Having said this, He breathed His last."* *Luke 23: 46 (NKJV)* **Note:** neither Stephen nor Jesus committed their souls to God, only their spirits. The spirit is kept safely by the Lord in some place and manner that we don't understand or have knowledge of until after our resurrection.

Suicide and Christian Beliefs

After the Lord's spirit went back to Heaven, to be with His Father, our God and Creator, the Lord's body/soul went back into the grave. There the body/soul, although still alive in God's eyes, slept and was conscious of nothing at all; at least, until God called Him forth and returned His spirit to Him to be united with His new heavenly body. So, at resurrection time, these elements of our being will be reunited as one whole being again. The only difference is that we will receive a body which will be indestructible and everlasting. There is unity in the body of Christ. *"But to each one of us grace has been given as Christ apportioned it. This is why it says: 'When He ascended on high, He led captives in His train and gave gifts to men.' What does 'He ascended' mean except that He also descended to the lower, earthly regions: He who descended is the very one who ascended higher than all the heavens, in order to fill the whole universe." Ephesians 4: 7-10 (NIV)*

GUESS WHO?

Suicide and Christian Beliefs

When some well-meaning minister, pastor or lay person, or even someone who is considered a terrific Christian, tries to tell you that when you die your spirit goes directly to Heaven to be with God, they are horribly wrong. If this were the case then there would be no need of Christ's death on the Cross at Calvary. He would not have had to die for anyone, sin or not. Why! Because there would be no example to be made for saving our us, nor any slate to be cleaned and cleansed, no blood needed to be shed, no death necessary for salvation and no need for a resurrection and judgment. It's just one quick trip to Heaven without the angels checking for our names in the Book of Life. How wonderful to skip all that and go directly to Heaven. Who are they kidding, only themselves. Think about it! Come on! What is there to think about? Two and two makes four, it always will, not one plus zero.

Suicide and Christian Beliefs

In terms of death and life, God will judge us as we have lived. In cases of suicide, He will also judge victims as they have interrupted His plan for them and died ahead of schedule. I, for one, would not want to be accused of interrupting God's schedule. Self-induced murder is very offensive to God. It speaks volumes to the Lord and tells Him there no longer existed any respect for His Gift of Life. We have God's promise that He will judge us sternly for our sins and iniquities from which we have never repented, nor for which we have never requested His forgiveness. *"Do your best to present yourself to God as one approved, a workman who does not need to be ashamed and who correctly handles the word of truth. . .God's solid foundation stands firm, sealed with this inscription; 'The Lord knows those who are His,' and 'Everyone who confesses the name of the Lord must turn away from wickedness."* 2 Timothy 2: 15, 19 (NIV) and *"Since the children have flesh and blood, He too shared in their humanity so that by His death He might destroy him who holds the power of death, that is, the devil, and free those who all their lives were held in slavery by their fear of death."* Hebrews 2: 14-15 (NIV)

There is no acceptable escape from the life of this world which is acceptable to God, other than by the means He provides to us. It is the order of a sovereign and organized God that tells us when to live and when to die. We are neither the architects, nor are we the orchestrators of our own lives, that right is reserved for God. It is by the power of the Lord and by doing His Will and not rejecting the gifts which He has given us, that we fulfill His purposes and our mission which He alone has dictated and determined. God has both the control and the power. Anything we do which is contrary to His Will, is not acceptable to the Lord. We must become a workman who doesn't need to be ashamed in the presence of God, whether while we live on Earth or eventually reside in Heaven, or in the New Jerusalem. Read my book, *Recognizing His Presence and Knowing His Perspective*, it about knowing God is always with you, viewing you with clear eyes. *". . .lo, I am with you always, even unto the end of the world." Matthew 28:20 (KJV)*

OH, MY! YES, THERE IT IS, I SEE YOUR NAME!
IT'S WRITTEN CLEARLY IN THE LAMB'S BOOK OF LIFE!

Suicide and Christian Beliefs

Suicide undermines the Lord's desires, plans and love for us. Therefore, we fail at our God-appointed mission when we cut short our road to glory and everlasting life with Christ. We may determine that the dead are now in Jesus Christ's keeping: those who fulfilled their saintly purposes will be resurrected to a life of glory, some receiving special crowns for their work on the Earth; but the wicked will remain in the grave until they are awakened and called by God to be judged. Woe to the wicked! Woe to those of us that believe some other gospel or story, or are convinced that grace covers all aspects of life without considering all of the warning scriptures.

Is your name written in the Book of Life?

Nobody can afford to put his or her life on the line by walking around inside some plastic bubble coated with infallible grace. Read God's Scriptures and see what Jesus warned us about: we can lose

Suicide and Christian Beliefs

His precious grace and forfeit our lives because we are ignorant of Scripture. Everything comes with a price, just as Jesus Christ had to pay a price for our lives. He warned us continually of what not to do and what to beware of, does this ring any bells? Once saved, always saved! I don't think so! Nice little statement but it's as erroneous as saying, "When I die, I am going directly to Heaven." Sorry, but we've been there already.

There are questions of various sorts which should be discussed that deal with the disposition of people who have died in Christ. **For example:** Do the saved saints, or born again Christian, go directly to Heaven? We are told that some souls have already gone to Heaven to be with God. *"When He opened the fifth seal, I saw under the altar the souls of those who had been slain for the word of God and for the testimony which they held." Revelation 6: 9* and *"Then another angel, having a golden censer, came and stood at the altar. He was given much incense, that he should offer it with the prayers of all the saints upon the golden altar which was before the throne." Revelation 8: 3 (NKJV)* These are saints that will go to Heaven prior to the Second Advent of our Lord Jesus Christ. They are the martyrs that will be in Heaven and they will be conscious, alive in the spirit but; but perhaps, to only the degree to which God permits a measure of awareness to occur to them. Maybe they are fully functional and aware of God's every move. It doesn't really matter. What matters is that they are in Heaven with the Lord and sooner or later, at God's appointed time, they will be fully transformed alive in their totally transformed bodies. These spirits are probably the saints who have laid down their lives while delivering the Gospel of Christ; those martyrs of Christianity who died willingly to proclaim the magnificence, glory and authority of God Almighty. In *2 Corinthians 5: 6-8* Scripture speaks to us about being absent in the flesh, yet being home with God.

Christians like to state these scriptures as such: when we are no longer "living" in our bodies, we will be "living" in God's presence. These scriptures do not claim, in any sensible way, that we suffer death, give up our earthly lives, and go directly to Heaven – even Jesus Christ, our Lord, stayed out of Heaven for 40 days!!! And we will not go directly to Heaven when we die, we will lay inert in our graces until commanded or called by God to arise and be judged. There is no fast track to Heaven between death and resurrection. The body/soul sleeps, we are not immediately rewarded, nor are we wickedly tortured. Such is not the way of a loving and merciful God. He has a very organized plan of transition for each of us – the good and the bad.

Suicide and Christian Beliefs

Prior to the First Resurrection, when saints who are raised by God come alive again, I note that certain souls have already been taken into the presence of God (when Christ was raised, so were an unknown number of saints; it has been estimated that more than 500 graves were opened and emptied without human resolve); perhaps these resurrected souls were Old Testament prophets or individuals God found worthy of resurrection and entrance into Heaven. Nobody knows for sure and I can only speculate as to who those individuals would be. So, if the First Resurrection occurs with the return of Christ to the Earth, then what resurrection occurred prior to the *Holy Bible's* First Resurrection? All I can be absolutely sure of is that there was some kind of a general resurrection of dead souls that were reunited with their spirits from Heaven and are there now with God.

"And I saw thrones, and they sat on them and judgment was committed to them. Then I saw the souls of those who had been beheaded for their witness to Jesus and for the Word of God, who had not worshipped the beast of his image, and had not received his mark on their foreheads or on their hands. And they lived and reigned with Christ for a thousand years. But the rest of the dead did not live again until the thousand years were finished. This is the first resurrection. Blessed and holy is

he who has part in the first resurrection. Over such the second death has no power. . ."
Revelation 20: 4-6 (NKJV)

God is the god of the living and not the god of the dead, as Jesus told us in *the twenty-second chapter of Mathew, verse thirty-two.* God will judge us, of that we can be certain. *"They give an account to Him who is ready to judge the living and the dead. For this reason the gospel was preached also to those who are dead, that they might be judged according to men in the flesh, but live according to God in the spirit."* *1 Peter 4: 5-6 (NKJV)*

Although the people we have known and have died, are considered to us to be in a death state, in the sense that we understand death, the bodies/souls of those individuals are actually resting in solitude in the grave, both wicked and dead. We stress and reiterate this point several times so that it cannot be missed or overlooked. This is important. These souls are still alive to God; that is why they are a "soul". **Don't forget:** we, as human beings, are composed of these parts: body/soul and spirit. At the last trumpet, those who are alive to God, although they are dead in their graves to us, will respond to God's voice, as will those living saints whom God has chosen to be with Him. The *Holy Bible* tells, in Paul's words, *"But let me tell you a* *wonderful secret God has revealed to us. Not all of us will die, but we will all be transformed. It will happen in a moment, in the blinking of an eye, when the last trumpet is blown. For when the trumpet sound, the Christians who have died will be raised with transformed bodies, and then we who are living will be transformed so that we will never die. For our perishable earthly bodies must be transformed into heavenly bodies that will never die."* 1 Corinthians 15: 51-53 (NLT) and *"Our bodies now disappoint us, but when they are raised, they will be full of glory. They are weak now, but when they are raised, they will be full of power. They are natural human bodies now, but when they are raised, they will be spiritual bodies. For just as there are natural bodies, so also there are spiritual bodies."* 1 Corinthians 15: 43-44 (NLT) and *"For we will not be spirits without bodies, but we will put on new heavenly bodies."* 2 Corinthians 5: 3 (NLT)

A BODY RISING AT THE SOUND OF THE TRUMPET! WILL JESUS
BE CALLING YOU?

Suicide and Christian Beliefs

So often people say how Scripture is so difficult to understand and so full of contradictions that everything can be argued evenly from one side or another. This is the only case when people that are not enlightened by the Holy Spirit attempt to pit their intelligence against those that have been blessed with a clear vision from God. Those that do not understand the disposition of death and dying, living and being translated into Heaven, still have that veil of restraint held over their eyes. When an individual has allowed God to enter into His or Her heart, God's supernatural power through the Holy Spirit jumps into action begins to reveal many wonderful messages to God's new saint.

Death is a subject that most people do not understand, and the majority of folks today hold to old notions of what they were taught as a child.

Suicide and Christian Beliefs

Others that do not understand have their own excuses for such ignorance. The truth is found in the *Holy Bible* and it can only be learned by picking it up, reading it, studying, closely examining its passages and meditating on what you read. Pray for guidance and wisdom to discern those passages. The Bereans eagerly read and studied God's Word daily. *". . .in that they received the word with all readiness, and searched the Scriptures daily to find out whether these things were so." Acts 17: 11 (NIV)* The truth of God's Word can only be learned by praying about the scripture that is read and having given one's life totally over to Jesus Christ. Unbelievers will never come to grips with biblical truth because they are light years away in their understanding of what God's holy words say. If you feed a Koala a rich diet beyond what it is use to consuming, it will choke on the delicacies it tried to digest. So do unrepentant sinners and people that do not know God in the fullest sense, as does the most elementary and discerning new Christian.

HELL IS WAITING FOR YOU MY FRIEND. IF YOU WON'T REPENT AND CONFESS YOUR TERRIBLE SINS, AND IF YOU REFUSE GOD'S FORGIVENESS, THEN HELL IS WAITING FOR YOU. YOUR PLACE IS SAVED IN THE OVEN! TEE! HEE! COME BAKE WITH US!!!

Suicide and Christian Beliefs

The wicked have absolutely no use for God's Word and reject it; they see it as a hindrance in their lives and that the *Holy Bible* is fable or myth and stultifies their profane behaviors. Christians living outside God's Will and laws, that are not being obedient to His dictates, are blinded to all sensibility due to their own refusal to allow God to have control of their lives – so they believe only what they want and choose to believe – mostly nonsense.

THE DARK UNDERWORLD.

Suicide and Christian Beliefs

JUST A LITTLE MORE HELL TO GET YOU THINKING AGAIN.

Christians should know that souls sleep in the security of God. If they do not know that, then it is essential that they pick up their *Holy Bibles* and start reading. God wants us to be prepared for His Kingdom. We cannot enter into that Kingdom as ignorant individuals that know nothing of His ways. Do you go to a job interview without researching the company to which you are applying for a job? If you do, you are highly remiss; you should know what you are getting into and with whom you may be associating; not to mention what they stand for and sell. Every business sells something. Life is a sales job – we are always selling ourselves, or should be always selling ourselves, in one way or another. Why? To gain some measure of results that is important to he or she that is selling. And, you need to discover and learn the purpose/s of that organization.

So it is the same with the Lord, He wants us to study His Word and become strong in its power. We must seek God's Will for us. People join cults because they haven't prepared themselves with any proper research or inspection of what a cult stands for and believes. They become hypnotized with the trappings of what appeals to their initial senses and feelings. If it tastes good, it must be good. It doesn't matter that the ingredients will eventually rot one's insides. Not knowing or understanding God's Word is a lot like sauntering through life without a hint of what it's all about. It amazes me how many people I meet, that live, from day-to-day, without the knowledge or love of the Creator in their heart. They suffer from any number of bad things happening to them and blame God, the God whom they do not know; that same God Who has never really been accepted into their lives, but yet is now an invisible and terribly misunderstood scapegoat. That's like blaming your earthly father for something that has occurred in your life, when you haven't seen him or been in communication with him for decades. How is he to blame for your problems? Can you explain that kind of thinking outside of generational curses which we can end.

Suicide and Christian Beliefs

**JUST WHAT ARE THEY THINKING?
OR ARE THEY?**

It's hard to fathom the depth of the thinking that some juries have when they agreed with some person that pushes the blame of their own actions upon a living or deceased parent. (This is much different than generational curses being passed on.) It's shameful while openly showing their lack of intelligent reasoning. You bet I am biased, as a Christian I cannot afford not to be unprepared and unknowledgeable. So, these lost folks misplace the blame; they only see God as some entity that is interested in them being unsuccessful, or sick, or a poor helpless victim. They are clueless – can you see how a suicide victim can put together a negative picture of his or her life, based on some of these misguided and ignorant assumptions? Those that commit suicide are clueless – clueless to God's mercy, forgiveness, and loving promise to provide them with refuge, comfort, and salvation. They only need to listen and obey. That clueless statement may be harsh, but it is factual. If they'd had a clue or two, they never would have succumbed to taking their own life. Had they truly known God and had a personal relationship with Him, He would not have allowed them to kill themselves. No relationship, no God, no clue, no life. . .and this scenario goes on. Without belief in God, we are doomed. This is not what God wants for us. *"For God so loved the world that He gave His only begotten Son, that whoever believes in Him shall not perish but have everlasting life." John 3: 16 (NIV)*

YES, JESUS CHRIST DID GIVE HIS LIFE FOR YOU. WHAT WILL YOU DO FOR HIM? WILL YOU ACCEPT HIS GIFT OF LIFE? IS SALVATION IN YOUR FUTURE, OR NOT?

Suicide and Christian Beliefs

Accidental suicides also fall into this category. If a person fools around with their own life in a careless manner, thinking that they want to end it all, and somehow, by accident, they do. . .well, that counts as a suicide. A very ungrateful and neglectful life has been lost at a price that will exact punishment forever. Yes, they are a candidate for the second death. Read on! However, if you only have a gracist's viewpoint, then you'll assume that person will be spared because of God's mercy, and it doesn't matter if he or she was saved or not – they're covered by mercy and grace. I don't think so! Go back and re-read the verses already presented to you for your information and knowledge. Don't be an ignorant *putz*!

SORRY, BUT I JUST CANNOT SEEM TO GIVE YOU TOO MANY GLIMPSES OF HELL. I HOPE THE SHOE DOESN'T FIT!

Suicide and Christian Beliefs

We have determined that all souls, including the wicked and evil, while dead will rest in the security of Christ, although this is while they are lying in the grave. Christ told us that, *If anyone keeps My word he shall never taste death."* John 8:51 (NKJV) Paul told us that King David's heart rejoiced joyously concerning the Lord, he had said in the New Testament, *". . .Moreover my flesh also will rest in hope. For You (GOD) will not leave my soul in Hades, nor will You (GOD) allow your Holy One to see corruption."* Acts 2: 26-27 (NKJV) Job had several things to say about dying, about which he was troubled and worried. *"But man dies and is laid away; indeed he breathes his last and where is he? So man lies down and does not rise. Till the heavens are no more, they will not awake nor be roused from their sleep. . .Oh, that You would hide me in the grave, that You would conceal me until your wrath is past, that You would appoint me a set time, and remember me. . .if a man dies, shall he live again?. . .you shall call, and I will answer You. . ."* Job 14: 10, 12-15 (NKJV)

It appears that Job will remain in the grave until after God's wrath and the plagues have been completed. See **Revelation 15: 1** Job knew that he would be dead in the grave but alive in God, so that the Lord would call him back to life when the appointed time arrives. Then he would receive his immortal transformed body. Our new bodies will be like those of the angels. So will the new body of Job. *"For in the resurrection they neither marry nor are given in marriage, but are like angels of God in Heaven." Matthew 22:30 (NKJV)*

Apparently we will need this new heavenly and indestructible body, as those of the angels, so we may live in the fullness of life as God has originally intended. So our resurrection body is a must, to be considered totally alive. Jesus told us concerning the resurrection of the dead, *". . .nor can they die anymore, for they are equal to the angels and are sons of God, being sons of the resurrection" Luke 20:36 (NKJV)* King David said, *"And I, in righteousness will see Your face; when I awake, I will be satisfied with seeing Your likeness." Psalm 17:15 (NIV)* David understood that when we receive our new bodies, we will be in the likeness of God, our Creator, and that our bodies would be like those of angels. The Apostle Paul further ensured us of that truth when he said, *"But our citizenship is in Heaven. And we eagerly await a Savior from there, the Lord Jesus Christ, who, by the power that enables Him to bring everything under His control, will transform our lowly bodies so that they will be like His glorious body." Philippians 3: 20-21 (NIV)*

Suicide and Christian Beliefs

THE FIRST RESURRECTION. WILL YOU BE RESURRECTED WHEN THE TRUMPET SOUNDS AND CHRIST CALLS YOUR NAME?

At the First Resurrection, we can safely deduce that our spirits from Heaven will be linked back up with our souls from the grave to form our new angelic spiritual body. This is a gift from God.

On the other hand, those wicked in God's sight, the evil ones of all past ages, those unsaved, and those that are lost in the grave from suicide, will be dealt with in a completely different manner. David, after starting, gets to the part of his song that deals with death and punishment. He says, *". . .How long will your wrath burn like fire? Remember how fleeting is my life. For what futility you have created all men! What man can live and not see death, or save himself from the power of the grave?" Psalm 89: 46-48 (NIV)* When God judges all of the dead, at the end of the Millennium (the 1,000 years that occurs following the Second Coming of Christ) at His Great White Throne Judgment, the wicked will suffer God's wrath during the Second Death, to which they will be assigned in exist in torment forever. The Second Death is the lake of fire and brimstone which is eternal punishment. **Remember:** this occurs after the Second Resurrection. But after the First Resurrection, when Christ returns, the following is said of the evil and wicked dead, *". . .This is the first resurrection. The rest of the dead did not come back to life until the thousand years had ended. Blessed and holy are those who share in the first resurrections. For them the second death holds no power. . ." Revelation20: 5-6 (NLT)* Hallelujah! Praise the name of the Lord! Scripture then says that the wicked will be cast into the lake of fire that burns with sulfur and those wicked and unrepentant souls will join Satan, the beast (antichrist), and the false prophet, and be tormented day and night forever and ever.

Yes, the final judgment of mankind is totally in God's hands, and all those lost souls and sinners that never repented their sins and rejected the Lord Jesus Christ as their Redeemer and Savior, will be in deep trouble, or like I used to say when I lived in Japan, "in deep *itai*" which means "hurts". The *Holy Bible* says the following: *"Then I saw a great white throne and Him who sat on it, from whose face the earth and the heaven fled away. And there was found no place for them. And I saw the dead, small and great standing before God, and books were opened. And another book was opened, which is the Book of Life. And the dead were judged according to their works, by the things which were written the books. The Sea gave up the dead who were in it, and Death and Hades delivered up the dead who were in them. And they were judged, each one according to his works. Then Death and Hades were cast into the lake of fire. This is the second death. And anyone not found written in the Book of Life was cast into the lake of fire." Revelation 20: 11-15 (NKJV)* This place of the Second Death is where eternal torment and separation from God exists. There is no going back, it is too late; and it is too late for repenting and asking for forgiveness. This is a place of death and destruction, not you get a second chance to make an acceptance of Christ's gift of life.

In suicide cases, the victims have entered into a place of death, not a place of life. Suicide victims will not have their names read from the Book of Life because there will be no entries for suicide cases, as they no longer exist now, their names will no longer exist in the Book of Life because they managed to have it erased. "If" it once appeared there, it has now disappeared. When a suicide victim takes his or her own life, he or she removes his or her own name from God's Book of Life.

HAS YOUR NAME ALREADY BEEN WRITTEN INTO THE LAMB'S BOOK OF LIFE? OR, NOT?

This is and has always been a personal choice of all suicide victims; leastwise, those that thought they knew God. Their ignorance or misunderstanding of God's love, mercy, and forgiveness is no excuse, nor will God consider it a forgivable offense. Based on the plethora of information contained in the *Holy Bible*, we believe that even those that suffer so-called mental disorders or sicknesses will also be grouped into the camp of those souls that will be lost and suffer forever. They were not born with a hatred of God, nor were they born with a proclivity to take their own life. . .that was learned and acquired by their earthly experiences and associations with evil and ungodly things, practices and/or people. It was a personal choice of how they lived and eventually died. Like homosexuality, it is a personal choice for one reason or another, but this choice was not influenced by God, because such behavior is appalling to the Lord and detestable to His sight, and Scripture promises they will not inherit the Kingdom of Heaven. *"The acts of the sinful nature are obvious: sexual immorality, impurity and debauchery." Galatians 5:19*

God tells the prophet Daniel the horrible news awaiting those who will be judged without a record worthy of salvation. God said, *". . .but at that time every one of your people whose name is written in the book will be rescued. Many of those whose bodies lie dead and buried will rise up, some to everlasting life and some to shame and everlasting contempt." Daniel 12: 1-2 (NLT)* and Jesus told us that, *"If your hand causes you to sin, cut it off. It is better to enter Heaven with only one hand than*

Suicide and Christian Beliefs

to go into the unquenchable fires of hell with two hands. If your foot causes you to sin, cut it off. It is better to enter Heaven with only one foot than to be thrown into hell with two feet. . .where the worm never dies and the fire never goes out." *Mark 9:43-46, 47 (NLT)* If your name does not appear in the Book of Life, at the time of the Second Death, you'll understand the punishment that will come your way. At this time, the first death will be abolished forever, which means your old body/soul which has been dead and rested, will now be destroyed forever in the lake of fire. Death and Hades will be thrown into this lake of fire and will be no more. Are you absent from the Book of Life?

As perhaps God views His human creations as extremely valuable, such could be His thinking for keeping these souls alive in the sense that they will never be destroyed completely. If they had no value to God, my guess is that He would annihilate and obliterate them totally, with no remaining existence for them at all. Existing in torment, in the lake of fire is, perhaps, God's way of retaining the essence of these created souls without giving them any perks. They deserve what they will get; they earned it by what they did or did not do, according to the Book of Life. Which is better? To be totally eliminated without any existence, or to live forever in a lake of fire, never to escape but to know that you are there because you rejected God and His Son? To live with that thought forever would be extreme punishment, cursing oneself during every second of torture and suffering. I think it's a kind of "gotcha." Tough bananas to all dimwits and nincompoops.

If I take the spirit, as considered as such in the New Testament, that would mean our mental disposition or attitude, then one of two things will happen to it. **One:** we are saved Christians, then our spirit has been sent back from God to meet with our resting/sleeping souls which will be revived and be transformed into a glorious Christ-like and angelic body. **Two:** if we have been wicked, then our attitude was one of rebellion and therefore, it will always be tormented as Satan (who was a literal being created by God – a spirit creature) will be tormented in the Second Death in the lake of fire. Satan will be destroyed as will all wicked souls, but Satan and his minions will all become ashes.

Any soul which is not considered to be part of God's Kingdom and the Lord's Holy family is considered to be unsaved and wicked. Their fate is a direct result of how they spent their lives and what kind of beliefs and attitudes they had. Were they in agreement with Christ and part of His saintly family or were they opposed to Jesus, by being lost and rebellious? Their final outcome is clear. The Second Death leaves little speculation as to what God has is mind for all those who have rebelled against Him and His purposes. That rebellion equates to: final annihilation, separation, and damnation – that sounds about right. As a Christian, I believe you would agree. If you are not a Christian, it is time to board the "eternal life train" (the tickets are freely given) and get Jesus in your heart today. It is interesting to note that the wicked have been judged by their deeds, where Christians are judged not be deeds but by their loving faith.

IS THIS THE ENTRANCE YOU WANT TO FIND AT THE DOORWAY TO YOUR NEW AFTER LIFE HOME? OR WOULD YOU LIKE TO FIND SOMETHING BEYOND DESCRIPTION THAT "BEAUTIFUL" DOESN'T EVEN BEGIN TO DEFINE?

Suicide and Christian Beliefs

Although the thought may be unbearable, it nevertheless is a reality and it is further proven in God's Word, just how rejecters of God's Word, and lost individuals will perish and suffer. They will suffer as Satan will suffer because they are recognized as being part of his unholy camp. Their suffering is based on their convictions, actions, behaviors, deeds, or lack of good deeds, beliefs, and in failing to love and accept God's beloved Son, Jesus Christ. This is what God says, *". . .I banished you from the mountain of God. I expelled you, O mighty guardian, from your place among the stones of fire. Your heart was filled with pride because of all your beauty. You corrupted your wisdom for the sake of your splendor. So I threw you to earth and exposed you to the curious gaze of kings. You defiled your sanctuaries with your many sins and your dishonest trade. So I brought fire from within you, and it consumed you. I let it burn you to ashes on the ground in the sight of all who were watching. All who knew you are appalled at your fate. You have come to a terrible end, and you are no more." Ezekiel 29: 16-19 (NLT)*

As Satan will be expelled and destroyed, ending up as ashes, so may all those wicked souls resting, find utter torment. They will be resurrected to find their names missing in God's Book of Life. They will faint with agony over their shortcomings and suffer humility shame and scorn, and be tossed into the lake of fire. Bottom line, where the proverbial rubber meets the road, there is nothing else for them and the worst part is that they chose their own path. They followed their own plan. They have nobody to blame but themselves and they have eternal torment forever during which to think about their errors. Their destiny was self-drafted, a foolish plan of contempt for God. Unfortunately, I believe suicide victims fall into this horrible class of tainted folks. There is no sidestepping the issues which God has with these lost souls. But, there is the temporary respite they get from suffering, as they sleep in the grave.

Suicide is only one form of death; it is only one form of bailing out on life; it is only one way to ruin the plans that God has carefully set in motion for one of His own beloved and precious beings. For any of us to take God's sovereign rights into his or her own hands, and declare that they are God, whether by spoken word or by mental thought, is a travesty of His wonderful gifts of love and life. The truth of the matter is that we are imperfect and make tragic mistakes, but the tragedy of giving our life away to a second-rate god named Lucifer, is even more abhorrent and unacceptable; it is an act of switching gods – from the best to the worst. It is an insult to God our Master and Creator; it is saying that He has no right to us, so we will give our life to Satan, the lying angel of the grave.

If we live for Christ, then we should die for Christ; but if we have no relationship with the Lord, then we will surely die and suffer the consequences. Will your name be in the Book of Life? Do you understand that suicide is a completely selfish act and deserving of death for all eternity? It is not a sacrifice that some brave men or women do for the saving of many lives by giving their own. As Christ said, *"Greater love has no one than this, that he lay down his life for his friends." John 15:13 (NIV)* This is an explanation for the difference between selfish suicide and unselfish sacrifice. I hope you see the difference. Please see the difference! Try hard to visualize it in your mind! It's your life today, tomorrow, and forever.

Alternative Considerations and Beliefs

There are other ideas about the disposition of the soul and spirit after death. Although a considerable amount of Christians believe that when a suicide occurs, the victim's soul/body will be quickly damned for all eternity, lying unconscious in the grave until resurrected for the Great White Throne Judgment, others don't believe that happens. There are other opinions which are weakly based on some Scripture and directed more by the heart than at the head. These personal stances declare that once a person has accepted the Lord as their personal Savior, he or she will be saved forever and cannot lose their salvation. If I agreed to this position or even gave it an iota of credibility, I would be sanctioning the act of suicide by vicariously saying that a saved Christian could commit suicide, for one reason or another. Like getting to Heaven immediately by skipping the resurrection and judgment, forgetting this world and its troubles, yet going on to be with the Lord, baring no holds.

no negative thoughts allowed

Suicide and Christian Beliefs

BAD THINKING – VERY BAD THINKING!!!

This warped thinking and venal egocentric action would eliminate the natural processes of living and dying and fulfilling God's plan, for one's life, by interfering with it and taking the suicidal path and matters into one's hands. I will not punch such a ticket for someone considering suicide; that is, for anyone to commit suicide because they think God will take them into Heaven no matter what they door whether they think they've been saved, or have not been saved! I just don't think it happens that way, and the more I read the Scriptures and study what they have to say, the more warning scriptures that pop up in front of me. Is there a message here?

God has not hit me over the head and said, "Say this or that." Such has not happened and I don't believe it will. According to most published Christian authors I know, and I am acquainted with many dozens of them, God is too busy giving them enlightenment and direction. It would be nice if He distinctly told me something solid, but He hasn't. What I write is based on what He has provided me in His Holy Word and by removing any veil or fog from my eyes, so I can discern His Word with skill and accuracy; however, there will be those that will argue that fact. Why?

BECAUSE THEY WILL CLAIM TO HAVE THE EDGE "FOR THE INSIDE TRACK TO GOD," OR HAVE CONTROL OVER THE CORNER OF UNDERSTANDING FOR THE JESUS MARKET.

Do you get this? Do you see the picture? If not, then go along with me on this issue, okay? I pray for inspiration along these lines, I do not claim to have two-way conversations with God. He likes me I am sure, and He loves me, but I haven't had any long or short talks with Him on my telephone. UPS® does not deliver any holy packages of information from the Lord. So with me, I guess it's really a prayer, study, read, evaluate, meditate, and write approach. I do pray that He gives me insight as to the findings I present, and I ask Him to prevent me from writing or publishing anything that would be blasphemous or inaccurate, as it would be in contradiction to His Word and purposes. All I ask from god is increase knowledge, wisdom, discernment and understanding of His Word and desires for me. Nothing else but god health is desired or expected, and what I do get is a bonus.

Now, once again, think about that scenario of God taking a suicide victim to Heaven because once, and maybe a very long time ago, when the person thought they knew God, and believed that He would forego everything else in their life and take them directly to Heaven. It's done that way anyhow – we already determined that. So, do you really think that a person would consider taking his or her own life because they think it is a fast track to Heaven? Unfortunately, I believe that truly happens very frequently. I believe that many Christians are naïve enough to believe those people have gone to Heaven or will go to Heaven. Where does it say that in the *Holy Bible?* Don't give me two or three verses you think that supports such thinking, give me some concrete discourse and sensible biblical proof. Don't waste your time! You'll be back to the "once saved, always saved" mental-midget-mind set.

Trust me, if God allowed every Christian suicide victim to go directly to Heaven, it would pervert His Scriptures, change their meaning, and say it was okay to wreck His plans for that person. There would also be a significant number of suffering and troubled Christians who wouldn't think twice about suicide as a way out. As long as they were sure that they would be joining Christ in Heaven. This position or belief is neither sound, nor solid; it is ignorant and absurd. Besides, it would leave a wide door open for especially weak-minded, weak-hearted, and/or weak-willed individuals to walk through. Such folks are looking for permission to do away with themselves and I am not giving that permission. Is your church or pastor giving that permission, or avoiding it like a plague because of the inability to make a biblical stand?

Shame on such people, they need some *Holy Bible* education and spiritual direction lessons. Be good to them and tell them so, before they have a chance to pass out suicide tickets. Even God with all His infinite mercy doesn't support this attitude or claim. If you doubt that, read on, and keep in mind that final cure for all: the Great White Throne Judgment.

If a person claims to have accepted Jesus Christ as their personal Savior and Redeemer, but keeps on doing what they have always done, sinning in the same manner, without making changes, then they have not truly believed what they openly professed and for that which they went through the motions. Their personal claim has been a sham. There are no gray areas with God. Suicide is not a gray area. People like these I have just mentioned say one thing, but do another.

When one accepts Christ into his or her heart, this act of turning one's life over to Jesus should be done in love and reverence, and in belief, with faith and hope of a better existence. The Holy Spirit's power, from the supernatural intervention and spiritual extension of God, then infuses one's body and the saved person begins to believe and act accordingly. They walk in obedience to God's way and little-by-little, they begin changing their lives to match the walk of Jesus Christ. They do not betray God unless they are unsaved and only they and God know the real answer to that question. This can be puzzling and perplexing. You are not changed *per*

Suicide and Christian Beliefs

se, but you have been exchanged for your Christ life, as He now dwells inside of you.

What about a saved person, or let's say a person who "claims to be saved," goes out and kills fifteen people, after they have committed their life to Christ; they could have committed their life to the Lord ten years ago, three weeks ago, two years and four months ago, and so on, but that doesn't matter. The time element is not important. What is most ultimately important is that they killed fifteen people. A truly saved individual, one who has accepted Jesus Christ with all their heart, spiritual awareness, and conviction, does not commit such an act. Argue about it all you may want to, but only those who have not really accepted Christ one hundred percent, as their own personal Savior, would be able to perpetrate such a horrible crime.

**WHO COULD BE SAVED AND THEN BEHEAD SOMEONE?
I'LL TELL YOU WHO – A LIAR!**

Suicide and Christian Beliefs

People who commit a multitude of murders are usually psychopaths and never meant to allow Christ into their heart to begin with, because their continuous obsessed need for control and self-absorbed warped personality disorder has never permitted anyone or anything to share their mental space, except for a satanic force. When a person is saved, they receive the power and indwelling of God's Holy Spirit which then directs, counsels, intercedes, and keeps the saved person from doing or behaving in an anti-God fashion. That is how the power of God's Holy Spirit works inside of us. *"He who does not love Me does not keep My words; and the word which you hear is not Mine but the Father's who sent Me." John 14: 24 (NKJV)* Who or what do you suppose is delivering those words? Scripture tells us that we have that guarantee of God's love and protection, by receiving the power of the Holy Spirit in our lives. *". . .and He will give you another Helper, that He may abide with you forever – the spirit of truth, whom the world cannot receive, because it neither sees Him nor knows Him; but you know Him, for He dwells with you and will be in you." John 14: 16-17 (NKJV)*

Suicide and Christian Beliefs

GOD'S SPIRITUAL ESSENCE: HIS SUPERNATURAL POWER VISUALIZED AS A REACHING HAND.

I'll tell you what, that is some powerful stuff my friend. Focus on the Spirit and the Spirit will guide you in God's ways. Focus on something bad, like suicide, and you'll probably end up serving the wrong god. Yes, we already covered that ground, we've been there, but if you are considering suicide, then I'll say it ten or twenty more times if that is what it takes to prevent you or someone from taking their own life. Focus on some God-thing, not on suicide. When a person focuses on something, they usually make it happen; leastwise, their chances of being successful (at achieving what they are focusing on) are considerably better. Their percentages are higher, much higher.

Suicide and Christian Beliefs

Also, some people recant their salvation vows while others just fall away and could care less about their promise/s to God. In fact, they take back their holy vows and forsake the Lord. There are people that do regret giving their lives to Christ and they totally turn their back on His salvation. They may be raised a Christian and become a Muslim. That is serving a different god. So, do you still consider them saved? If you said, "yes," get real! They are serving another god, not Jesus Christ. The Lord is pretty clear about not having other gods before Him. So, don't tell me, "once saved, always saved". Myopic thinking like that is imprudent and immature. In fact, it could get someone to commit suicide without thinking twice about anything else.

People curse God and accuse Him of all kinds of things which they personally caused to happen in their own lives. They no longer love or want God and they give Him back their once coveted and received salvation, as it has become totally worthless to them. Sounds bad, I know, but there are many that fall away, or even use Jesus as a swinging gate when it's convenient for them to do so. I believe salvation no longer wanted by them, because they never committed all the way in their hearts and mind. God knows, they know, but I don't know, so I cannot, nor will I personally judge them. I will only theorize and guess. God will adequately handle those cases. Let's move on!

There are saved Christians that are not going to stop sinning, yet it does mean they are forgiven by the grace of the Lord. Christ's sacrifice washed away our sins. My son use to pray for forgiveness before he commit a sin, I heard him, as he prayed out loud. Well, as silly as it seems, he was forgiven as soon as he transgressed against God. That is what grace is all about. It is an unconditional love gift from Jesus. But people may accept a gift with one face, because it is "politically correct" to do so in front of another, yet behind his or her back they choke on the gift because they don't truly like it. This happens all the time and it happens with people who do not wholeheartedly allow Christ to truly come into their life. It is called lip service, or looking good, but there is no real committal on their part to follow through with their public vow. Some people make that commitment to win the love and affection of some other person – by saving they've been saved. Oh dear! This is a horrible decision and actually has attached consequences of damnation attached to it. Don't lie to God, as only a fool would do this. *"A fool's mouth is his ruin, and his lips are a snare to his soul." Proverbs 18:7 (ESV)*

Christ paid the ultimate penalty for every person in the world. Our sins have been washed away forever; however, that is not our "free pass" to act unlike a Christian and commit acts which are truly sinful with our own prior and ongoing knowledge of such sinfulness. "Once saved, always saved" doesn't cover this kind of willful sin. So, can we lose our salvation? I believe certain people won't necessarily lose their salvation, because they cannot lose what they never had. Scripture does tell us that, *"Once people have seen the light, gotten a taste of heaven and been part of the work of the Holy Spirit, once they've personally experienced*

the sheer goodness of God's Word and the powers breaking in on us – if then they turn their back on it, washing their hands of the whole thing, well, they can't start over as if nothing happened. That's impossible! Why, they've re-crucified Jesus! They've repudiated him in public!" **Hebrews 6: 4-6 (The Message)**

One should not forget that numerous folks do not walk the Christian talk; they wear the cross around their neck while saying the right words, but Jesus is not in their minds. Faith Movement adherents and advocates preach gospels and understandings of gospels which are nothing like what the New Testament teaches us. They openly and defiantly blaspheme God by making a mockery out of His simple teachings about faith. They will not be forgiven this sin; Scripture says that, *"He who is not with Me is against Me, and he who does not gather with Me scatters abroad. Therefore I say to you, every sin and blasphemy will be forgiven men, but the blasphemy against the Spirit will not be forgiven men. Anyone who speaks a word against the Son of Man, it will be forgiven him; but whoever speaks against the Holy Spirit, it will not be forgiven him, either in this age or in the age to come."* **Matthew 12: 30-32 (NKJV)** And, yes, these blasphemers are many, too many to count!

Suicide and Christian Beliefs

Look at what Oprah Winfrey is touting to millions of ignorant listeners. Her New Age religion is trying desperately to redefine and destroy our traditional Christianity as we know it today. In an article titled *Moral Decline (no author listed)*, I found the following information:

"Did you know that the New Age religion she so tirelessly promotes is 100 percent opposed to the foundational beliefs of Christianity found in the Scriptures? Did you know that Oprah does not believe that Jesus came to die on the cross? Did you know that Oprah is teaching that there is no need for salvation? Did you know that Oprah is teaching that there is no heaven? Did you know that Oprah is teaching that there is no hell? Did you know that Oprah is teaching that you are God, she is God, "the light" is God and just about anything else you want to call God is God? Did you know that Oprah is teaching that the Bible is not any more important than a whole bunch of other "religious" books? Did you know that Oprah is teaching that killing babies through abortion is a good thing? Did you know that Oprah is teaching that homosexuality is wonderful, and that those who say homosexuality is sin are those who are evil?"

Go figure! These are words directly from the perverted heart, mind and mouth of Satan. This is about as blasphemous as a person can be, and the claims of this religion are some of the worse I've even encountered. These assertions fly directly in the face of our Christian God Jehovah and His Son Jesus Christ Whose prerogatives and declarations are divinely holy, not man-made and concocted out of inspired satanic thinking. We will see more of a trend for this during this time period in which we are living. Prophetically speaking, it's inevitable.

DO DROP IN, WE'VE LOTS OF JUNK FOR YOU TO BECOME ACQUAINTED WITH AND INCORPORATE INTO YOUR LIFE!

Suicide and Christian Beliefs

The list of these New Age religions is unbelievably long – Satan has been at work and he is in a hurry! I considered providing a list of these New Age travesties of thought, but the list would have included hundreds of names and their offshoots. Millions of souls are involved in these false religions and their beliefs are direct affronts to God. I truly pity those folks participating in the utter nonsense that they "all" believe. This list of names is so long that it has opened my eyes like never before as to the rapidity in growth taking place today. Satan is scurrying to overthrow a God that he never will be successful in doing; unfortunately, he is going to take many unsuspecting and foolish people with him.

IS THIS THE TYPE OF THING THAT YOU BECOME INVOLVED IN AND ENJOY, AND ALLOW INTO YOUR LIFE? TOO BAD, BECAUSE YOUR FUTURE IS VERY DIM AND WITHOUT THE REAL GOD OF LOVE TO COMFORT AND SAVE YOU. YOU ARE DOOMED!!!

Suicide and Christian Beliefs

There are people that use the Lord and His teachings by perverting the clear meanings of Scripture, while trying to make something out of them that doesn't exist. They claim to be saved, but they are dead in their works. If they had been saved and infused with the Holy Spirit, God's Protecting Force would not have tolerated such blasphemy to occur, nor permitted profane sacrilege and irreverent vile words to roll off their tongues. Only children and followers of a satanic persuasion, including atheists and agnostics, and those that worship another false god would slander and ridicule God and His Holy Word. This is complete Christian heresy. These are unforgivable sins. And if they were saved folks, God says, "that's just too bad," you are not forgiven child. For you have committed the big one! Saved or not, you won't escape judgment on this issue.

SO MANY PEOPLE BLASPHEMOUS AND DON'T KNOW IT!

Suicide and Christian Beliefs

Suicide is similar, in that it slaps God in the face by saying, without actually verbally espousing such, that God is not worthy to be trusted. *"Although I may have accepted you and been baptized, I really don't have the Holy Spirit in my body. He never entered when He learned I hadn't truly given You my life. Just look at how I act. Do I look like I'm trying to emulate Christ?"* This is the possible type of thinking that a potential suicide victim may roll over in his or her mind prior to killing himself or herself. Get real here!

GOD'S PRESENCE & PROTECTION

The indwelling of God's Holy Spirit is sent to be with us to protect us forever when we bring Christ Jesus into our hearts as our Savior. Did you read that part where it said, the Holy Spirit is sent to protect us? Sure God's power comforts and heals, but it protects us as well. If God sanctioned suicide, then He must be giving His Holy Spirit the day off and going against His own holy dictates, when someone chooses to forget his or her deal with God. That is, the part about really trusting and believing in Him. We must assume that either God is going against His own Word, or that the person committing suicide was not one hundred percent saved, only part way, and that is not enough; it is never enough. God wants a total commitment for eternity. It's all or it's nothing.

This life is short, and if suicide victims cannot give God a full commitment while they are here on Earth, for only a very limited time, then why should He trust them with an eternal commitment which is forever? This type of commitment does not get us into Heaven, or bring us anywhere close to God's Kingdom. That's a fact and a promise. Stupidity is not an excuse to God just like ignorance is no excuse in breaking the law – it is not as bliss as you might want it to be. He tells us that, *". . .the wisdom that comes from Heaven is first of all pure; then peace loving, considerate, submissive, full of mercy and good fruit, impartial and sincere. . ." James 3: 17 (NIV)* Therefore, it is quite possible that the suicide victim was not in class the day that lesson was taught: from hooky, to heartache, to eternal catastrophe. Lord forbid!

Suicide and Christian Beliefs

Getting to know God and His ways, through Christ, is a personal blessing which transcends earthly relationships, it is a relationship which grants us wisdom to know wicked from evil, good from bad, justice from injustice, and intelligence from stupidity and so forth. God-serving Christians don't purposely, did you get that, "don't purposely" do stupid things. If you have God on your side, His Holy Spirit in your body, the temple for your spirit and soul, and the Lord Jesus Christ in your heart and mind, then you won't do something inane. Committing suicide is one of those things. Truly saved people do not commit suicide. I hear excuses that the saved person was under the influence of drugs so they committed suicide. Sorry, that is an excuse that just doesn't fly! If the power of God's Holy Spirit was truly working in his or her life, then they wouldn't be on drugs. Quit making excuses for those people, their new god is the god of getting "high", not the god who is on High.

HER GOD IS IN HER COKED UP NOSTRILS, UP HER NOSE, AND IN HER FANTASYLAND!

Suicide and Christian Beliefs

Yes, we can be guilty of doing ignorant things, for one reason or another, but suicide quite often takes planning and thought; it's not always a spontaneous behavior. I am sorry to say, a truly saved person will not commit suicide.

IF A PERSON DOES COMMIT SUICIDE, I SUPPORT THE CLAIM THAT IT IS NOT THEIR FREE COUPON TO HEAVEN, BUT THAT THEY'VE ONLY STAMPED THEIR PASSPORT INTO OBLIVION.

Sometimes the truth hurts, so there it is, like it or not! There are no free passes. Committing suicide is not good, it is a bad deed performed without God's sanction and bad deeds are judged by the Lord at the Great White Throne Judgment. Men of faith that believe in Jesus and have made Him the core of their lives are not judged by deeds or words. They are judged for their faith and commitment. But only evil men and women are judged for their works and deeds. Suicide is an evil act not inspired by God, but brought about by demons and the god of darkness. *". . .The dead were judged according to what they had done, as recorded in the books." Revelation 20:12 (GN)*

There are those that use the saving grace of Christ as a hoax for their own evil needs, or they misuse His loving grace for their own wicked convenience.

Suicide and Christian Beliefs

These people put on a good act of being contrite and changed in their behaviors, attitudes and beliefs, but their true value system hasn't changed one iota. Oftentimes, we hear about prisoners that are inmates serving sentences for their criminal acts, and that claim to have seen the light and have recanted, repented, and mended their evil ways. But let the vast majority of them out of prison, and they will go right back to the gutter again where their original roots have always been. Not all of them, but a significant number of them. This behavior is a betrayal of God's gift of Christ to all of us, and it is a travesty of life in general. There is no Holy Spirit alive and well among any liars or con-artists. It's a shame, because it is these sinners, just like all of us again, that truly need Christ in their/our lives and functioning in their/our hearts. But such evil folks mock the Lord, by using Him and rejecting Him at their own convenience. They blaspheme His all-powerful name and being; they slander His grace by playing deceitful and lying games with it.

Suicide and Christian Beliefs

"Those who live according to the sinful nature have their minds set on what that nature desires; but those who live in accordance with the Spirit have their minds set on what the Spirit desires. The mind of sinful man is death, but the mind controlled by the Spirit is life and peace; the sinful mind is hostile to God. It does not submit to God's law, nor can it do so. Those controlled by the sinful nature cannot please God. You, however, are controlled not by the sinful nature but by the Spirit, if the Spirit of God lives in you. And if anyone does not have the Spirit of Christ, he does not belong to Christ. But if Christ is in you, your body is dead because of sin, yet your spirit is alive because of righteousness." Romans 8: 5-10 (NIV)

Let's face it, people who love the Lord and walk in His ways, do not commit crimes. If they are liars and profess how they love the Lord and have gone through the motions of acceptance and even baptism, they may have done such for some reason or reasons other than the real purpose of taking Christ into their hearts. This is not salvation; it is "show and tell" and nothing else. Such folks conjure up a lie for themselves and then try to live it and yet, they also continue living in the same sinful way as they did prior to accepting Christ as their Redeemer. Read the last part of the verse above. It says that *if Christ is in you, your body is dead because of sin, yet your spirit is alive because of righteousness.* Did you get that part about your body being dead if Christ is in you, and that your spirit is alive because of righteousness? What more can be said?

There are also those who give their lives for others, or surrender their lives to God in unconventional ways. The *Holy Bible* tells us that if we give our life for another, assuming the reason is a good one, then God looks at that unselfish act favorably. *"Greater love has no one than this, that one lay down his life for his friends." John 15: 13 (NASV)* Often has been the time, usually in war during combat, when one soldier gives his life to protect and save others. We have all heard of soldiers who have dived on top of hand grenades and sustained fatal injuries by cushioning the horrible blow. The explosion would have taken lives had the sacrificing soldier not acted so unselfishly. God says there is no greater love, no greater gift from one man or woman to another, as there is no greater gift of life that comes from Jesus for His ransom sacrifice upon the Roman cross.

AS THE BLOOD OF CHRIST PROVIDES US WITH NEW LIFE IN THE FATHER, SO IS THE BLOOD OF A HERO (REPRESENTATIVE OF HIS OR HER SACRIFICE) SO OTHERS MAY CONTINUE TO LIVE.

However, this scripture *John 15:13* does not say that God will automatically or even eventually take that gallant and honorable person into His presence because of their unselfish and loving act, as He did His Son Jesus Christ. But we do believe such individuals, that were not saved in Christ, will rest in peace until they are called back to life by God to be judged at the Great White Throne Judgment. Sacrificing your life for the good of others seems to be acceptable to God, as a great act of love; in fact, it's a final act of one's character, honor and moral fiber. Hmmmm! I wonder why? Why do you think that is so? Could it have anything to do with the ransom sacrifice of our Lord Jesus Christ?

THE GREAT WHITE THRONE JUDGMENT

Suicide and Christian Beliefs

Remember: there is a difference between giving up one's life for the love and for the good of others; by protecting them against imminent harm from an evil source, such as an enemy or his weapons in war, and that of simply killing oneself to spare others potential harm from oneself. Sorry! That doesn't count. Such a person still has time to find Jesus and let Him carry that burden; that is partially why He died for us. This is a very weak defense for leaving this life and God will judge it as such, and of this, I have no doubt. Stand back and look at the whole picture. Common sense will guide you wisely.

Another thought concerns those who suffer horribly from disease, from painful inflictions, wounds and mental disorders. Many Christians say God is merciful and will accept them into His loving hands as soon as they give up their earthly ghost. Don't kid yourself! *"A fool takes no pleasure in understanding, but only in expressing his opinion." Proverbs 18:2 (ESV)* Can you tell me where God has promised to do that? Sure, God is all merciful and mighty and He forgives us for many deeds which fall outside His normal arena of being acceptable. But suicide, once again, is not one of those things. I believe God will also judge these people, at the Great White Throne Judgment, those who take their own lives due to illness and suffering. I believe all those who are resurrected back from the dead, and appear before God for judgment, will have their time in court, so-to-speak, and that is when God may show His bountiful mercy in providing some other means or escape, to those who took their own lives. If you are considering suicide, I still wouldn't be too eager to test those waters.

The Great White Throne Judgment

"And I saw the dead, small and great, stand before God; and the books were opened: and another book was opened, which is the book of life: and the dead were judged out of those things which were written in the books, according to their works." Revelation 20:12

"And whosoever was not found written in the book of life was cast into the lake of fire." Revelation 20:15

There are other solutions. That old statement, "haste makes waste" is all too easy to put into force, take it slowly and reconsider such decisions of finality because, "patience is a virtue" and those who find God and come to Him, will learn that He will bring all things together for the greater good of all. *"And we know that in all things God works for*

Suicide and Christian Beliefs

the good of those who love Him, who have been called according to His purpose. For those God foreknew He also predestined to be conformed to the likeness of His Son. . ." Romans 8: 28-29 (NIV) The likeness of His Son is not the likeness of a suicide victim. That is no comparison between Jesus Christ and that of a suicide victim. The Apostle Paul was quite clear about that in the previous verse. There is a reason for the well-known statement that "suicide is a permanent solution for a temporary problem." It is permanent in more ways than one. Don't let it be your third strike, or your final out of your last inning.

I have tried to provide you with some answers and some stimulating thought in this section. I believe I have done my job. Keep in mind, there are many sides to most subjects, suicide is somewhat limited in its biblical scope of discussion because so little is really said about it. Like homosexuality, very little is said, but what is said about homosexuality speaks volumes. Besides, homosexuality is a sin; it is perversion, not necessarily a sickness, or mental disorder, as some of my clinical friends (misguided Christians or not) would like you to believe and accept. It is also considered as a curse to the society that condones its lifestyle – it is abhorrent and detestable to God. It is so despicable that He destroyed Sodom and Gomorrah to get His point across. My guess is He will also destroy any country, any place, any city, or any group of people that practice and condone this lifestyle.

We can read in **Romans** and **Leviticus** about God's feelings about homosexuality and we do not have to read much to understand what He means. But it is obvious to the most basic animals that do not practice unnatural sex, as suicide should be to the most casual observer of life, without much being said in the Scriptures about it. It is wrong and is not acceptable to the Lord. What is there to figure out? However, when you put all the pieces of the suicide puzzle together, you are able to form a partial picture of what the artist has attempted to render. You may have a puzzle with missing pieces, so you will have to fill in the gaps with answers to the picture/s which satisfy you and give you peace of mind.

Test the spirits and test the validity of what you experience. If you are considering suicide and some voice tells you that it is okay, remember that voice is not from God. Suicide has never been part of His plan, He loves you and wants you to live and flourish, to experience His awesome love and to complete the blueprint He has for your life, not the one you or someone else has been drafting. Give yourself a chance; give God a chance. Only He is the real architect of your life! What you are going through is only transitory and it too will pass as have other issues and problems in your life.

GIVE GOD A CHANCE WITH YOUR LIFE! HE LOVES YOU!

Additional Thoughts

In spite of trying to find answers that will soothe our spirits and comfort us when we begin to contemplate where the spirit of our loved one may have gone, as a result of suicide, it is folly to think that his or her spirit is floating around in "Never Never Land" without a care. This is not the case. As I did my research, I quickly discovered that to come up with Scriptural references supporting the idea and notion that a lost spirit would be in the bosom of God, well, such evidence was and is extremely weak. We all want to think that our God of mercy would welcome and cradle the suicide victim's spirit in love and understanding, but there just isn't anything tangible to make that a valid claim, only extreme wishful thinking, and the hopeful slogan, "Once saved, always saved". The soul our dead body, as previously stated, lies in the grave aware of absolutely nothing. This state of nonbeing includes no horrible punishment, and no heavenly presence. It is not conscious of anything.

Remember the easy formula: Die, remain in the grave, get resurrected, be judged and go to the lake of fire (the Second Death), or receive God's mercy and compassion and join body/soul and spirit together in a state of harmony with God.

On the other hand, there is a multitude of material dealing with the springs of living waters that the Lord tells us about, in so many ways, throughout the *Holy Bible*. It doesn't say specifically "that" in so many words, but what it does is show us the small picture of death through suicide and also the conceptual view of death, as it related to the "Big Picture" God has provided and planned for us.

In my interpretation, I believe this wholeheartedly. God is very specific when He tells us what He will and will not tolerate. He tells us that He has a plan for our success, and has had that plan from before we were born, and before He even created the world and mankind, as we know it today. God has been a long range planner for eons. Read my book, *The Plan.* We are not a fleeting thought in the mind of God Almighty. We are His child whom He loves.

Suicide and Christian Beliefs

It is His various undisclosed purposes that He wants us to fulfill, there is a difference in how we live our lives and how we measure up to God's desires and Divine Plan for us. His Divine plan is totally individualized; it demands that we walk in righteousness and obedience to His Perfect Will. His Will for us is to oblige Him and accomplish what it is that He has intended for us to achieve. Fulfilling God's purpose/s is and should be our chief objective – like saving souls. When we duck out on His overall program for us, we cheat God of fulfilling His purpose/s through us. So we deny His majesty and supreme authority as our Creator. This insults God when we reject His Son's sacrifice, His gift of grace and His precious gift of life that He so lovingly bestowed upon us. *Our interruption is our corruption! Our disconnection is His rejection!*

Suicide and Christian Beliefs

Turning one's back on Our God Who has the sovereign authority of the universe to decide for us, heal us, help us, guide us, direct us and choose the manner in which we live and die, is displaying a final statement which says Jesus can't do what He claims. It is indirectly calling God Jehovah a liar and comparing Him to Satan. It purports an attitude of nobody can help me, my position is totally helpless and there is no friend in Jesus. Even prior claims to being saved will not let the suicide victim off the hook. Scripture once again tells us we cannot return to where we have once been in the trust of Christ, if we have walked away from His salvation and/or not taken it seriously enough to be truly saved.

Much can be said by people that think they have given their life to Christ, but then consciously live a life style which is contrary to walking with Christ. Being saved and then finding oneself in a quagmire of doubt, shame, guilt, depression and so forth, may be because the heart that was given to the Lord was unconvinced and not convicted. Trust in the Lord is an ongoing activity, it is real and it is lived daily. Our conviction and commitment is in the proof of the pudding. Is it acceptable fruit produced on that vine, or is there nothing there but withered vines to be piled up and burned? These thoughts and words come from Scripture. They were from the example that Christ taught us. We cannot deny the claims and words and commandments of Jesus Christ. Christ came to resolve our guilt and wash away our sins – and that He did and of that there is no doubt!

CATHOLIC PURGATORY! UNFORTUNATELY THIS NOTION IS NOT SCRIPTURAL AND CAN ONLY BE FOUND IN THE CATHOLIC DOUAY- RHEIMS VERSION OF THE HOLY BIBLE IN 2 MACCABEES 12:42-46.

Where the spirit goes is the most important piece of information people seek. Folks want to know if the spirit has been accepted by God and found to be righteous enough to enter Heaven because of his or her state of grace with Christ prior to dying. Or has the spirit gone to some place called Paradise to be with other saints that are waiting for their time to be with the Lord? Or, is there really a Purgatory where they must wait until they have been prayed for enough and finished their complete penance to get out? Prayers for the dead are useless and fruitless – you can't score runs when the ball game is over.

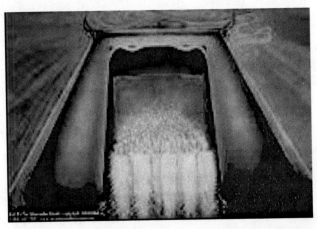

SOULS WHO HAD BEEN SLAIN FOR TESTIFYING TO THE WORD OF GOD, NOW FOUND UNDER THE ALTAR OF GOD.

We do know that the spirits of those under the altar of God, in Heaven, have an existing relationship with Him which is not the same relationship that other dead spirits have. I believe the "souls under the altar" are the spirits of those dead saints who were martyred for their preaching of the gospel which will occur during End Times. They are waiting for their time of justice and revenge to be carried out by the Lord; therefore, they'll be able to completely enjoy God's full presence when they are no longer confined under the altar. Maybe that place under the altar is simply a secure waiting place of somewhat comfort and peace for those special saints, even though they seem to clamor for God to take revenge for their deaths. This is my explanation for that heavenly scenario.

Here in *Revelation 6:9-11(ESV)* it is said that *"When he (the Lamb – Jesus Christ) opened the fifth seal, I saw under the altar the souls of those who had been slain for the word of God and for the witness they had borne. They cried out with a loud voice, "O Sovereign Lord, holy and true, how long before you will judge and avenge our blood on those who dwell on the earth?" Then they were each given a white robe and told to rest a little longer, until the number of their fellow servants and their brothers should be complete, who were to be killed as they themselves had been."* Saying that they had to rest a while longer is rather indicative of these martyred saints being in the soul state of sleep. But now they have been temporarily awakened to witness Jesus Christ opening the seals and this informs them that their time of resurrection is very near and He has claimed victory over death.

Also, we read about the Apostle John observing the temporarily conscious living immortal souls (of martyred Christians who lost their lives for preaching or sharing the Gospel of Jesus Christ with others) in direct conversation with the Lord. Oddly enough though, these "souls" not "spirits" are underneath an altar. Where this altar is, is not openly stated, but the assumption by those that believe in an immortal soul is that this altar must be in the heavenly temple of God.

THE ALTAR OF GOD JEHOVAH OUR FATHER.

Why the martyrs are described as being "under the altar" must be for protection. Obviously, if this assumption is true, the altar of incense in heaven must be extremely large in order for thousands of martyrs to be there. That would be a literal interpretation, and makes about as much sense as all the dead saints literally going to Abraham's bosom, see *Luke 16:22-31 (ESV) "The poor man died and was carried by the angels to Abraham's side. The rich man also died and was buried, and in Hades, being in torment, he lifted up his eyes and saw Abraham far off and Lazarus at his side. And he called out, 'Father Abraham, have mercy on me, and send Lazarus to dip the end of his finger in water and cool my tongue, for I am in anguish in this flame.' But Abraham said, 'Child, remember that you in your lifetime received your good things, and Lazarus in like manner bad things; but now he is comforted here, and you are in anguish. And besides all this, between us and you a great chasm has been fixed, in order that those who would pass from here to you may not be able, and none may cross from there to us.' And he said, 'Then I beg you, father, to send him to my father's house— for I have five brothers—so that he may warn them, lest they also come into this place of torment.' But Abraham said, 'They have Moses and the Prophets; let them hear them.' And he said, 'No, father Abraham, but if someone goes to them from the dead, they will repent.' He said to him, 'If they do not hear Moses and the Prophets, neither will they be convinced if someone should rise from the dead.'"*

Many people are hardheaded and simply don't understand that which is of God and that which is not of God. We know that miracles will be done by many false figures claiming to be Christ, during our

End Times, but they are not of God. Even the elite will be deceived, and that it why it is so important that we entertain only God's Word and know it thoroughly.

Will lost spirits or those saved become Mr. and Mrs. God, as some so-called "Christian cults" believe? This term "Christian cult" is really an oxymoron: the two words are opposites and do not match. I've gone through the various religions of the world and I find several different beliefs concerning the state of a dead soul/body and spirit. The faith we speak about is called Christianity and Christianity is very clear about many things. Other teachings are only revealed as the saved Christian begins to walk closer to God, enjoying a new wealth of knowledge and understanding. Take the beliefs of the Church of the Latter Day Saints (LDS or the Mormon Church). This is but one example of what people are told, claiming it is the truth of Our Living God, yet is obviously not. We've been warned in *Revelation 22:18-19, Deuteronomy 4:2* and *12:32* and again in *18:20-22* not to add or take away from God's Scriptures. God doesn't undo or reverse His words or commandments – He remains steadfast in what He says. However, *The Book of Mormon* along with *Doctrine and Covenants*, and *The Pearl of Great Price* do exactly that and nothing stated in any of these three books can be proven.

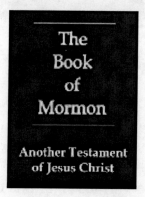

BEWARE OF ANY FALSE TESTAMENT OF JESUS CHRIST.

If *The Book of Mormon* contains all the ordinances and principles that pertain to the Gospel of our Lord, Jesus Christ, then why don't LDS esoteric doctrines show up in it? The doctrine that God is nothing more than an "exalted man with a body of flesh and bones" is not found in the *Book of*

Mormon; nor does their LDS doctrine of Jesus Christ being the "spirit brother" of Lucifer. Nor do the doctrines that men can become gods, and that God the Father has a god above him, who has a god above him, *ad infinitum.* The Mormon founder taught that faithful Mormon men can ascend to divinity. In the *King Follett Discourse*, Joseph Smith said, "My Father worked out his kingdom with fear and trembling, and I must do the same. And when I get to my kingdom [godhood], I shall present it to my Father, so that he may obtain kingdom upon kingdom, and it will exalt him in glory. He will then take a higher exaltation, and I will take his place, and thereby become exalted myself." On so onward and upward the progression continues. Eventually all Mormons will become gods; thus, Mr. and Mrs. God, as they also retain their original status of marriage in Mormon heaven. And that could get confusing because there may be more than one wife, and we know that our real God Jehovah is not a god of utter confusion. Is he?

Clinically speaking, I would refer to Joseph Smith as being considerably narcissistic with his grandiose sense of self-importance, a desire for excessive admiration, a sick sense of entitlement to God's throne, and needing friends that would support him in his fantasies. Oh, yes! I should also say He was narcissistic because he did exploit others, many to their deaths, his need to fulfill his envy for other men's wives, and his apparent arrogance and haughtiness mentioned in his various behaviors. I do believe he had 33 wives!!! In *Jacob 2:24-30*, in *The Book of Mormon*, conveniently written by Smith, you'll find his basis for having so many wives. What a game player! Enough said.

YOUR VERY WORST NIGHTMARE – LUCIFER!

In any discussion with a Mormon about Mormonism's conflicting teachings on the nature of God, you must cut away their apparent camouflage. You have to get to the central facts. It's simple, really. Just show them how the *Book of Mormon* conflicts with Joseph Smith's later teachings. If he was right about God, when was he right? Take your pick, but you can't pick both, and neither can a Mormon, except if he uses doublethink and presents to you doubletalk! When a Mormon chooses either false teaching as being correct, he or she must reveal that the other teaching has to be wrong; therefore, Joseph Smith's credibility as a prophet collapses, and you know what God's *Holy Bible* says that you do with false prophets! Read my book, *Moroni's Message*, it deals with the hoax of the Mormon religion.

One night in September of 1954, or thereabouts, I found myself cuddled up under a table in our living room in Guam. My father was stationed on the navy base above Agana, and we had just moved into base housing. It was made of sturdy cinder blocks and was not like the Quonset huts others on base live in. When the typhoon hit that night, it was scary, and we had twenty some adults and kid-lings safely secured within our stone walls. One family was Mormon, and they witnessed their beliefs to all of the adults that were present. I had lain on the floor listening with intend and interest, but as a baptized Christian, I understood, even at ten years old, that what I heard was directly opposed to what my *Holy Bible* teaching had taught me.

That was my first taste of false religion, Joseph Smith, and Bring'em Young. Scripture says this about false teaching. *"I am astonished that you are so quickly deserting the one who called you by the grace of Christ and are turning to a different gospel— which is really no gospel at all. Evidently some people are throwing you into confusion and are trying to pervert the gospel of Christ. But even if we or an angel from heaven should preach a gospel other than the one we preached to you, let him be eternally condemned! As we have already said, so now I say again: If anybody is preaching to you a gospel other than what you accepted, let him be eternally condemned!"* Galatians 1:6-9 (NIV) and then again *"Therefore I tell you that no one who is speaking by the Spirit of God says, 'Jesus be cursed,' and no one can say, 'Jesus is Lord,' except by the Holy Spirit." 1 Corinthians 12:3 (NIV)*

THIS JUNK IS MAINLY THE ASSORTED WRITINGS AND STORIES OF ADULT FAIRY TALES WITH DEADLY ENDINGS. ABSOLUTELY NOTHING HAS BEEN PROVEN TO SUBSTANTIATE THEIR WILD CLAIMS.

Suicide and Christian Beliefs

There are no truly misunderstood mysteries or myths in Christianity which cannot be decently explained, verified and substantiated, or cause us to stumble and/or be misled; and although there are some mysteries mentioned in the *Holy Bible*, a time will soon come when even those mysteries of the revelations of the Apostle John will be made clear and understandable to all believers. Tagging our faith with false claims or assumptions is ludicrous. Secular scholars and religious philosophers have done this for hundreds of years, they just never learn. Their ego and learning has clouded their eyes to the true wonders of God. They view the *Holy Bible* as a book of fairy tales and they do not have a simple clue as to the truth of His Word.

The majority of mankind believes this way, or has accepted another way of thinking about God's

Suicide and Christian Beliefs

Universe and the possibilities of there being no god, or many gods, or about a god that does not live within the confines of the Christian concept of holiness. Nor can this concept be found in the *Holy Bible*, anywhere among its pages; and such ignorant men and women also have no understanding of the Christian concept of dying, salvation or being lost. Scripture says, ***"The unfailing love of the Lord never ends! By His mercies we have been kept from complete destruction. Great is His faithfulness; His mercies begin afresh each day."*** *Lamentations 3: 22-23 (NLT)*

When we do things that cause the Lord to become angry, we pay a very high price. When the Israelites turned their back on God, He poured out His wrath upon them. Children were treated like pots of clay, and parents turned their backs on them and gave them nothing to eat. People searched for food among the garbage pits. Their guilt was much greater than that of Sodom and we know about that story of sudden disaster. A whole city of sick and unrepentant, perverted homosexuals were wiped out in a flash by God. Can you imagine a whole city of homosexuals lusting after you and your family? Abraham couldn't even find ten good righteous men among the perverts of the city, so God, as he had promised, cleaned their slate – nothing was left standing, only smoke could be seen, rising like it was coming out of a furnace.

SINNERS FLEEING FROM SODOM AND GOMORRAH.

GOD DIDN'T MESS AROUND WITH THE DEBASED SICKIES OF SODOM AND GOMORRAH. HE DESTROYED THEM FOR THEIR PERVERSION AND DISGUSTING BEHAVIORS AGAINST HIS WORD, HIS COMMANDMENTS AND NATURE.

Suicide and Christian Beliefs

In *The Book of Lamentations, Chapter Four,* there are four distinct sections about Jerusalem's punishment: one part is about the suffering of Jerusalem's children; another part is about God punishing Jerusalem's religious leaders; another part about the power of Jerusalem's enemies; and finally, the end of Jerusalem's suffering. The Israelites' children were even consumed and eaten by their mothers in verse ten. How awful and wicked was this terrible cannibalism. Jerusalem was burned to the ground by the Lord. Folks, God doesn't mess around, He is a very serious Creator who destroys what He finds detestable. Only then, after the city was burned did the Lord feel satisfied. This happened because innocent blood had been shed and defiled. But in the end, God said, *"Oh Jerusalem, your punishment will end; you will soon return from exile." Lamentations 4: 22 (NLT)*

I cite this above scripture because the Lord speaks of his anger for the sins of Jerusalem and the Israelites, and for the unspeakable evils they blatantly committed. Yes, part of those terrible evils was the shedding of innocent blood. So, maybe there is the possibility that the Lord, in all of His infinite mercy, will give sinners who have taken their own life, a second chance somewhere in His perfect scheme of things. We are under a New

Suicide and Christian Beliefs

Covenant with God, and that covenant provides grace which was absent during Old Testament times. The New Covenant began with Christ paying the price for sin on the cross. When His blood started to flow, the Old Testament times were at an end and the New Testament times began.

If Jerusalem can be forgiven, then just maybe there is hope for suicide victims to receive a second chance. Maybe suicide victims will be given tasks to do or finish; tasks that were similar to the skills or talents they developed and used there on earth. With the Lord, anything is possible. However, I do not see much substance in this kind of thinking. How many mansions does Jesus have? How many heavens are there? Does a lost spirit go to one of those heavens to be reeducated and given a second chance to know God? Jesus, in spirit form, did descend into Hades and preach to the spirits in prison (those wicked in the grave). See *1 Peter 3: 18-19.* Consider the vision of the Apostle Paul, who was considered a very reliable guy, he said, *"I was caught up into the third heaven fourteen years ago. Whether my body was there or just my spirit, I don't know; only God knows. But I do know that I was caught up into paradise and heard things so astounding that they cannot be told." 2 Corinthians 12: 2-4 (NLT)*

Suicide and Christian Beliefs

SCRIPTURE TELLS US THAT CHRIST PREACHED TO THOSE SPIRITS IN PRISON AND DECLARED HIS VICTORY OVER DEATH. BUT HE DIDN'T SHAKE HANDS WITH THE DEVIL!!!

God offers us not only grace and salvation, but He offers us a hope that we infuse our faith in His ways and promises. *"What is faith? It is the confident assurance that what we hope for is going to happen. It is the evidence of things we cannot yet see." Hebrews 11: 1 (NLT)* Perhaps this is God's way of saying that what we truly do hope for, like the spirit of a suicide victim eventually going to Heaven, is a possibility. How much hope do we need for that to have occurred, or to have happen at God's appointed time? Will our hope be honored, or is there some other meaning in the words of this scripture? We that are left behind grieving search desperately for answers. We try to put the pieces of this puzzle together. Nobody, and I mean nobody, can discern the truth of this matter. Even though the weight of the evidence leans towards a negative conclusion, such may not be the truth of God. There is a scripture that is heavy in its essence and may be taken to heart in a very bitter sense, but it comes from the Apostle Paul again, as he has called us all to persevere. *"Think how much more terrible the punishment will be for those who have trampled on the Son of God and have treated the blood of the covenant as if it were common and unholy. Such people have insulted and enraged the Holy Spirit who brings mercy to His people."* *Hebrews 10:29 (NLT)*

Another thought also comes from the scriptures in the *Book of Hebrews*. This is a warning about drifting away from the message of the Lord, and turning our back on Christ's salvation and His gift of grace. Scripture says, *"So we must listen very carefully to the truth we have heard, or we may drift away from it. The message God delivered through angels has always proved true, and the people were punished for every violation of the law and every act of disobedience. What makes us think that we can escape if we are indifferent to this great salvation that was announced by the Lord Jesus Himself?"* *Hebrews 2: 1-3 (NLT)* Another heavy message from the Apostle Paul can be found in the ***Book of Titus***. Paul's message is, *"Everything is pure to those whose hearts are pure. But nothing is pure to those who are corrupt and unbelieving, because their minds and consciences are defiled. Such people claim they know God, but they deny Him by the way they live. They are despicable and disobedient, worthless for doing anything good." Titus 1: 15-16 (NLT)*

Although our grief may be too much to deal with when a loved one commits suicide, we can find peace in the comfort of the Lord. His words may be harsh, but He is God Almighty, and only He can say the things He does and show us His Perfect Truth. The lost are usually remembered for their good deeds and accomplishments, their sacrifices and their kindness, their gentleness, and compassion, their laughter and their tears. Sometimes they are remembered for their compromised dedication to the principles of Christianity and their love of Jesus Christ and His redemption. We hope and we allow our thoughts to linger in a state of harmony or bliss,

Suicide and Christian Beliefs

tragedy and sorrow, or a blend of all these emotions when we bring our loved one to mind. We want to assume the best for his or her spirit that has departed from our lives and we want to not make judgments about where his or her spirit may be.

Therefore, we trust in God and His holy ways and means to bring acceptance (closure for clinicians) to our hearts and minds, while applying His gracious mercy to the lost spirit that is seeking peace and perhaps is within the clutches and grasp of the Lord. Our final prayers are a petition and plea to God for Him to show His mercy to that spirit and grant him or her everlasting serenity. With many bad behavioral acts, such as suicide, I say there is never complete closure, because somewhere in our minds we will leave a crack in that doorway, or a slight lift between the window and the sill which allows for a continuance, no matter how small or slight, to exist. We may forgive complete, but there is never total closure – ever! Why? It's rather simple to consider, but even one small fleeting thought about that act of suicide will prove there has been no full closure. Why again? Because that thought will almost always be one of fatalism and despair, grief or sadness, or any emotions which is less than positive. Yet, we can choose to not remember; this effort is more than possible, in fact, you can make it work.

Suicide and Christian Beliefs

It may be that our Loving Father will show His grace to believers no matter what sins they have committed, but I feel this is really wishful thinking. **Remember:** everyone who commits suicide will be resurrected and judged, of that we can be certain. In the *Book of Isaiah, Chapter 55*, God shows us a free offer of His many blessings. Maybe there is hidden mercy in His blessings. For sure, these blessings are for everyone. That is, those folks that are still alive. You must want to partake in these blessings. What this means as regards suicide is not mentioned. However, *"Any city or house divided against itself shall not stand." Matthew 12: 25 (KJV)* God does not set us up for failure – we commit to that scenario all by ourselves. If Christ is truly in us, then we've received God's mercy, forgiveness and love. If we've abandoned the Lord, and trespassed against His Will and plan, then we should not be surprised at God's judgment when He proclaims us a sinner that will be separated from Him forever.

Suicide and Christian Beliefs

SUICIDE MAKES GOD NOT ONLY DISAPPOINTED, BUT VERY ANGRY. SUICIDE VICTIMS MESS UP GOD'S PLAN FOR HIS OR HER LIFE. DON'T YOU GET UPSET WHEN SOMEONE WRECKS YOUR PLANS THAT HAVE TAKEN A CONSIDERABLE AMOUNT OF TIME, WORK AND EFFORT TO PUT TOGETHER, ESPECIALLY FOR SOMEONE ELSE?

However, this offer of mercy may be viewed as hope for suicide victims because God says, *"For my thoughts are not your thoughts, nor are your ways My ways . . ." Isaiah 55: 8 (NKJV)* God is letting us know that we just may think differently than He does and this opens a potentially whole new perspective on how God may view life and death. An opposite thought which may cancel out such hope, is found in the *Book of Exodus* wherein God says He will blot a sinner's name out of His book. *". . .Whoever has sinned against Me, I will blot him out of My book."* *Exodus 32:33 (NKJV)* Maybe the grace we get from Jesus will nullify and eradicate God's statement to Moses because we were under the Old Covenant at that time. But in *Revelation 3:5 (NIV),* it says *"He who overcomes will, like them, be dressed in white. I will never blot out his name from the book of life, but will acknowledge his name before my Father and his angels."* Then again in *Psalm 69:27-28 (NIV)* it says. *"Charge them with crime upon crime; do not let them share in your salvation. May they be blotted out of the book of life."* Therefore, if you cannot overcome evil, and if you decide to commit suicide, your name will most definitely not appear in Christ's Book of Life. That seems sensible, reasonable and just to me. If it doesn't to you, then perhaps a re-examination of the Holy Scriptures is in line and should be done quickly.

ALL FINAL HOPE FOR SALVATION RESTS IN THE MERCIFUL, HOPEFUL, LOVING AND FORGIVING ARMS OF JESUS CHRIST THROUGH THE TRULY WONDERFUL SACRIFICE HE LAID DOWN ON OUR BEHALF. THE FINAL JUDGMENT OF A

LOST SPIRIT WILL ALSO BE IN THE HANDS OF GOD. HE AND ONLY HE WILL MAKE THE ULTIMATE RESOLUTION TO THE DISPOSITION OF A SUICIDE CASE. ALL LIFE WILL BE JUDGED AFTER DEATH BY THE LORD ALMIGHTY...AND HIS WORD IS THE FINAL AUTHORITY. BY CHRIST'S GRACE THROUGH OUR FAITH ARE WE SAVED. THANK GOD FOR HIS MIGHTY MIRACLES AND SENSE OF JUSTICE EVEN WHEN AND IF WE SLAP HIM IN THE FACE.

SUICIDE

What lies on the other side of darkness, what
lies in the black abyss?
Did I hear a silence so deafening, or was it
rumbling in the pit?
I did not have to surrendered all, my soul I
could have saved,
But was my decision of foregone thought, a
simple road I paved.

It's troubled me how I have planned, yet it
took so long to do.
I fooled my family, I fooled my friends, I
even fooled you too.
You thought my love was strong and
faithful, but I knew my heart was weak.
And when I planned to destroy my spirit, I
could hardly even speak.

I had no peace, I had no meaning, my life
was nothing but pain.
So when I chose to extinguish my breath, I
felt no loss just gain.
My soul floated amidst some vacuum, in a
space without a side.
As I tumbled, I fell then quickly it ended,
that horrible fatal slide.

Suicide and Christian Beliefs

I don't like it here, it's empty, it's quiet, it's
nothingness to me.
I regret that decided to leave my life, that
precious misery.
My suffering was bad, my pain was great,
and my mind was always shattered.
But at least I had some air to breath, and
that's what really mattered.

Dahk Knox
September 25, 2002

Chapter Four
Biblical Warnings

Personal Preparation

When I first started reviewing the various biblical scriptures which I intended to use to build a case for suicide as a final destruction, I began reacquainting myself with verses that seems to jump out at me off the pages of the *Holy Bible*. I had read these scriptures before, but now they were new and had added meaning. Each time I read a verse, new clarity would come forth. I would stop and pray about what I thought I was learning, and more new information, and more new scriptures kept coming to me. It seemed like each time I opened the *Holy Bible*, one verse would send me to another. That new verse would link up with another part of the *Holy Bible* and so forth. I was totally amazed at the amount of material I had garnered so quickly. I felt like I was directly linked to some invisible source of information that was being specifically sent to me from somewhere beyond my comprehension. Things like that don't happen to me. I have not been instructed by God or any other heavenly being, to receive information and write about it. I instigated my own need for writing this book. My only communication with God is through prayer. I do talk to Him and I hope He listens. If He talks to me it is by some other means which I am totally unaware of, and that is the truth. I see His beauty and majesty all around me and there is no question of His existence in my mind. However, I truly do believe the Lord can and will lead us in certain directions, for His reasons and glory. Finding these new verses with their warnings or reading old verses and discovering their full meanings is exciting. What will follow in this section are my comments on various verses I have found to be quite prophetic in their warnings to each of us. Read from this point onward with a completely open mind and try to assimilate what I will be sharing with you.

God tells us to keep what we initially learn as a new Christian in our hearts and not to drift away. If we do drift away from His Word and Will, we will be the losers for such abandonment. *"Be sure, then, to keep in your hearts the message you heard from the beginning. If you keep that message, then you will always live in union with the Son and the Father. And this is what Christ himself promised to give us – eternal life."* 1 John 2: 24-25 (GN) and *". . .evil persons and impostors will keep on going from bad to worse, deceiving others and being deceived themselves. But as for you, continue in the truths that you were taught and firmly believe. . .you have known the Holy Scriptures, which are able to give you the wisdom that leads to salvation through faith in Christ Jesus."* 2 Timothy 3: 13, 15 (GN)

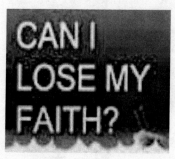 **YES! YOU CAN!**

When others are able to persuade you to abandon your faith, you end up paying the price. One must remain steady in his or her faith in the Lord as such faith guarantees your salvation. Don't play games with your faith because it is the key to your eternal life with God. You need faithful retention if you are to continue in the saving grace of Jesus. *"My righteous people, however, will believe and live; but if any of them turns back, I will not be pleased with them." Hebrews 10: 38 (GN)*

YOU MUST HAVE FAITHFUL RETENTION OR YOU WILL LOSE YOUR CONTINUED WALK IN GRACE WITH JESUS CHRIST. AS GOD IS FAITHFUL TO YOU, SO DOES HE EXPECT YOUR FAITHFULNESS TO HIM. RECIPROCITY IS EVERYTHING.

Scripture constantly affirms that our faithfulness, in our walk with God, is the true fruit of which real faith is the very root. Even the Apostle Paul understood the potential for disqualification in the eyes of the Lord. He knew he could be rejected by God for his inadequacies of faith. See *1 Corinthians*

9:27 (NLT), it says, *"I discipline my body like an athlete, training it to do what it should. Otherwise, I fear that after preaching to others I myself might be disqualified."* Can you imagine the Apostle Paul being disqualified in God's eyes? This verse is not about Paul not having the qualifications for ministering anymore, but it was Paul's personal fear of losing his own salvation, not rewards for his service to the Lord. Like the vine, Christ said that those who are true believers, those who are totally faithful, can ultimately abandon faith and fail to abide in Him; therefore, they are thrown off and withered and, eventually burned.

Alexander Maclaren said, in his *The True Branches of the True Vine,* the following:

". . . even at that moment, our Lord, in all His tenderness and pity, could not but let

words of warning – grave, solemn, tragic – drop from His lips. This generation does not like to hear them, for its conception of the Gospel is a thing with no minor notes in it, with no threatenings . . .but Jesus Christ could not speak about the blessedness of fruitfulness and the joy of life in Himself without speaking about its necessary converse, the awfulness of separation from Him, of barrenness, of withering, and of destruction. Be on your guard against the tendency of the thinking of this generation to paste a bit of blank paper over all the threatenings of the Bible, and to blot out from its consciousness the grave issues that it holds forth. One of two things must befall the branch, either it is in the Vine or it gets into the fire. If we would avoid the fire, let us see to it that we are in the Vine."

When you read the Parable of the Law of Forgiveness, found in **Matthew 18: 21-35**, something new rings a bell that may not have been rung before.

Robert Shank in his book *Life in the Son* states:

"Jesus here teaches that the forgiveness of God, through fully and freely granted in

pure mercy and grace to undeserving sinners, nevertheless remains conditional, according to the individual's subsequent response to the gracious forgiveness which he has received. This is the point of His parable. To demy this is to deny that the parable has meaning."

Also in *Life in the Son*, Dr. Shank writes:

". . .He enunciated cardinal principles governing man's spiritual relation to God which are as valid today as at the moment of utterance. One of these principles, according to His teaching in the Parable of the Law of Forgiveness, is that true repentance toward God is inseparably associated with our attitude toward our fellow men and cannot exist apart from a charitable, forgiving spirit toward others.

"Such true repentance, like sincere faith and the faithful retention of the saving word of the Gospel, is necessary – not merely for a fleeting moment at the occasion of one's conversion, but continually and habitually, as an essential condition of forgiveness and salvation. 'So likewise shall my heavenly Father do also unto you," warned Jesus, *'if*

ye from your hearts forgive not ever one his brother their trespasses.' It is possible warned Jesus, that Peter and others who have known the forgiving grace of God might forfeit that forgiveness. The forgiving race of God cannot dwell in bitter, unforgiving hearts. He who refuses to forgive his brother has no real sense of need for the forgiveness of God and no just claim on His gracious forgiveness. 'Forgive us our debts, as we forgive our debtors.'"

As Christians, we have learned that we are either in the camp of Jesus Christ, or we are not. If we have Christ in us, then He will have us in Him. Christ gives us life, if we reject life, we will not have life in Him. ***"The testimony is this: God has given us eternal life, and this life has its source in his Son. Whoever does not have the Son of God does not have life." I John 5: 11-12 (GN)*** That is very clear. So is the Lord's stance for us to repent all of our sins to God, and having faith in His Father. Consider the following written by *Dr. Robert Shank*, in *Life in the Son*, it says:

"Many believe that saving faith is the act of a moment – one great moment in which the sinner humbly acknowledges his sin in repentance toward God and accepts Jesus

Christ as his personal Savior. They believe that one grand and holy moment of decision ushers on into an irrevocable state of grace in which he is conditionally secure. But others are persuaded that the moment of holy decision is but the beginning, and that the state of grace is not irrevocable in our present earthly sojourn in God's moral universe in which 'the just shall live by faith.' They are persuaded that saving faith is not the act of a moment, but the attitude of a life."

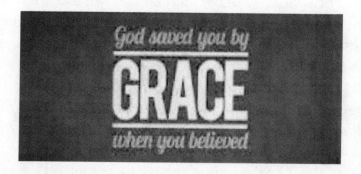

What about unconditional security? I am told and led to believe, by most Christians, that what Christ said in the Gospel of John is full proof that grace covers everyone forever. I find it to be not true. This scripture mentions conditional behaviors, not guarantees of total full grace coverage; but for those conditional behaviors, we may have grace. Let's read this verse together, slowly and carefully, not allowing ourselves to be pumped up into the process of unconditionally being saved. *"Verily, verily, I say unto you, He that heareth my word and believeth on him that sent me hath everlasting life, and shall not come into condemnation, but is passed from death unto life." John 5: 24 (KJV)*

Consider this: hearing and believing are not a momentary thing, but are a continuous behavior (an active and on-going conduct) to be performed throughout one's Christian life. No one-time shot will allow anyone or anything to continue as such for an eternity, performance is constantly required – "God-expected" Christian performance. If Alex Rodrigues, star outfielder for the New York Yankees, hits a bottom of the ninth inning walk-off home run to win the World Series, then that doesn't mean that home run will be good to win all future World Series Championships. Hey, it didn't work that way for Bill Mazeroski and the Pittsburgh Pirates in 1960. The following year the Pirates lost twenty more games than they did in 1960 and ended up in sixth place out of eight teams. One home run, like a one-time confession for accepting Christ is not what *the Holy Bible* says. God demands your full attention and devotion all of the time. He does not want your part-time love, He wants your full love all of the time, and that's a good thing. Like *Henry Alford* says in *The Greek Testament:*

". . .where the faith is, the possession of eternal life is, and when the one remits, the other is forfeited." Robert Shank says, in *Life in the Son, "Contrary to the assumption of many, John 5: 24 does not present a privileged position which, once attained, is forever irrevocable. Quite to the contrary, our Savior's words depict a privileged position directly governed by the specific condition of habitually hearing a believing. Jesus declares that the happy circumstance of deliverance from present condemnation and of standing passed out of death into life is the privilege only of such as habitually hear His word and believe the Father. It is only on the basis of a present hearing and believing that one shares the eternal life of God and enjoys deliverance from present condemnation and spiritual death."*

This position only makes good sense. We all want an ongoing great relationship with God. We want open communications to be part of that relationship, but as a marriage between man and woman may come to an end, due to no communication, the relationship is no longer sound, and it falls apart with each person choosing to go their own way. So it is with your relationship with God. You do not get to choose an on and off again relationship – you must be doers, hearers and believers of the word every day. There is no other acceptable way.

New Testament gospel tells us that eternal life with the Lord is only ours now, on the simple condition of our daily faith in Christ, and not based on some single moment's act of faith in our past. That single act of faith, accepting the Lord as my personal Savior, was not an irrevocable consequence on my one time action as a seven year-old. If it was, I sure fooled God or fooled myself, because there were those torrent years that I almost forgot all about my personal relationship with Him, as I sure didn't live my life with Him abiding inside, and there were obvious vacancies in my temple while other rooms were occupied with less than Christian ideals.

AGAIN AND AGAIN YOUR FAITH MUST REMAIN CONSTANT IN TRUSTING THE LORD FOR YOUR WELL-BEING AND SALVATION. IT IS PARAMOUNT IN YOUR LIFE! DON'T EVER LOSE YOUR FAITH IN GOD!

Suicide and Christian Beliefs

However, He did tell me that if I received Him (in faith) and if I trust in Him and His Holy name, then I will be given the privilege of becoming a child of God. *"But to all who believed him and accepted him, he gave the right to become children of God. They are reborn—not with a physical birth resulting from human passion or plan, but a birth that comes from God. John 1: 12-13 (NIV)* It is hard to understand, but I realize there are many people who haven't an iota or scintilla of a belief in what I am saying, and why Scripture is so important to me, and should be to you. It is because that is how God is able to show His thoughts, messages, and proclamations in written form. As we read, we meditate and pray over His Word, and we learn and gain wisdom. You become knowledgeable in His Word.

PRAYER IS SO VITALLY IMPORTANT. NEVER CEASE PRAYING AND TALKING TO GOD. HE WANTS TO HEAR FROM YOU TODAY AND EVERY DAY. I PROMISE!

Suicide and Christian Beliefs

When I accepted God, although very young, at that particular moment, I became born of the Spirit. I consciously and deliberately chose to follow God for the rest of my life, so I started to pray every day and every evening. When I closed my eyes, my final prayer each night ended with *Psalms 23:6 "Surely and goodness and mercy will follow me all the days of my life and I will dwell in the house of the Lord forever." (KJV)* Sixty years later, I still end my prayers with this verse. Trusting in God is an everyday decision. Accepting Him as Redeemer needs constant attention and maintenance, it is all part of the manual. . .read it and see for yourself! *Dr. Edwin Dargan* states in his written work, *The Doctrines of Our Faith*:

> *"Men sometimes make the mistake of taking this initial act of repentance and faith as if that completed all that man had to do in order to be saved; and in a sense this is true, provided that faith and repentance be continued; but the Scriptures show that there must be this continuance, and this is what we call perseverance."*

Our Lord tells us, *"He that endureth to the end, the same shall be saved." Matthew 10: 22 (KJV)*

Suicide and Christian Beliefs

And remember that we are also called to be holy, and not just part time but all the time. That is what God demands from us – total obedience to His ways and desires. If we comply, He assures us of our salvation for all eternity.

"Therefore, preparing your minds for action, and being sober-minded, set your hope fully on the grace that will be brought to you at the revelation of Jesus Christ. As obedient children, do not be conformed to the passions of your former ignorance, but as he who called you is holy, you also be holy in all your conduct, since it is written, "You shall be holy, for I am holy." And if you call on him as Father who judges impartially according to each one's deeds, conduct yourselves with fear throughout the time of your exile, knowing that you were ransomed from the futile ways inherited from your forefathers, not with perishable things such as silver or gold, but with the precious blood of Christ, like that of a lamb without blemish or spot. He was foreknown before the foundation of the world but was made manifest in the last times for the sake of you who through him are believers in God, who raised him from the dead and gave him glory, so that your faith and hope are in God. Having purified your souls by your obedience to the truth for a sincere brotherly love, love one another earnestly from a pure heart,

since you have been born again, not of perishable seed but of imperishable, through the living and abiding word of God..." 1 Peter 1:13-23 (ESV)

For us to abide in Christ we must live with and for God. It is the same throughout the scriptures. A loving and awesome God calls His people into a very personal relationship with Him. If they will stay in that relationship He promises they will experience His faithful love, have an eternal intimate relationship with Him, and gain rewards both now and forever. Abiding is both a call and a command. In order to stay in relationship with God one must strive to live as Christ lived. This includes obeying His commands, loving one another, remaining faithful to the truth of the gospel, and refraining from any evil. We are to stay in Christ, not yielding to the world around us. In being firm and immovable in our walk with God, we will experience the love of God lived out through our lives. Our hearts become His dwelling place and His ours. Christ is our only living source of love and life. Our life is His and His life is ours to cherish.

CHRIST IS OUR ONLY LIVING SOURCE OF LOVE AND LIFE. OUR LIFE IS HIS AND HIS LIFE IS OURS TO CHERISH AND TREASURE.

Chapter Five
Debunking the Myths of Grace

"He who has the Son has the life; he who does not have the Son of God does not have the life." 1 John 5:12 (NASV)

Grace Space

What is "grace space"? It is a term for Christian thinking that believes that once a person is saved, they are always saved no matter what they do or what happens in their life. Such is the common opinion usually and automatically accepted and taught without the merit of an ounce of good sense or biblically based proof and scriptural understanding. A simple study of biblical canon will clearly show anyone that is truly interested in learning about grace and what the Lord has freely given, through His sacrifice on the cross, what grace is really all about. Grace is a "blanket-coverage" for our past, present and future sins, but it has its limitations. Scripture makes us aware of those parameters. Unfortunately naïve Christians and even those who pastor churches just gloss over the issue of grace. When Christians become so set in their beliefs, they become blinded to the significance of many core

Suicide and Christian Beliefs

Scriptural concerns and assume what they have always known to be true, is the truth. . .when it is not. Such is a perversion of Holy Scripture.

Never, in all of my studies have I had a closed mind to the Will and Word of God. He, on many occasions, has made me aware of His holy words and their meanings. I have not vacillated in my personal thinking, nor have I changed any of my basic beliefs or central core convictions acquired from my Christian training, educational studies, and upbringing. But I have become more in tune with certain Christian beliefs which "are not founded" on good biblical principle. Most changes in thought have come about from studying the cults. These wicked teachings bend Holy Scripture and turn it into religious garbage. Pick a cult, better yet, choose a cult exposed in *The Kingdom of the Cults* by the late Walter Martin. During my early years with California Western University, as a Ph.D. Program Mentor and Graduate Student Field Advisor, I had the privilege of meeting Walter

Martin and becoming his dissertation chairman and advisor. Walter's work was not only superior in its research and compilation, it was a vanguard effort of revealing the evil works of Satan and his demons in book form. It is from cultic thinking that many people are led astray from the truth of Christ. Many perverted text translations have blossomed because of the ignorance of those that had fallen victim to their distorted messages.

CULTIC THINKING CONDEMNS AND KILLS BOTH THE BODY AND THE SOUL. WHAT DO YOU THINK?

It is well known that the uneducated and unbalanced in knowledge, manage to twist Scripture to achieve what they want. . .it is to their own destruction that they do this. If anyone falls victim to these lawless individuals, such may be their own undoing and an utter calamity of faith will follow. See what Peter said, *". . . (there are) some things hard to understand, which the untaught and unstable distort, as they do also the rest of the Scriptures, to their own destruction. You therefore, beloved, knowing this beforehand, be on your guard lest, being carried away the error of unprincipled men, you fall from your own steadfastness, but grow (instead) in the grace and knowledge of our Lord and Savior Jesus Christ. . ."* 2 Peter 3:16-17 *(NKJV)*

CONSIDER THIS STATEMENT BELOW:

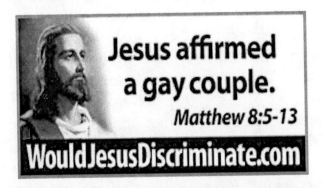

SEE HOW THESE VERSES ARE TWISTED BY THOSE WHO ARE PERVERTED AND TWISTED THEMSELVES?

Suicide and Christian Beliefs

UNFORTUNATELY, THESE SCRIPTURES, MATTHEW 8:5-13 HAVE ABSOLUTELY NOTHING TO DO WITH BEING HOMOSEXUAL, BUT HAVE EVERYTHING TO DO WITH SHOWING "GREAT FAITH" AND "BELIEF" IN CHRIST AND HIS HEAVENLY HEALING POWER. OF THAT, THERE IS NO DOUBT – BUT DO YOU SEE HOW THESE SCRIPTURES CAN BE TWISTED BY FALSE TEACHERS, AND WHEN THEY ARE, THEY MAKE NO SENSE AT ALL. FINDING THIS STATEMENT BY CHRIST TO BE CONDONING OF HOMOSEXUALITY AND PERVERSION, IS SUCH A FAR STRETCH THAT EVEN THE BEST OF MOUNTAIN CLIMBERS WILL FALL OFF THE MOUNTAIN TRYING TO REACH OUT THAT FAR.

Christianity apart from the cults and their misleading messages has to be representative of God's true Word; therefore; we must be careful of what we teach in our churches, small groups and schools. We will be held accountable to God for distorting His truth. If grace were the catch all, end all, and the "final word" to the mercy and forgiveness of Jesus, then the *Holy Bible* would not be filled with other warnings about the possibility of us falling short with respect to God's wonderful grace. *"Christ (was faithful) as a son over his own house; whose house are we, if we hold fast the confidence and the rejoicing of the hope firm unto the end. For we are made partakers of Christ, if we hold the beginning of our confidence steadfast unto the end." Hebrews 3: 6 and 14 (NKJV)* Note the "if" and what is said about us remaining steadfast (true) to the end of our days. This does not mean we can meander from our Christian walk, turn our back on God, and expect that everything will be just fine and dandy. God demands obedience to His ways and not just our partial or conditional behavior. *"If we endure, we shall also reign with Him: if we deny Him, He also will deny us."* *2 Timothy 2:12 (NKJV)*

SEEK THE GOOD SHEPHERD AND HE SHALL BE THERE FOR YOU – ALWAYS! HE PROTECTS YOU, COMFORTS YOU, LOVES YOU AND CARES SO DEEPLY FOR YOU THAT HIS HEART ACHES WHEN YOU WANDER AWAY FROM HIM AND BECOME LOST.

God's Word seems pretty clear. If you purposefully wander off and go astray after being in His loving and protective fold, then He will no longer be your Shepherd. . .He will deny you! Continual abidance in the Lord is essential towards one's salvation. We need to have perseverance. *B.F. Wescott* says in his work, *The Gospel According to St. John,* says:

> *"The doctrine of 'final perseverance' has been found in the passage (Matthew 10: 6 and Luke 15: 4). But we must carefully distinguish between the certainly of God's promises and His infinite power on the one hand, and the weakness and variableness of man's will on the other. If man falls at any stage in his spiritual life, it is not from want of divine grace, nor from the overwhelming power of adversaries, but from his neglect to use that which he may or may not use. We cannot be protected against ourselves in spite of ourselves."*

PERSONAL NEGLECT OF OUR OWN SPIRITUAL LIFE, DUE TO OUR OWN SEPARATION FROM GOD AND HIS DIVINE GRACE, IS AN ACT OF DELIBERATE SELF-DENIAL OF OUR TRUE AND ON-GOING ACCEPTANCE OF GOD'S MERCY AND ETERNAL SALVATION.

Don't misunderstand me, I believe in God's gift of grace. It is free to all of us, but we can also misuse it and misunderstand how to properly accept it if we have some hidden agenda or covert reason other than simply accepting the Lord's grace genuinely.

Suicide and Christian Beliefs

People accept Christ as their risen Savior and King, but some folks just flat out fail to take this commitment seriously. They make a public display while they are not sincere in their heart. The heart is where God dwells. Your body is your temple and if you are a sincere Christian and truly have accepted Christ as your Messiah, then you will not be going out and purposely committing sins. Why? Because the supernatural power of God's Holy Spirit is living in the temples of those that truly believe and the Spirit shields us from Satan's enticing sins. Those strong in the Lord do not fall away, but those that are weak do. Christians claiming to be saved, yet partake in unscriptural sin, deny the Lord and His commandments and expectations. Scripture says, *"Fear not them which kill the body, but are not able to kill the soul: but rather fear Him which is able to destroy both soul and body in hell. . .Whosoever therefore shall confess me before men, him will I confess before My Father which is in heaven. But whosoever shall deny me before men, him will I also deny before My Father which is in heaven. Matthew 10: 24-26, 28, 31 and 32 (NKJV)*

SORRY! YOU CANNOT TURN YOUR BACK ON GOD AND EXPECT TO BE SAVED BY THE GRACE OF CHRIST. GOD WANT'S YOUR HEART AND SOUL/BODY, AND SPIRIT, NOT YOUR BACK.

Suicide and Christian Beliefs

Scripture says, *"Whoever disowns the Son, the same hath not the Father. Let that therefore remain in you which ye have heard from the beginning. If that which ye have heard from the beginning shall remain in you, ye also shall remain in the Son, and in the Father. And this is the promise that He hath promised us, even eternal life. 1 John 2: 23-35 (KJ)* Countless verses tell us of the folly of leaving the presence and good graces of God. "Once saved, always saved!" Dream on, I don't think so. Statements like this are usually made by Christians that were taught this message early on in their newness to Jesus. They never grew beyond their small borders of Christian learning, personal *Holy Bible* discovery, and a hearty concerted study seeking the truth.

In the ***Book of Jude***, we are told to keep ourselves in the love of God and to have some mercy on those who continually doubt, saving them from the fire. Yes!!! You can slip away from God's grace, but that is your choice. So choose wisely. God has "made book" literally, on His claim against the unbelieving gracist. He has said, *"But my righteousness one shall live by faith; and if he shrinks back, My soul has no pleasure in him. But we are not of those who shrink back to destruction, but of those who have faith to the preserving of the soul." Hebrews 10: 38-39 (NAS)*

Do you forfeit your faith and an eternity with the Lord? This scripture is to warn Christians of what may be, not what has to be. Keeping your faith is what guarantees you the freedom of being with God and enjoying His grace. Faith is a biggie here. Scripture says, *"For by grace are ye saved through faith, and that not of yourselves: it is the gift of God; not of works, lest any man should boast." Ephesians 2: 8-9 (KJ)* If you keep believing you will be saved as promised, but if you stop believing in God's grace, then you may well lose it. *"But we believe that through the grace of the Lord Jesus Christ we shall be saved, even as they (the disciples)." Acts 15: 11 (KJ)*

YOU MUST BEAT SATAN AT EVERY TURN BY KNOWING THAT YOU ARE SAVED AND PROTECTED BY THE POWERFUL AND UNBREAKABLE GRACE OF GOD; THAT IS, UNLESS YOU REJECT HIS GIFT OF LIFE AND HIS ETERNAL PROMISES.

Suicide and Christian Beliefs

Bible Study

THIS IS WHAT YOU DO TO GET TO KNOW GOD'S WORD AND UNDERSTAND IT FULLY AND COMPREHENSIVELY. IT IS LITTLE-BY-LITTLE YET WHAT YOU LEARN STAYS WITH YOU!

Some individuals will continually try to assure other Christians that they are unconditionally secure forever. This is without contingency despite the numerous warnings and admonitions written in the Scriptures. Pastors often claim that such statements are only the Lord's way of motivating His saints to remain faithful to His ways and to constantly persevere. Pastors that teach the truth about these scriptures are said to be doctrinally off their trolleys, utterly confused, and not in touch with the reality of understanding that salvation comes from total grace. This is fallacy. Many ministers are deadly wrong and what they teach you could kill you, if you believe what they teach.

YOU ARE NOT UNCONDITIONALLY SECURE FOREVER. YOU MUST FULFILL GOD'S EXPECTATIONS TO BE PART OF THE CLUB! A MISGUIDED FAN ONLY LOSES.

Suicide and Christian Beliefs

Warnings are given in Scripture to remind each saint that falling away or failing in their faith is a deadly peril to be faced. *"If people have escaped from the corrupting forces of the world through their knowledge of our Lord and Savior Jesus Christ, and then are again caught and conquered by them, such people are in worse condition at the end than they were at the beginning. It would have been much better for them never to have known the way of righteousness than to know it and then turn away from the sacred command that was given them. What happened to them shows that the proverbs are true: 'A dog goes back to what it has vomited' and 'a pig that has been washed goes back to roll in the mud.'"* 2 Peter 2: 20-22 (GN)

THERE ARE NO PLASTIC BUBBLES OF PROTECTION FROM EVIL AND/OR SUGAR-COASTED PROTECTION FROM THE WRATH OF GOD. YOU'RE EITHER WITH HIM IN GRACE, OR AWAY FROM HIM IN DISGRACE AND WITHOUT MERCY. THE CHOICE IS ALL YOURS!

How can any thinking Christian read a scripture like this and still think they will always be saved? How many warnings do the Scriptures need to give us before we understand? The protective covering of grace is a marvelous and truly wonderful gift, but it is like a fragile plastic bubble. It can burst in our face if we continue to float in cactus patches or allow our hearts and minds to ride the wind like a cloud without purpose or direction. When we settle down with our free gift of grace, we need to treasure it for its preciousness, endless worth, and terrific value. Never has there been a freely purchased gift which was given without a need for compensation, yet paid for with the most sacrificial blood ever shed. Never, ever, ever, or will there be again!

"Grace is not a thing which can be infused and there are no gifts of grace which, so to speak, can be lodged bodily in the soul. Grace is the attitude of God to man which is revealed and made sure in Christ, and the only way in which it becomes effective in us for new life is when it wins from us the response of faith. And just as grace is the whole attitude of God in Christ to sinful men, so faith is the whole attitude of the sinful soul as it surrenders itself to that grace. Whether we call it the life of the justified, or the life of the reconciled, or the life of the regenerate, or the life of grace or of love, the new life is the life of faith and nothing else. To maintain the original attitude of welcoming God's love as it is revealed in Christ bearing our sins – not only to trust it, but to go on trusting – not merely to believe in it as a mode of

transition from the old to the new, but to keep on believing – to say with every breath we draw, 'Thou, O Christ, art all I want; more than all in thee I find' – is not a part of the Christian life, but the whole of it."

The above insert is taken from *James Denney's* book entitled, *The Christian Doctrine of Reconciliation.*

A warning, a very urgent warning from the Apostle Paul states, ***"And you, who were in time past alienated and enemies in your mind by wicked works, yet how hath he reconciled in the boy of his flesh though death, to present you holy and unblameable and unreproveable in his sight: if ye continue in the faith grounded and settled, and be not moved away from the hope of the gospel which ye have heard."*** *Colossians 1: 21-23 (KJV)* Also see, *2 Corinthians 4: 14*. When reading *John 8: 43-47*, we are told by Christ that those of us that are not of God will not hear, obey, nor understand His words. **Why? Because God is not in us, as God is also not in the heart or mind of a suicide victim.** If God or His Holy Spirit's power dwelled inside the temple of the suicide victim, then there would be no suicide. He that doesn't hear or believe is not part of God and the Lord is not part of

Him, but that person is part of his father the devil, as Scripture says he is.

IS THIS YOUR PERSONAL CUP OF TEA? IS THIS WHERE YOU THINK YOU BELONG? DOES THIS GIVE YOU THAT MYSTERIOUS KICK YOU NEED, OR WOULD YOU CONSIDER TRADING IT FOR GOD AND ACCEPTING THE MIRACLES HE'LL DO IN YOUR LIFE?

When we lose our trust and faith in God, we do devilish things. Suicide is a devilish thing, it is not a God-thing and no manner of such thinking is justified with God. Faith is the key. *Franz Delitzsch*, says in his book, *Commentary on the Epistle to the Hebrews*:

Suicide and Christian Beliefs

"The just man, the man accepted before God, lives by faith; but if he loses his faith, and faithlessly draws back from the right path, his acceptance is forfeited. That such apostasy is possible even for those who have been truly justified, i.e., for Christians who have had more than a superficial experience of divine grace, is one of the main points of instruction in this epistle. To teach this lesson, the clauses of the prophetic utterance are inverted. The second, as it stands here, is a warning as from the mouth of God Himself, a warning in a high prophetic tone. But the writer, as twice before, resumes the language of comfort and encouragement after words of the saddest foreboding. He proceeds, with pastoral gentleness and wisdom, to encourage the fainthearted and establish their wavering by rousing their Christian confidence, and associating himself with them as exposed to the same dangers, and courageously defying them."

People like myself, may very easily be labeled as a heretic, or being confused about biblical doctrine, unsound of mind and biblical understanding and so forth. But I do believe in salvation by grace and I expect to be castigated by men of limited learning and enlightenment that follow false beliefs, for the warnings of the *Holy Bible* which I have written about. Remember this verse? ***Proverbs 18:2 (ESV)*** *"A fool takes no pleasure in understanding, but only in expressing his opinion."*

Robert Shank says:

> *"Wisdom is justified of her children; but only eternity will reveal the full measure of the tragedy of this popular fallacy and the inevitable inconsistency of all who embrace it."*

OUR SIN IS GREAT
GOD'S GRACE IS GREATER

We are talking about the way grace is taught in churches today with the watering down of the warning verses and the claims of "Once saved, always saved!" Listen to what the Apostle Peter has to say about losing one's salvation. *If people have escaped from the corrupting forces of the world through their knowledge of our Lord and Savior Jesus Christ, and then are again caught and conquered by them, such people are in worse condition at the end than they were at the beginning. It would have been much better for them never to have known the way of righteousness than to know it and then turn away from the sacred command that was given them."* 2 Peter 2: 20-21 (GN) Also, *". . .pass the time of your sojourning here in fear."* 1 Peter 1: 17 (KJV) and *"Let him who feels sure of standing firm beware of falling."* 1 Corinthians 10: 12 (KJV)

And finally, *"Of how much greater punishment, suppose ye, shall he be thought worthy who hath trodden underfoot the Son of God, and hath counted the blood of the covenant, wherewith he was sanctified, an unholy thing, and hath done despite unto the Spirit of grace?. . .We shall not escape if we turn away from Him from heaven."* Hebrews 10: 29 and 12: 25 (KJV)

"When it came to the Law, God gave His finger but when it came to Grace, God gave His whole body."

We have no time to bask in self-assuredness; how totally ignorant of the value of grace and how conceited to think as such. We should fear what the Lord can do to us, if we betray His love and grace. *". . .spend the rest of your lives here on earth in reverence for Him." 1 Peter 1:17 (GN)* Sometimes we become much too smug and we believe we have it made, and then we forget to give the Father the glory which He deserves by simply forgetting the price paid for our grace. We manage to take it for granted and think that whatever we do will be okay, even if it is a small sin. But to God, each sin is awful and it is weighing on us when we think Jesus has cleared the slate for us, and that we have the presence of God's Holy Spirit is us, so anything we do will be forgiven because we are saved. I do not need to fear the Lord when it comes to grace. Do you say to yourself, "I think I will go sin, why not? I am saved!" Sorry, it just doesn't work that way.

Suicide and Christian Beliefs

I would not suggest you get too comfortable with how well planted and protected your feet are in that cement foundation you have built around yourself. **Remember: pride comes before a fall.** Just because you claim to be a saved Christian, does not give you some super untouchable voucher to eternal life. You may not have to earn it (that measure of grace you have been given), but you do have to use it as Jesus meant for it to be used. *"If you think you are standing firm you had better be careful that you do not fall." 1 Corinthians 10:12 (GN)*

Let me put it this way, because this is about as clear as I can get, *"For there is no longer any sacrifice that will take away sins if we purposely go on sinning after the truth has been made known to us. Instead, all that is left is to wait in fear for the coming Judgment and the fierce fire which will destroy those who oppose God!" '. . .What, then, of those who despise the Son of God? Who treat as a cheap thing the blood of God's covenant which purified them from sin? Who insult the Spirit of grace? Just think how much worse is the punishment they will deserve!' For we know who said, 'I will take revenge, I will repay'; and who also said, 'The Lord will judge His people.' It is a terrifying thing to fall into the hands of the Living God!" Hebrews 10: 26-31 (GN)* Those who don't see and understand this, are living in "grace space";

and that is not on the inside but on the outside of the perimeters of God's Word. Let this be a wake-up call to all gracists that reside on the planet earth, but are not in tune with the Creator's warnings concerning the precious spilled blood of His Son Jesus Christ as it relates to our "blanket coverage" of grace.

Don't get so tightly wound up and rolled up in that blanket that you lose all perspective of God's truth **AND** become blinded to the reality of grace and how it really works. We are warned again, *"Be careful, then, and do not refuse to hear him who speaks. Those who refused to hear the one who gave the divine message on earth did not escape. How much less shall we escape, then, if we turn away from the one who speaks from heaven!" Hebrews 12: 25 (GN)*

READ BELOW!

Suicide and Christian Beliefs

"ONCE SAVED, ALWAYS SAVED? DON'T MAKE ME PUKE WITH THAT LINE OF GARBAGE. READ YOUR SCRIPTURES AND SEE WHAT WILL REALLY HAPPEN TO YOU. LEARN WHAT YOU CAN AND CANNOT DO!

Several years ago, a friend of mine who knows my thoughts on grace and suicide, made an interesting comment to me. He said something like this. *"For years, I heard people say, 'Once saved, always saved' and I remembered that I had unconditionally accepted that same attitude many years before. Why? Because my minister thought and taught that way; he had learned that belief from another minister and so forth."* I think most ministers today have just accepted that belief and attitude because they were taught to think the same thing. So many preachers have done that without doing any kind of real research which when coupled up with a tad of common sense and what the Scriptures really say, something different is learned. All it takes is a little effort to check things out and consider the logic and intelligent approach to what Jesus taught us. How hard can that be? I fear that the majority of Christians learn a certain way of thinking; they accept church dogma and doctrine unconditionally, and also ingest it without fully thinking it through. Basically, they are too lazy to open the scriptures and read them! Is that you?

Suicide and Christian Beliefs

God has a purpose for you
that is held in His heart.
God has a path for you that
is paved with

HIS GRACE.

For years, I believed the same way. Then I wondered about things I heard people say. Things that didn't add up, or make sense. They would either misquote the Scriptures or twist the meaning. I will probably be accused of the same thing by those traditionalists that won't take the time to check things out as I have, and that is why I have taken the time to include all of these important scriptures into the text of this book – for your easy convenience of not having to look them up. My research doesn't make me right, but it does show that there is more meaning and understanding to suicide and grace than what is usually said and believed. I find it hard to believe that mass murders get to go to Heaven, or be somewhere in the presence of God, because they have been saved. I just don't think so, and no amount of that type of babble on suicide and grace is going to change my mind. God did give us common sense! Use it!

Suicide and Christian Beliefs

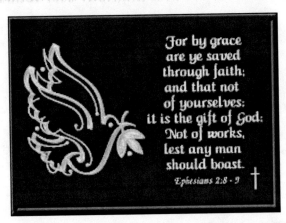

For by grace are ye saved through faith; and that not of yourselves: it is the gift of God: Not of works, lest any man should boast.

Ephesians 2:8 - 9

Stop and think about this. Do you really think you can be saved and baptized and then turn your back on God and His Holy Spirit that is fully functioning inside of you and directing you? I don't think you would go out and commit murder, believing that you may get caught and punished by man, but that God will forgive you because at one time in your life you bothered to accept His grace. *"Do you not know that your body is a temple of the Holy Spirit, who is in you, whom you have received from God? You are not your own; you were bought at a price. Therefore honor God with your body."* *(NIV)*

If you are having trouble with these messages I am relating you, then get fully acquainted with what our *Holy Bible* says – that's all I am saying.

Suicide and Christian Beliefs

YOU MUST KEEP HOPE, BE REPENTANT AND ASK FOR HIS MERCY. CONFESS TO THE LORD YOUR SINS AND ASK HIM TO RELEASE YOU FROM THE CLUTCHES OF SATAN AND THE THINKING WITH WHICH HE HAS HELD YOU HOSTAGE. REMEMBER: FORGIVENSS IS ALREADY YOURS, THAT PRICE HAS BEEN PAID IN FULL. DON'T EVER FORGET THAT!

God's Holy Spirit is not supposed to let those who are saved do this type of thing. When you give up on God, He doesn't give up on you. He loves you. But there is also a limit as to how far you can go and still be acceptable to Him. People like those mentioned above usually don't truly repent their crimes and ask for forgiveness simply out of courtesy to the Lord. They have already lost hope and abandoned God. It was their decision to cash out. Only they and God know the truth.

Suicide and Christian Beliefs

Some final thoughts about grace and suicide which are good to reiterate: when an individual commits suicide, he or she falls outside of grace by sinning as such. As a sinner, doing such a deliberate act, is without having God's Holy Spirit in their heart. It is an act of transgression against God and His commandments. *"For if we sin willfully after we have received the knowledge of the truth, there no longer remains a sacrifice (Christ's death for the forgiveness of all sins) for sins, but a certain fearful expectation of judgment, and fiery indignation which will devour the adversaries."* *Hebrews 10:26-27 (NKJV)* Suicide smacks of insult to Him and is a rejection of God's gift of life and of His grace. Punishment in death follows this act of selfishness, and there are no comforting scriptures which say what has happened will be forgiven or undone. It is what it is!

"Of how much worse punishment, do you suppose, will he be thought worthy who has trampled the Son of god underfoot, counted the blood of the covenant by which He was sanctified a common thing, and insulted the Spirit of grace?" *Hebrews 10:29 (NKJV)* One must do the Will of God to receive His promise. *"Therefore do not cast away your confidence, which has great reward. For you have need of endurance, so that after you have done (His will) the will of God, you may receive the*

promise." *Hebrews 10:35-36 (NKJV) Ephesians 2:8 (NKJV)* says, *"For by grace you have been saved through faith; and that not of yourselves, it is (grace) the gift of God."* Folks, the gift of grace, as the scripture says is through faith that one is saved. Suicide victims had no faith and showed no faith by their act of self-murder to receive grace and be saved. No faith, no grace, no saving. Gracists go spastic when confronted with such statements. Why? Because their answer is: grace covers all sin, subject closed. Sorry, this grace thing is easy and it is a "God-thing" and it is good, but you can lose salvation. As one rejects any decent gift (from another person or from God), it is an individual choice to spurn and/or not accept any gift given, with or without conditions.

SUICIDE VICTIMS HAD NO FAITH AND SHOWED NO FAITH BY THEIR ACT OF SELF-MURDER TO RECEIVE GRACE AND BE SAVED. NO FAITH, NO GRACE, NO SAVING. ONLY OBLIVION AND ETERNAL DARKNESS! SUBJECT CLOSED!

Commentary of Salvation

What do the experts have to say about the warnings of Scripture? Where do those men that are well-learned and educated in religious studies, and especially the study of the Holy Scriptures, truly stand? Do they agree with the findings, attitude and my personal theorizing written in this book, or are they proponents of some other beliefs? Let's examine their thoughts, writings and concepts. I have not chosen any particular order for these submissions, but rather I have placed these insertions where and how I felt they would best make a difference to the reader. I consider them to be a conglomeration of excellent statements about the doctrine of perseverance and eternal security.

Robert Shank's book, *Life in the Son*, says the following:

". . Calvin declares that 'God has at heart the salvation of all. . .yet it does not therefore follow that he has not determined with himself what he intends to do as to every individual man' – some of whom He created for salvation, and others for perdition. Again, as so often with Calvin, the left hand giveth, and the right hand taketh away. 'God has at heart the salvation of all (and) invites all to the acknowledgement of his truth.' But He also has at heart the everlasting perdition of men whom He created for no other purpose or destiny – men to whom, from before

creation, He utterly denied all prospect of arriving at the acknowledgment of His truth and salvation. "God has at heart the salvation of all' – and the damnation of most! Without regard to anything in men, god is pleased to consign to everlasting perdition many whose salvation He 'has at heart.' Why! Perhaps to confirm the logic of Calvin's theology."

Robert Shank further says:

"That Calvin resorts to similar exegetical artifice in his interpretation of passages which affirm that Christ died for all mankind. For example, according to his interpretation of 1 John 2:2, John did not mean that Jesus is actually the propitiation 'for the sins of the whole world." Instead, he meant only that He is the propitiation for the sins of the elect wherever they may happen to be throughout the whole world, and in whatever generation they may happen to live on earth."

John Calvin, Commentaries on the Catholic Epistles, says:

Suicide and Christian Beliefs

". . .the design of John was no other than to make this benefit common to the whole Church. Then under the word all or whole, he does not include the reprobate, but designates those who should believe as well as those who were then scattered through various parts of the world. For then is really made evident, as it is meet, the grace of Christ, when it is declared to be the only true salvation of the world."

Although thought to be unscriptural by many believing Christians, limited atonement is still part of the Calvinist religious philosophy today. For many it is an acceptable belief although most Calvinists that believe as such are considered to be off base with Scripture. They are considered to be illogical. For example, *Robert Shank*, again in *Life in the Son,* writes:

"Quite inconsistent are moderate Calvinists who reject a limited atonement while advocating an unconditional election. Why should Jesus bear the sins of men who have no prospect of forgiveness and whose inevitable destiny, by decree of God, is eternal perdition? Why should God sacrifice His Son for men whom He does not desire to save and whom He does not love?

Or, how is it true that god loves men whom he deliberately creates for no other end and purpose than everlasting estrangement form Himself?

"The only claim guilty sinners have on the mercy of God is the gracious character of God Himself. That claim was enough to send Jesus to Golgotha and to a shameful death as the propitiation 'for the sins of the whole world.' The guilt of men who persist in disobedience is compounded many-fold by the fact that Jesus 'gave himself a ransom for all' and God desires that none perish, but that all come to repentance and to the knowledge of His truth and saving grace."

Unfortunately many believers think that to be part of the Church and its beliefs is enough and that one's faith may wane and cause one to wander away, but they will still be saved. Scripture tells us that we must remain in continuance with God's Word and not let false doctrines or apostates lead us in the wrong direction away from the true God. We have to have a faith that remains in us from beginning to end; and we must remain in the Son and in the Father. This is what God promised us if we want to gain and keep eternal life. Once again read *1 John 2:24-25; Timothy 3: 13-15* and

Suicide and Christian Beliefs

Colossians 1:21-23. Jesus Christ taught us that when we first accept His Word and gospel, as an elect of God, we will not only know and recognize God's truth, but that we must follow His Word and do His Will through our continued obedience and with faithful retention. If any of us are to continue in the saving grace of Christ and the eternal life of God, then this is our directive.

Chapter Six
Forgiveness and Suicide

What is This Forgiveness Issue?

Forgiveness can be a tough cookie to digest, especially for someone that has normally been a spiteful and hateful person. If that is you, then you have to let go of the grudges you hold against others. Or you have to simply forget what transgressions have been committed against you and make a self-commitment of not hating, despising, or disliking the person or persons that have hurt you either physically or mentally. We must carry mental trash into Heaven. Mental garbage has to be dropped in the "forgiveness mind-dump" here on earth. Like I have said in other books, you can be bitter or better. A pastor-friend, Dr. Ben Sigman, once put it very nicely during one of his moving sermons in church. He said, *"Resentment is either rehearsed or released."* Resentment can eat you up inside and do more to upset you and hurt you than what was caused by the initial pain you suffered somewhere in the past. Can you really imagine having a few seconds of ill-sent hurt that have caused you unlimited resentment and mental anguish? If you suffer from this now, and have not let the pain go, then you must. It has controlled you long enough and has probably been the ongoing seed of many long moments (minutes, hours, days and so forth) of receiving a fiery dart wound from another person. Get over it! Get beyond it! Give forgiveness! That is easily said, I realize that, but it must be said and it must be done. God wants you to forgive all those that need your forgiveness. This is what Scripture says, *"If you forgive those who sin against you, your heavenly Father will forgive you. But if you refuse to forgive others, your Father will not forgive your sins." Matthew 6: 14-15 (NLT)*

Must you be forgiven before you'll be forgiven by God – is that the rule? I thought we were already forgiven with Christ's death on the cross. Let's not forget that is when He began His New Covenant with us, and we were already forgiven our sins. Hmmmm? I call this condition **"The Forgiveness Dilemma."** Let's discuss that question and learn the proper scriptural answer. Then you can learn the truth and keep it steadfastly in mind. Don't allow some imbecile to rent space in your head and then go on living in it without even paying rent! Come on! Do yourself a big favor and get over it! Wake-up and move on! Let's examine what the scriptures really say.

Suicide and Christian Beliefs

It's vitally important that you understand that various scriptures are taken out of context and used as some particular religious belief wants to use it. It becomes part of their religious dogma, or incorporated into their church doctrine. At any rate, it is their philosophical understanding of what has been instructed to the church body of what they should believe to be biblical truth. Unfortunately, we are taught many mistruths about what a scripture means and what it does not mean. This is a case, my case, of how the forgiveness scripture, as I refer to it, is misinterpreted.

That Scripture is, *"For if you forgive others their trespasses, your heavenly Father will also forgive you, but if you do not forgive others their trespasses, neither will your Father forgive your trespasses." Matthew 6:14-15 (ESV)* When God gave His commandments and His expectations, rules, precepts and so forth to those under the Old Covenant (Old Testament Times), He expected them to be obeyed. But when Christ "died" on the cross, the New Covenant began. Anything He said prior to that time was still under the Old Covenant, not legalistic *per se*, but under old Jewish Law. When He expired, the New Covenant came into being with its new sets of understanding and obligations. Christ's words were aimed at the Hebrews and Jews of His day. Those words were intended to bring those Hebrews and Jews to a place where they could experience their own spiritual needs without the necessary of their priests. His words about forgiveness were only to magnify their demands found in their Law, oh so legalistic still. Jesus simply wanted those Jews and Hebrews to comprehend and realize their need for a Redeemer, a Savior, and that He was there to fulfill Scripture.

For example: our forgiveness has already been grounded and set in Christ's sacrifice through the shedding of His blood for everyone. We've been forgiven already and not forgiving others will not keep us out of heaven, nor will it mean the God won't forgive us because He already has through the ransom sacrifice of His Son Jesus Christ. How much more do we need? We are under a New Covenant. Christ's death inaugurated our New Covenant and brought the Law (the Old covenant) to its termination. Everything was totally changed at the cross! Check out this scripture: *"For this reason Christ is the mediator of a new covenant, that those who are called may receive the promised eternal inheritance—now that he has died as a ransom to set them free from the sins committed under the first covenant. In the case of a will, it is necessary to prove the death of the one who made it, because a will is in force only when somebody has died; it never takes effect while the one who* *made it is living. This is why even the first covenant was not put into effect without blood."* *Hebrews 9:15-18 (NIV)* I not only bet that you didn't know that or understand it, but that you still don't want to believe it – so, let's go a little further with some meaningful verse. The Old Covenant is obsolete and we now experience God differently.

The night before Jesus was crucified, He took His cup and He passed it to His disciples saying these words: *". . .he took the cup, saying, "This cup is the new covenant in my blood, which is poured out for you."* *Luke 22:20 (NIV)* Did you catch those important words which said "new covenant"?

ITEMS JESUS PROBABLY USED IN THE LAST SUPPER WHEN HE DISCUSSED HIS NEW COVENANT WITH HIS DISCIPLES, AND THE COVENANT IS MEANT FOR US, TOO.

Here is why the New Covenant is so very important and why the Law was done away with and replaced by Christ's sacrifice. Read these scriptures slowly and understand that what is for Israel is also for us. Under the Old Covenant the Law was for the Hebrews and the Jews, but now Judah and Israel share the New Covenant with all of us Christian Gentiles. Read: *"The point of what we are saying is this: We do have such a high priest, who sat down at the right hand of the throne of the Majesty in heaven, and who serves in the sanctuary, the true tabernacle set up by the Lord, not by man. Every high priest is appointed to offer both gifts and sacrifices, and so it was necessary for this one also to have something to offer. If he were on earth, he would not be a priest, for there are already men who offer the gifts prescribed by the law. They serve at a sanctuary that is a copy and shadow of what is in heaven. This is why Moses was warned when he was about to build the tabernacle: 'See to it that you make everything according to the pattern shown you on the mountain.' But the ministry Jesus has received is as superior to theirs as the covenant of which he is mediator is superior to the old one, and it is founded on better promises. For if there had been nothing wrong with that first covenant, no place would have been sought for another. But God found fault with the people and said: 'The time is coming, declares the Lord, when I will make a new covenant with the house of Israel and with the house of Judah. It will not be like the covenant I made with their forefathers when I took them by the hand to lead them out of Egypt, because they did not remain faithful to my covenant, and I turned away from them, declares the Lord. This is the covenant I will make with the house of Israel after that time, declares the Lord. I will put my laws in their minds and write them on their hearts. I will be their God, and they will be my people. No longer will a man teach his neighbor, or a man his brother, saying, 'Know the Lord, because they will all know me, from the least of them to the greatest. For I will forgive their wickedness and will remember their sins no more.' By calling this covenant "new," he has made the first one obsolete; and what is obsolete and aging will soon disappear.'" Hebrews 8:1-13 (NIV)* Hmmmm!

Personally I think that these scriptures are rather profound and crystal clear. If you already know and believe this too, then what is your stumbling block?

Suicide and Christian Beliefs

Do you still refuse to give up what you are holding onto for dear life, that misunderstanding which has become a blight, a fallacy that you claim as God's truth? If so, then look at these scriptures, keeping in mind that we don't forgive to be forgiven – that has already happened. *". . .he predestined us to be adopted as his sons through Jesus Christ, in accordance with his pleasure and will—to the praise of his glorious grace, which he has freely given us in the One he loves. In him we have redemption through his blood, the forgiveness of sins, in accordance with the riches of God's grace that he lavished on us with all wisdom and understanding." Ephesians 1:5-8 (NIV)*

And once again, read these verses: *"When you were dead in your sins and in the uncircumcision of your sinful nature, God made you alive with Christ. He forgave us all our sins, having canceled the written code, with its regulations, that was against us and that stood opposed to us; he took it away, nailing it to the cross. And having disarmed the powers and authorities, he made a public spectacle of them, triumphing over them by the cross." Colossians 2:13-15 (NIV)* and also, *"Since God chose you to be the holy people he loves, you must clothe yourselves with tenderhearted mercy, kindness, humility, gentleness, and patience. Make allowance for each other's faults, and forgive anyone who offends you. Remember, the Lord forgave you, so you must forgive others." Colossians 3:12-13 (NLT).*

There is considerable clarity in when we were forgiven and why we don't need to forgive others to be forgiven – let that myth go away as it did when the New Covenant with Christ came into effect. *"And do not bring sorrow to God's Holy Spirit by the way you live. Remember, he has identified you as his own, guaranteeing that you will be saved on the day of redemption. Get rid of all bitterness, rage, anger, harsh words, and slander, as well as all types of evil behavior. Instead, be kind to each other, tenderhearted, forgiving one another, just as God through Christ has forgiven you." Ephesians* 4:30-32 (NLT) **Remember:** The Apostle Paul told those he ministered to that they should forgive others just as Jesus had forgiven them, but not so that God would forgive them – that's been done!

Suicide and Christian Beliefs

Let's face it – we simply forgive others because it feels good to do so and we know that Christ has forgiven us already; besides, who are we to not want to forgive someone when God, Our Loving Creator, Who is OVER us, has forgiven us unconditionally of everything that we have done, are doing, or may do?

So, in light of what has been said over the past few pages, what does forgiveness have to do with suicide? We have discussed in earnest the ramifications of suicide. We have discussed what works and what doesn't work as far as what Scripture says is acceptable and what isn't acceptable. Hopefully you have become aware that suicide is not an acceptable option to God, even if you are a gracist in belief, and some of those gracist beliefs are hard to reconcile and admit to. Such thoughts go against the gain of your religious training or education. So, with your gun now loaded with ample ammunition for any discussion about forgiveness and what you personally feel and think about a suicide victim's disposition. . .well, it's your call. Think it through and find out what you're comfortable with thinking and believing.

Guess what? It is okay to allow your mind to open up to another idea about the location of a suicide spirit once they have chosen to leave this realm. I am not Catholic, but this is one area where they are probably closer to the truth than are most Protestants. Suicide victims should not be consecrated or buried in hallowed ground. Why? They have trespassed against God's Will for them and have never accepted total forgiveness for their sins against others, or for their resenting attitudes against others, or his or her life. That is why they probably killed themselves, in most cases, granted there could be some other dumb reasons.

Yes, suicide is dumb. But some of you will say, *"They didn't know what they were doing. They were high on drugs or had been taking drugs for a long time, and all those other lame reasons."* I hate to tell you this, but wake up! They killed themselves and there is no special place for them in God's cutting edge book, the *Holy Bible*. There are no special allowances for such suicides. If you think so, do your own research, find where that "out" or "option" is mentioned or detailed in the *Holy Bible* and let me know. I want to see it, read it and learn from it. However, don't waste your time, it's not there. ***"Watch out that you do not lose***

Suicide and Christian Beliefs

what you have worked for, but that you may be rewarded fully. Anyone who runs ahead and does not continue in the teaching of Christ does not have God; whoever continues in the teaching has both the Father and the Son. If anyone comes to you and does not bring this teaching, do not take him into your house or welcome him. Anyone who welcomes him shares in his wicked work." 2 John 1:8-11 (NIV) Yes, trying to rush yourself into God's holy presence doesn't really work, not according to Scripture. Suicide is just one way of doing that, isn't it? You will have no reward for stopping God's instruction and teaching, and especially if you allow someone else to be your influence into doing what isn't Godly and acceptable to the Lord. Confess, repent and seek mercy and understanding, as you've already been cleansed by Christ's blood.

YOU HAVE FORGIVENESS AND YOU'VE ALREADY BEEN CLEANSED BY THE BLOOD OF JESUS CHRIST.

Suicide and Christian Beliefs

Remember this is old thinking about forgiveness – get past it: Again, suicide victims have left this earth without totally forgiving those who have put them in the position to weakly give up and settle for death over life. Circumstances can cause such behavior also, but there are still options like hanging in there and getting tough to the situation, seek counseling or meet the troubling problems head on. Yet, God says if we do not forgive others, then we also will not be forgiven, and that means forgiven our sins. Christ died to forgive our sins, so who are we not to forgive others? Like I said above, get past this old thinking about forgiveness still being needed to be in God's presence – it's not needed.

Christ died in horrible pain and agony, sacrificing His life so that we may be forgiven our sins and obtain a greater life in Him who has died for us.

Suicide and Christian Beliefs

You've already read about Christ's crucifixion outlined in this book. So, who are we not to forgive others but slide out the back door with our rent unpaid? We are just another grudge holder. God is our landlord and we are accountable to Him. He says He has sent His Son to pay for our sins and grant us the possibility of eternal life in His Kingdom, but some folks reject that wonderful gift and allow Satan's forces to be successful and win. What a shame! What a crying shame! **God does forgive our sins even if we haven't forgiven others.** So, then what happens to our spirit when we die? It depends upon how and why we died. *"Lord, I confess my sins openly to you and in written form, I forgive anyone and everyone who I have held resentment against and I release those feelings and thoughts."* There! Was that so tough? Just mean what you have said – if you say it.

Suicide and Christian Beliefs

People go to their graves hating others. They allow others to win by taking their own lives and not facing up to their greatest fears. It is the easy way out. It is the coward's way out. It is sending your spirit to someplace it probably doesn't want to be. Has such a person jumped out of the proverbial frying pan into the fire? Quite possibly yes. If God has not forgiven the sins of an unrelenting suicide victim, then where is their spirit? We know where their body/soul is, but just where is their spirit? I can tell you this much, it is not with God, nor is it in some Heavenly place where there is peace and harmony. Don't kid yourself, the suicide victim doesn't deserve such comfort, they interrupted God's plan and imposed their own; they turned their back on God's forgiveness and let their own sins go unchecked; they rejected Christ's sacrifice and made an "evil and unacceptable to God sacrifice" of their own. We have learned in the Old Testament how unacceptable sacrifices were treated by God. They were **unacceptable, an abomination and they that did so were destroyed.** Point made!!!

Scripture was not written to be rejected or shuffled around to meet the personal or group needs of individuals and organizations, choosing to set up their own interpretations of God's Word. Scripture was written and recorded to be understood and used as guidelines to live by and to live with, in God's terms. Scripture gives reasons to be Christians showing, us how to have a relationship with the Lord. The *Holy Bible* is all about relationships, it is not a book that is meant to be confusing and bog us down with words we do not comprehend. Scripture may be composed from another language or two, but that does not mean we go and get lost in Scripture by trying to point out every word in an ancient language and dissect it to death. That is not only boring to the most casual reader, but it is only exposing the root of a word whose meaning has most likely already transcended its original significance and proper usage.

When we read Scripture, we should be reading it with an open heart and mind, just as we worship and accept our Lord. Because we love to read and study prophecy, being so exciting and stimulating, we do not, or should not, go and get lost in its world of eschatology titillation. **We should focus on saving**

souls; that is our chief job. **We should focus on doing good to and for others and leading them to the Father.** *"Do nothing from rivalry or conceit, but in humility count others more significant than yourselves. Let each of you look not only to his own interests, but also to the interests of others." Philippians 2:3-4 (ESV)* We should focus on being obedient to God's ways, those things which matter the most and are important to the Lord, and by not allowing ourselves to become caught-up into, or lost in any maze of Scriptural intellectualism. Such intellectualism stagnates most biblical enthusiasts, as they try to look educated and scholarly. I mention all this because most Christians would allow this to happen without attempting to discover truths on their own.

Unfortunately, most Christians hear what they want to hear when they listen to some teacher they believe to be reputable, but he or she really isn't. Most Christians do not test the spirits or examine the facts laid down by some minister that they, in all cases, unconditionally believe. *(Beloved, do not believe every spirit, but test the spirits to see whether they are from God; because many false prophets have gone out into the world." 1 John 4:1(NIV)* This is sorrowful because we are told to examine the Scripture daily as did the Bereans, to see what was true and what was not. *"Now these were more noble-minded than those in Thessalonica, for they received the word with great eagerness, examining the scriptures daily, to see whether these things ere so."* Acts 17: 11 (NSAV) Do you personally do this? If not, maybe that is why you might be easily duped into believing and accepting something that you should have examined first – on your own. Prayer and supplemental reading are powerful tools.

I implore you to examine the Scriptures yourself. Suicide is a touchy subject and everyone that loved the suicide victim wants to believe the best about their final ethereal existence. Is it celestial and safe? Are they in the bosom of the Lord, or are they simply condemned to a future existence in oblivion? If you are a gracist, then I ask you too, to go examine what Scripture says, in total, not just a verse or two that makes you feel good and makes you sure that you have the right answer. Look at the other side of the bread to see how it is buttered and what it tells you to be aware of and how to prepare for unexpected tragedy. Make forgiveness a part of your daily life. Don't think twice about it, and don't hesitate to forgive quickly. We are all human and make mistakes, we even do rotten things on purpose, but we do deserve personal forgiveness, as Jesus has given us unconditional forgiveness for our sins through His propitious and holy sacrifice. Get

Suicide and Christian Beliefs

straight with the Lord now and know that you do not hold grudges or resentment against any other person. Check your bitterness out today and maybe you'll find a more peaceful and fulfilling life if you decide to get rid of it. I personally don't allow others to rent space in my head. People like that are little people and don't deserve my head room. Do they deserve yours? No! I didn't think so. Then do something about it if you are so haunted by them.

YOUR JOB IS TO READ AND STUDY THROUGH THE HOLY SCRIPTURES AND LEARN WHAT THE LORD HAS FOR YOU TO MEDITATE UPON AND INCORPORATE INTO YOUR LIFE!

Without our forgiveness of others, and hopefully our forgetting what they have done, we cannot satisfy God with our attitude towards others, and our bitter behavior. . .and eventually, what does that mean salvation-wise, or what does that do to the condition and state of our spirit? It's not hard to figure out. God doesn't have to give you a step-by-step journal which says, "Do this, don't do this. Believe this, don't believe this," and so forth. I think you get the picture. Use your common sense, this is God you are dealing with, not some unknown and incomprehensive entity. God is clear and if you are still confused, then go to Him in prayer and ask Him to talk to you about your concerns. He is Our Living Heavenly Father Who truly wants to discuss our concerns with Him. This is called having faith in God and trusting Him to do right by you. Would He do anything else? I don't think so!

Two parting thoughts: first, don't rest your beliefs and laurels on one or two scriptures you think sum up any issue of major importance in God's gospel; secondly, be quick to forgive and forget. Get rid of the pressure and let God's Holy Spirit live in your temple and do His Godly work. It will be magnificent, and of this I can assure you.

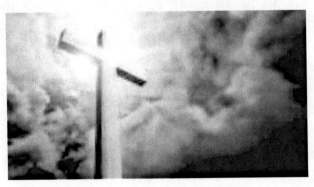

Hell: Something to Believe or Not Believe

When I first attended church I never heard much about Hell that I fully, or even partially understood. Just getting to know who Jesus was and that Paul was a great apostle and a guy named Jonah got swallowed by a whale or some relatively large fish was about all I could digest. Then Moses came along and Joseph with his coat of many colors and some character named Hulk Hogan . . . no, it was Samson, a super star of combat who could kill a thousand enemy soldiers with the jaw of an ass. Well, there were evil women like Jezebel and Delilah, but there were neat ladies like Ruth, and Esther who gambled her throne. A little boy named David slew a great giant, but there were bigger giants than Goliath. The stories just went on and on. Then I heard about Revelation and that totaled confused me. I was told that it was mainly symbolism and I figured that was a good thing because I didn't understand how whores could eat their own flesh. And I didn't know what symbolism meant either. Mystery Babylon was a mystery, as was the 144,000 and my need to get my name recorded into some Book of Life, which I remember figuring that I had already done because I was alive. That was no connection there with reality, but I was

306

a kidling, totally ignorant of what the *Holy Bible* was all about, but it had my attention and I was learning and memorizing and sharing with others.

HE WAS NOT SAVABLE, IN THAT, HE JUST COMMITTED SUICIDE AND CHOSE HIS OWN DESTINY. BAD CHOICE!

So along came Hell and that scared the devil right out of me. What I pictured in my mind was some really high level scary stuff. For some period of time after learning about Hell, I was a model saint. Where and when that mind-set changed, I don't know, but probably about the time I became an independent and know-it-all teenager. By then I realized how I truly knew everything but Hell wasn't part of that equation. Guess what? Hell is still scary and lots of folks see Hell differently. Some religions even reject the whole thought of it.

Suicide and Christian Beliefs

Like those guys who pick and choose what is good for their cult and what isn't. Unfortunately, I am pretty mainline Christian and I believe there is a Hell and I want to discuss the concept and reality of Hell with you. Oh, yes! This will have something to do with suicide, you betcha!

One thing I quickly recall is that Jesus said in the *Book of Matthew* that there was eternal fire and punishment. *"Then He will also say to those on His left, 'Depart from Me, accursed ones, into the eternal fire which has been prepared for the devil and his angels'. . .and these will go away into eternal punishment, but the righteous into eternal life.'" Matthew 25:41 and 46 (NASV)* Jesus spared us nothing, and he cut us no slack when it came to talking about Hell. The Lord told us, *"the sons of*

the Kingdom shall be cast out into the outer darkness, in that place there shall be weeping and gnashing of teeth." **Matthew 8:12 (NASV)** In another scripture in **Matthew 13:42** Jesus says that Hell is like a furnace of fire and in **Matthew 3:12** Christ says its fire is unquenchable. In **Revelation 20:10** Hell is described as being a place where there will be fire and brimstone and torment day and night forever and ever. Hell is a lake of burning sulfur with eternal separation from God's glorious presence. *"And these will pay the penalty of eternal destruction, away from the presence of the Lord and from the glory of His power. . ."* **2 Thessalonians 1:9 (NASV)**

JUST ANOTHER REMINDER THAT HELL EXISTS!

The worst of all this is the everlastingness of Hell. It never ends, it never goes away, it's suffering and pain felt by each person therein, is forever, without a break or a short duration of relief – Hell is eternal and that scares me to no end. Hmmmm! Yes, to no end. . .that is exactly what makes it so bad. . .there is no respite, no end. . .it just goes on and on. And we got to choose to go there, if we end up there. There is no one to blame but yourself. Hell is where the hammer meets the nail for everyone that was too busy to listen to Jesus and decided not to be a responsible and accountable person. If you go to Hell, you earned it! It's somewhat like being the losing pitcher in a ball game, in that, you earned it – you gave up the runs that caused you to lose. And, if you score no runs with Jesus while playing by His rules – well, you lose again.

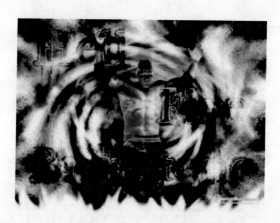

WHO IS THAT STANDING IN THE HELLFIRE? ISN'T THAT A SUICIDE VICTIM? WHY YES, IT IS!

Suicide and Christian Beliefs

R.C. Sproul says in his book titled *Essential Truths of the Christian Faith* that:

> "...their problem (those in Hell) will not be separation from God, it will be the presence of God that will torment them. In Hell, God will be present in the fullness of His divine wrath. He will be there to exercise His just punishment of the damned. They will know Him as an all-consuming fire."

R.C. Sproul believes as I do, that the eternal continuousness of Hell is the worst part of being there coupled with its horrors and suffering.

Hank Hanegraaff says, in his book titled *Resurrection:*

> "The horrors of Hell are such that they cause us instinctively to recoil in disbelief and doubt."

There must be balance in God's universe, without it we haven't any choices and are forced to accept whatever the Will of God is for us. That means no freewill to choose to be good or to be evil; to select an eternity with God or an eternity with Satan. We must have balance; it only makes good common sense. Evil is like communism: both seek a complete domination; there is no middle ground and no choices in anything else. A one-way system would be false and forced, it would lack complete love for our Savior and those that did want to be in the Holy Presence of God would suffer a different eternal fate – one of closeness versus their choice of full separation from God. It stands to reason, if there is a place of eternal bliss and happiness, there must be a place of suffering and torment, a universe of balance dictates such. So, eternal Heaven (being in God's presence and probably in the New Jerusalem) is balanced with being in Hell (a place of complete separation from God forever).

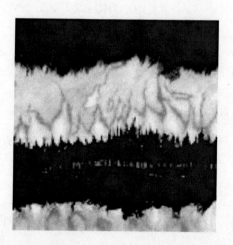

HELL IS A VERY BIG PLACE AND THERE SEEMS TO BE A WHOLE CROWD DOWN THERE TODAY!

Suicide and Christian Beliefs

If there were no Hell, there would be no reason for anyone to obey God. If God is just, true and merciful, then there must be a Hell to give justice to those that suffered at the hands of those that were evil. You don't get to break God's rules and get off that easy; God said that revenge was His and He will exact every correct and perfect measure of it for Himself and those that suffered at the hands of evil and rottenness. Hell is essential for God's justice to be imposed and controlled; God is an organized God and He would not allow any confusion to exist between evil and goodness. Without Hell we would not have any true justice for evil committed against us and those that committed the evil would be free of the Lord's wrath.

Sorry, this scenario of allowing folks to choose their own destiny and not have to answer for a life of crime, hatred, and injustice against innocent people, just doesn't equate. God has always announced His intentions and He has always gotten His revenge. Why should God not have a place like Hell for those who choose to go there on their own, or due to their earthly behavior and demerits? It's simple, salvation leads to a heavenly place of contentment in the presence of God, and sin not repented and unbelief leads to a journey into the nether regions of darkness and turmoil. They say great minds travel in similar circles. Well, my mind isn't great by a long shot, but let's examine a couple of beliefs of two great thinkers: Jonathan Edwards and Peter Kreeft. *Edwards* says in, *The Works of Jonathan Edwards:*

> *"It is a most unreasonable thing to suppose that there should be no future punishment, to suppose that God who had made man a rational creature, able to know his duty, and sensible that he is deserving punishment when he does it not; should let man alone, and let him live as he will, and never punish him for his sins, and never make any difference between the good and the bad; that he should make the world of mankind and then let it alone, and let men live all their days in wickedness, in adultery, murder, robbery, and persecution, and the like, and suffer them to live in prosperity, and never punish them, that he should suffer them to prosper in the world far beyond many good men, and never punish them hereafter. How unreasonable is it to suppose that he who made the world, should leave things in such confusion, and never take any care of the government of his creatures, and that he should never judge his reasonable creatures! Reason teaches that there is a God and reason teaches that if there be he*

must be a wise and just God, and he must take care to order things wisely and justly among his creatures; and therefore it is unreasonable to suppose that man dies like a beast, and that there is no future punishment."

So, what does *Kreeft* say? In his book entitled, *Everything You Ever Wanted To Know About Heaven,* he writes about how our current mind sets have been clouded by credulity and not common sense, and that we have given up our belief and understanding about common sense distinctions concerning evil and good. We have lost the meaning and difference of the two through growing in humanism and allowing the ways of the world to rule over what should be a clear sensible understanding of God's initial wisdom implanted in our hearts and minds. *Kreeft* says:

"They (Eastern religions), like we, do not believe in sin or Hell. This entails loss of belief in free will, for free will can choose only between two really distinct objects. If all roads lead to the same place, we can only accept the not reject; all are inevitably blended into one Heaven. That is also why totalitarianism, collectivism, [Islam – my comment] and communism are popular

today; as in Eastern religions, the individual and his terrible burden of responsibility and freedom are removed. . . . We think of ourselves as having progressed in our appreciation of the value of love. But this is counterbalanced by our subjectivizing and sentimentalizing of love as mere kindness or tolerance. Thus we think of love as the rival of justice, and forget the necessity of justice. It is true that justice without love is hardness of heart; but love without justice is softness of head."

I really love that!

I visualize a Hell where there is justice, God's justice, and it varies in degrees of punishment. That makes crystal clear sense to me. *J.P. Moreland* and *Gary Habermas* in their book, *Beyond Death: Exploring the Evidence for Immortality,* make some points which are extremely valuable and make one think about the state of those in Hell. They say:

"It would be wrong to destroy something of such value just because it has chosen a life it was not intended to live. Thus, one way God can respect persons is to sustain them in existence and not annihilate them. Annihilation destroys creatures of intrinsic

value. . . and since God cannot force his love on people and coerce them to choose him, and since he cannot annihilate creatures with such high intrinsic value, then the only option available is quarantine. And that is what hell is." Hmmmm, could be!

I THINK THE LORD DESIRES TO METE OUT HIS JUSTICE TODAY. SOMEBODY TICKED HIM OFF REAL GOOD! RESTITUTION TIME!

Degrees of justice would be equally meted out to those who have transgressed God's laws and failed to make restitution – they have not repented their sins, they do not claim to know God as their Savior, or even recognize His supreme authority and majesty as their Creator and Lord – they have sinned continuously and expect no penalty for their crimes and blasphemies; in fact, they think when they died, the whole scene of life was over. We all know people who are evil and are prosperous at the expense of others. They laugh at the world and the agony and suffering their greed and selfishness causes, yet they continue on and appear to be getting richer and getting away with their awful behavior. However, with a God of justice and mercy ruling over us, they will be judged and found wanting. God will have His retribution for us.

THEY WILL BE JUDGED AND RESURRECTED TO A LIFE OF TORMENT AND SEPARATION FROM THE GOD WHO THEY DENIED AND HATED; THEY WILL BE PUNISHED IN ACCORDANCE WITH THEIR DEEDS AND THEY WILL AGONIZE.

As Christians, our gift of grace is free. We do not have to do anything to receive it, it is a gift. It is that simple. But, on the other hand, those that rejected grace and continue to sin, or those that have chosen a life of crime and dementia, will be given penalties according to their sins and crimes against the Lord and against man. Do you think a serial murderer that has killed a dozen people will be let off easier than one who committed petty crimes throughout his or her life and rejected the Lord's offer of salvation? I don't think so! A petty thief would probably be considered by God as a low stage degree of criminal compared to a Ted Bundy monster that destroyed people for pleasure.

God may not torture these individuals in Hell, but He certainly would pour out His Divine wrath upon them and make them suffer by tormenting their minds; therefore, making their existence utterly miserable and incomprehensibly intolerable to the understanding of us that are living. Flash! Suicide victims have therefore committed similar low-degree indignities toward the Lord and His plan for their life. They have tried to cheat the system but they have lost and fallen into that dark chasm which is death and perhaps, Hell. Their spirits will be resurrected and consigned to Hell. They were never repentant. Read this statement below and then think carefully about it, especially if it concerns you.

REPENTANT PEOPLE DO NOT KILL THEMSELVES AND WHEN SOMEONE DOES TAKE THEIR OWN LIFE, THEY CANNOT REPENT WHAT THEY HAVE DONE, IT IS TOO LATE. IS THE MESSAGE BECOMING CLEARER?

Suicide and Christian Beliefs

You cannot ask God to forgive you and repent your sins, then expect God to make everything all right after you kill yourself. Please, get real!!! Common sense is the key here. Where do you think your spirit goes when you die? And don't say Heaven, we already know we have to be in soul rest before we can be resurrected and judged? Where do you suppose a suicide victim goes after they are resurrected and judged? To the same place you will be going? Balance and equal justice are served by God, and you will not be in the same place, or in a similar situation, as a person that committed suicide, if you have not. But if you have been really bad, then you just may go to Hell and find that the plane of existence upon which you will dwell is based on your transgressions and unrepentant sins. Oh, yes, and lack of salvation.

THE CHOICE IS YOURS: HELL OR HEAVEN. DAMNATION AND PUNISHMENT, OR LIFE EVERLASTING AND JOY. SEPARATION FROM GOD FOREVER, OR IN HIS DIVINE PRESENCE FOR ETERNITY. WHAT'S TO CONSIDER?

God is merciful and He is just, and He will distribute His judgment with His Divine wisdom and balance, with Divine mercy and justice. Don't you think He won't do so because He will? Justice and fairness are elements of God's Divine attributes and He will share it with you. *"Masters, grant to your slaves justice and fairness, knowing that you too have a Master in heaven."* *(Colossians 4:1) (NASV)* We are expected to worship the Lord in righteousness and when we do, He is merciful and loving toward us. When we balk at His system, He is angered and disappointed with us, yet His steadfastness for justice and mercy remains the same. *"But let justice roll down like waters and righteousness like an every-flowing streams."* *Amos 5:24 (NASV)*

GUESS WHERE?

Suicide and Christian Beliefs

Let's say this thinking is very simple and quite easy to understand about the concept and reality of Hell. Without Hell there is no need for Jesus Christ, our Savior and Redeemer, there is no need for salvation and redemption. Obviously God made Hell for those folks that choose or chose not to be on His team and continually committed sins without remorse, or asking His forgiveness which they should have known that they already had. Because Hell exists, and because God is a merciful Creator, He gives all mankind a second chance to accept His statutes and ways; to believe in Him and worship Him with reverence and respect, as He is so-deserving and due. When man fails to recognize their Creator, sin occurs in such a manner that most sinning people embrace their sinful way of life and go about forgetting God. These folks continue as usual with their daily lives, without any fear of what awaits them in eternity. Their ignorance will cause them to suffer and writhe in pain both mentally and physically for all eternity. Big time bummer!!!

GOD KNEW THE BIG PICTURE AND HE KNEW THERE WOULD BE MORE PEOPLE REJECTING HIM THAN WOULD BE ACCEPTING HIM, SO HE GAVE US HIS BELOVED SON, A CO-EQUAL IN THE GOD-FAMILY GODHEAD, NAMED JESUS CHRIST TO BE THE PERFECT HUMAN RANSOM FOR OUR SINS AND TRANSGRESSIONS AGAINST HIM.

322

Suicide and Christian Beliefs

God Jehovah commissioned His Son to become a man in the flesh and sacrifice Himself to cleanse all the sins of mankind. Because there is a Savior and the offering of salvation, it stands to reason there must be a Hell. There would be no reason or purpose for having Christ's propitious ransom sacrifice on the Roman cross, if there was no place of eternal torment and suffering. Without Hell, why would God want Jesus to be sacrificed, and for what possible purpose/s? There is no other answer than to save souls from the belly of Hell and damnation before they go there forever. How does one get there? For all the above reasons already discussed. How do we stay out of Hell? For all the reasons already discussed as well.

HEAVEN OR HELL? WHICH IS IT? COME ON, CHOOSE NOW! THIS MIGHT BE YOUR LAST CHANCE. IT'S WAKE UP TIME!

Suicide and Christian Beliefs

When an ordinary man or woman thinks about the possibilities of there being a Heaven and a Hell, then various images have to be conjured up within their minds. It is clear that even the least educated or curious person would not be cognizant of some greater power. How can we not be aware that there is a God? I do not think that the trees I see, or the flowers I smell, or the ocean I enjoy just happened. I do not believe that things evolve into something else unless it is by the Divine hand of God working within that process of transformation. Osmosis is a God-thing! If you doubt that you are not in tune with the Lord Who so lovingly created you.

Suicide and Christian Beliefs

You may as well be pantheistic and worship some plant, shell, rock or insect. God is in nature, He is nature, but we do not worship nature, we worship God. There is a huge difference. Unless you are a Wicca adherent, and do not see the difference, then Satan could easily be the cause of such a lack of vision because he has clouded your ability to discern the godliness and order of the Lord's presence, being and involvement in your life. Yes, Wicca can and will do this to you.

THAT AUTHORITY WOULD BE GOD! OH! NEVER MIND! GOD ALREADY KNOWS ABOUT HIM.

I have a friend of over fifty years who utterly rejects the whole notion and concept of God. His approach to life is staggering – he makes himself the god of his life and cannot see beyond his own expectations of himself. His education is limited, but even with what he has accumulated in baseline knowledge over the years; he has still not learned one new thing to help him see past his outstretched arms. His belief that the major premise of Christianity is built on a hoax, and that Christ did not rise from the dead, is coupled with his theory that most of Christianity and any and all other related God theories are bunk because they were fabricated by Josephus, whom he considers the world's biggest liar and a drunk!

IT'S NOT THAT I'M AN ATHEIST, BUT RATHER THAT I'M A MEMBER OF GOD'S LOYAL OPPOSITION.

Anybody with a fundament class or two which discussed the writings of Josephus understands his life and his reasons for writing what he did. But my friend sees only the negative mercenary motives for Josephus to record what he did, by saying the things he reported in the manner in which he wrote his works were prejudiced. More goes into the life of Josephus and the lives of other contemporaries than what is simply stated on the surface and superficially stated about them in text books. It takes some research and considerable reading to truly discern the nature of their works and what they were really based on in total. You do not take a piece of something and think you understand its whole. I use the example of this man because the ignorance displayed in his thinking is commonplace in the world today. Unfortunately, most people haven't any clues as to who God is or what He means to us. The world is filled with unbelievers and those that cannot be bothered with worshiping a God Who loves them and extends a gift of salvation to them. How can folks live in darkness without any hope of an afterlife? It beats me and is beyond my comprehension of only bleakness to come and nothing at all to look forward to after death. Well, unless I come back as a holy Hindu cow either this time or next time, or the time after. You get my point, how could you not?

Our associate minister said something like this during his sermon. A couple came to him and asked to have their relationship blessed. The minister said, "Are you living together unmarried?" He thought they were. They said they were. He then asked if they were having a sexual relationship with each other. Again they answered yes. He told them that he could not bless a relationship which God forbids. It states in the Holy Scriptures, God's attitude and laws about such relationships. God wants holy relationships, the kind of relationships which are working in conjunction with His ways.

The *Holy Bible* is a book all about relationships. I use this example because it clearly demonstrates our society's current thinking about how we live our lives. As simple as God's rules are, man has changed his thinking about God a hundred and eighty degrees over the past fifty years. God has been taken out of the classroom, out of the American Pledge of Allegiance and out of our lives. God has been shuttled quickly off into oblivion by American atheists (a vast minority of our American population) that enjoy the freedom and liberty which our government provides them (to say and openly believe what they do).

I DON'T THINK SO! I REALLY DON'T THINK SO!

Suicide and Christian Beliefs

It is not hard to understand why my friend of fifty some years thinks the way he does. He manages to get great support for his infectious beliefs by almost everyone around him. It is because he will probably never accept God or His Son Jesus Christ, because he feels he is too superior and intelligent for such nonsense, and that there is no God who has had to set up a place like Hell. That is also why we have Jesus as a ransom sacrifice and His salvation as a plan for our redemption and peace of mind. I guess we need Hell. We need Jesus and we need His salvation.

The place called Hell will be the final resting ground and abode of all those spirits that have not only thought as my friend thinks, but have thought as such over the dozens of past centuries. Hell is where the sinners of this world will end up, that is why it is there. . .a place where unrepentant sinners will remain forever. A place where suicide victims will bide their time for eternity and wonder why it was so necessary for them to cut their lives so short, only to spend "forever" in a place they probably thought didn't exist, or to where they felt they would not be going. Surprise! Surprise! Surprise!

Chapter Seven
Understanding One's Purpose on Earth Can Eliminate Suicide

"The Lord has made everything for His own purposes, even the wicked for punishment."
Proverbs 16:4 (NLT)

I think it would be nice to know when you're not alone in a sea of delusion.

Is there any help for people who are considering suicide? What can be done to prevent suicide from taking place? Are there any answers? Yes, there are answers to these questions that make very good sense, but you have to start at the beginning, that is, your beginning with God. He knew us before we were even born. *"You saw me before I was born. Every day of my life was recorded in your book. Every moment was laid out before a single day had passed." Psalm 139:16 (NLT)* And again read, *"Since his days are determined, and the number of his months is with you, and you have appointed his limits that he cannot pass," Job 14:5 (ESV)* If you are not interested in establishing a relationship with God, than you have next to no hope for anything in your future. Without God in your life-equation for preventing suicide, there is no real or true hope of keeping one from committing suicide if they so desire to do so. Why? Because even if you provided a depressed person some temporary help, the potential for their suicide is still there; especially without any clinical or Christian counseling efforts or treatment. Those feelings of despair and hopelessness have never gone away and the door remains open for a suicide attempt as soon as treatment is over. . .ineffectual treatment, and/or as soon as they can get alone without any encumbrances or hindrances.

Such a person may last for a few weeks, months or years even, but the opportunity for suicide is still there lurking in the darkness of his or her mind. Their mind was never totally healed, so it still has pockets of mental disease left which could fester and be set off at any time. To live a life without suicide ever occurring is very nil, especially if God is not part of that healing formula. And this is where I do part ways with many of my clinical colleagues. Oh, well. I'm just sayin'.

Suicide and Christian Beliefs

SUICIDE COULD HAPPEN OR NOT HAPPEN, BUT THE RISKS AND CHANCES FOR IT HAPPENING ARE MANY AND GREATER WITHOUT GOD, AND WITHOUT KNOWING AND/OR DOING HIS WILL.

So, what do we do? We begin learning about God, and accepting Him as our Creator. **We are responsible to Him for all we do, can do and are allowed to do.** If this basic premise is not set, then there exists no opportunity for what I am about to tell you. Start by being completely open to God and accepting the Lord Jesus Christ as your personal Savior. It is my personal mission (ordained by God), for me and for other Christians to save lives for Him – as many as is possible during our lifetime. The Lord has a place for us to go when we leave this life and it is not where the suicide victim will end up abiding! What is our heavenly dwelling? Scripture says, *"For we know that if the tent that is our earthly home is destroyed, we have a building from God, a house not made with hands, eternal in the heavens. For in this tent we groan, longing to put on our heavenly dwelling, if indeed by putting it on we may not be found naked. For while we are still in this tent, we groan, being burdened—not that we would be unclothed, but that we would be further clothed, so that what is mortal may be* *swallowed up by life. He who has prepared us for this very thing is God, who has given us the Spirit as a guarantee. 2 Corinthians 5:1-6 (ESV)* and as a message for those that may be considering suicide, *"For we must all appear before the judgment seat of Christ, so that each one may receive what is due for what he has done in the body, whether good or evil." 2 Corinthians 5:10 (ESV)* Or, let's say this another way: *"For we must all stand before Christ to be judged. We will each receive whatever we deserve for the good or evil we have done in this earthly body." 2 Corinthians 5:10 (NLT)* Self-destruction (suicide) is evil and has been inspired by evil thought and direction form an evil source, most probably Satan. There is no heavenly persuasion involved with such an unholy act, and to think otherwise is not using one ounce of wisdom that God most likely has given, but won't be used.

Suicide and Christian Beliefs

Initially you must realize, after accepting the Lord into your heart and giving Him free reign of your life, that you should have just experienced His protection and the indwelling of the power of His Holy Spirit. Well, this is a truly great beginning, and now you must understand God's holy purposes and intensions for you, as we all must learn about this plan.

There are several objectives, all Godly, and they are very important. The Lord's first purpose is to give Him the worship He so claims and desires. Because God created us for Him pleasure, we must focus on pleasing our Creator. *"You created everything, and it is for your pleasure that they (we) exist and were created!" Revelation 4:11 (NLT)* So, we should be worshiping Him always with all of our heart and soul. *"Go to the Lord for help and worship Him continually." Psalm 105:4 (GN)* Our job is to get to know the Lord. Get acquainted with Him and establish a relationship with Him. He only wants you to love Him and know Him better. When you do this, you won't have any time to be thinking about committing suicide. So, if the shoe fits!!!

Are you communicating with Our God of love, or are you not communicating with Him? Who do you attempt to communicate with that you think of as your god? Is your god different from Jesus Christ?

Suicide and Christian Beliefs

I PREFER HEAVEN FOR MY FINAL DESTINATION. WHAT ABOUT YOU? HAVE YOU THOUGHT IT THROUGH YET? DON'T LET YOUR TIME RUN OUT ON YOU.

Thoughts of suicide will not even be on your personal agenda anymore, you'll be much too busy getting to know God, your Creator, and Satan your enemy and destroyer. Who will you listen to? Who will you follow? *"I want your constant love. . .I would rather have my people (you and me) know me. . ."* *Hosea 6:6 (GN)* If you know God, you will not be wanting to do away with yourself by committing suicide. That doesn't happen when you truly know God because He simply will not let go out of His hand. What Father would hold onto his child's hand over a bottomless pit and then let go of him or her for any inane reason? God will not let you go either, unless you decide of your own free will to let go! You are a part of the Lord's greater family which He created and you have a place within that structure and there is a heavenly plan for you. Is that what you truly want to screw up? If you do, and turn your back on God, there is no turning back; you are really gone for all of eternity.

Listen closely to what I say, *"You have been protected by the Lord and sealed in His protection forever, if you abide in His Perfect Will and love, walk in obedience to His dictates, and commandments, and live your life as a holy living sacrifice for Him."* This is what He tells us and guarantees those of us that believe in Him, trust in Him and have 100% faith in Him. He says, ***"And you also were included in Christ when you heard the word of truth, the gospel of your salvation. Having believed, you were marked in him with a seal, the promised Holy Spirit, who is a deposit guaranteeing our inheritance until the redemption of those who are God's possession—to the praise of his glory." Ephesians 1:13-14 (NIV)*** Scripture also tells us, *"And do not grieve the Holy Spirit of God, with whom you were sealed for the day of redemption." Ephesians 4:30 (NIV)*

WE ARE SEALED BECAUSE GOD OWNS US. AS WE GAVE OUR LIVES TO THE LORD, HE GRACIOUSLY COLLECTED THE DEEDS TO OUR LIVES; THEREFORE, HIS SPIRIT LIVES IN US, AND WE ARE SEALED FOR OUR OWN PROTECTION BY THE LORD. HOW GREAT IS THAT LOVE?

His Word guarantees this disposition of safety from Satan, the world, and from oneself. Suicide victims don't have this consolation, because God was never offered the deed to their hearts and minds. Anything you saw or heard outwardly from such people was all show and talk with no true substance or they'd still be living.

Here on earth is where God has designated His training ground to exist, as I have already mentioned earlier in this book. It is here, on this planet in space, that we undergo our character development, during our apprenticeship for becoming whatever it is that God has planned of us. This is practice time for when we are resurrected to be with God and have to play the game for real. Are you on the mound pitching for God, or did you not even make into the dugout because you never got out of the minor leagues? Bummer!!! You see, if you have shirked your duties here on earth, or are in the process of not participating as proscribed by God, you will not be trusted with greater assignments elsewhere in the Lord's realm. You won't even be a closer or a saver! Hmmmm, nice play on words!

In JESUS' Name

We Play

GUESS WHO IS PITCHING TONIGHT? NOT ME, I AM NOT IN THE ROTATION JUST YET. IS IT ANYONE YOU KNOW?

If we duck out the door, any of us, our destiny is with Satan in his hideous kingdom of evil and torment with complete and utter separation from God and His love and mercy. This choice is totally ours. So, one of our purposes is to have a relationship with the Lord and dedicate ourselves to that end. To be His friend and live forever in His blessings is our free gift from God. I would like to accept it, and I have already. *"Offer yourselves as a living sacrifice to God, dedicated to His service and pleasing to Him." Romans 12:1 (GN)* For such unselfishness, God will reward you mightily when you reside with Him in His home. One of those mansions is yours. It is best for you to keep partaking in God's Bread of Life so you don't become satanic toast! I am sure you get the message, how many comparisons do you need?

If we are to reside with God, in His home, then we are part of His greater family. We belong to a group of millions that have exercised His Word and His Will, saving the lost; they completed their missions and will soon play the real God-game in His presence. It blows my mind to think that I can be a part of that team, that special group, that celestial family of God. I believe that best part is that it goes on forever and ever. For me, it's like getting to eat my favorite ice cream cone that has a never-ending bottom, or going to The Olive Garden® and ordering a never-ending pasta bowl! WOW!!! That's like being in Noodle Lasagna Heaven. Consider this scripture: *"Just as our bodies have many parts and each part has a special function, so it is with Christ's body. We are many parts of one body, and we all belong to each other." Romans 12:4-5 (NLT)*

YUM, YUM! I DO LOVE MY PASTA!

When we accepted Jesus Christ as our personal Savior and Redeemer, something fantastic happened. We became infused with the Spiritual power of the Lord and we joined together with all other Christians in belonging to God's Holy family. *"He predestined us to adoption as sons through Jesus Christ to Himself, according to the kind intention of His will, to the praise of the glory of His grace, which He freely bestowed on us in the Beloved. In Him we have redemption through His blood, the forgiveness of our trespasses, according to the riches of His grace which He lavished on us. In all wisdom and insight He made known to us the mystery of His will, according to His kind intention which He purposed in Him with a view to an administration suitable to the fullness of the times, that is, the summing up of all things in Christ, things in the heavens and things on the earth. In Him also we have obtained an inheritance, having been predestined according to His purpose who works all things after the counsel of His will, to the end that we who were the first to hope in Christ would be to the praise of His glory. In Him, you also, after listening to the message of truth, the gospel of your salvation—having also believed, you were sealed in Him with the Holy Spirit of promise, who is given as a pledge of our inheritance, with a view to the redemption of God's own possession, to the praise of His glory." Ephesians 1:5-14 (NASV)*

The only time we are to give our lives up for God, is when it is specifically for the benefit of others and not for ourselves. Suicide with that bit of scripture alone is a mute subject no to be messed around with in any manner. It is an deliberate act of self-destruction that is unsanctioned by the Lord, and an ungodly act of violence and self-annihilation.

Suicide and Christian Beliefs

"Christ gave His life for us. We too, then, ought to give our lives for others. . ." 1 John 3:16 (GN)

Understand this: Jesus' path to the Roman cross marks the selfless, self-giving way of life to which his followers have been called. It is our Christian duty to act in accordance with His dictates, emulate His examples, and fulfill His wishes. However, we do not take our life because we have evil thoughts of hurting or doing harm to others, yet some people unwisely and without foundation, think by taking their own life they will not have a chance to injure or hurt someone else. This is ludicrous thinking with no foundation for making any sense whatsoever. It's more like a lie that becomes a final attention getting device, at the expense of the person that commits suicide. This is not a good idea! Ever!

THIS IS FAULTY THINKING AND THIS IS NOT SCRIPTURAL AT ALL. IT IS IN THE ISLAMIC NATURE AND WAY OF THINKING AND PRACTICE, TO DO SO, BUT NOT SO WITH CHRISTIANS.

Witness for example, the suicide bombers of the world and their beliefs of receiving perverted sexual rewards from a bloody god who demands murder/s and sacrifices. For these behaviors, he offers and gives nothing in return, because that god has no such power to do so, but fools trust that god of lies.

Suicide and Christian Beliefs

ISN'T THIS PERSON BRAVE? WOULD YOU LIKE TO BE JUST HIM OR HER? WHY NOT? IF YOU PLAN TO SUICIDE, WHY NOT MAKE A STATEMENT FOR YOUR CAUSE? DON'T BE SUCH A JERK! YOU'LL GO TO HELL AND EVENTUALLY BY JUDGED BY GOD. DON'T MESS UP HIS PLANS! IF YOU'RE SO PROUD TO DO SATAN'S WILL, THEN TAKE OFF YOUR COWARDLY MASK AND SHOW YOUR FACE!

This nature of belief is of Satan, obviously, who does nothing for the good of humanity, but only is interested in destroying human lives. And, who would be better to do his filthy dirty work than foolish and brainwashed human beings. Satan will get you every chance he can. He is very much alive and well in the Middle East, and they are waiting for the return of their *Mahdi*, the Islamic Anti-Christ. You see, their Jesus is not the same as our Jesus. And nowhere in their *Qur'an* or in *The Hadiths* is there any mention of God being loving or showing love. Hmmmm? Seems pretty evident to me who is in control in their daily lives. This god of Islam is the same god that sends chills down the back of Christians and others. He is the god a suicide victim will listen to, he is the god that makes his followers prostrate themselves five times daily, starting early, so he can be sure of their worship and enjoy that hardship he puts upon them. The real god, our Lord Jesus Christ, only asks that we worship Him with all our heart, mind and soul. Our faith and belief is enough, as His grace is enough for us. Allah has none of this action, nor does he represent it.

JESUS CHRIST IS LORD AND DON'T YOU FORGET IT! ANY OTHER GOD IS SATANIC AND FALSE AND WILL ONLY LEAD YOU TO HELL IN A HAND BASKET, OR SO IT IS SAID!

He doesn't demand that we bow down to Him even once during the day, but He does ask for and seeks our respect and adoration however we are willing to give it to Him. This is the Christian god of mercy and love, and not a pagan god of unmerciful hatred that nudges people to take their own life. Allah has only demons serving him and those ignorant lackey humans that follow through with the his satanic evil orders. *"And no wonder, for Satan himself masquerades as an angel of light. It is not surprising, then, if his servants masquerade as servants of righteousness. Their end will be what their actions deserve. 2 Corinthians 11:14-15 (NIV)* Don't ever give Satan any air time in your thinking network. Don't contemplate anything ungodly, it leads to disaster.

God created us to become like His Son Jesus Christ. Yes, we are all different and have dissimilar personalities, spiritual gifts, competencies, abilities, capabilities, deep passions, education and experiences, but such is life. . .ain't it great? God loves variety; we cannot all do the same thing/s and accomplish the same goals/s. If everyone was the same, we would all be doing exactly what everyone else would be doing. BORING!!! That is not what life is all about, and that is not what God intended for us – ever! We are not mindless clones existing for His entertainment. Our individuality is pure.

GOD HAS WONDERFUL PLANS FOR YOU. DON'T YOU LIKE FABULOUS SURPRISES? HIS SURPRISES EVEN PROVIDE A HINT OF WHAT IS TO COME AND A GLIMPSE OF ETERNITY WITH HIM IN PARADISE.

Suicide and Christian Beliefs

"Now there are varieties of gifts, but the same Spirit; and there are varieties of service, but the same Lord; and there are varieties of activities, but it is the same God who empowers them all in everyone. To each is given the manifestation of the Spirit for the common good. For to one is given through the Spirit the utterance of wisdom, and to another the utterance of knowledge according to the same Spirit, to another faith by the same Spirit, to another gifts of healing by the one Spirit, to another the working of miracles, to another prophecy, to another the ability to distinguish between spirits, to another various kinds of tongues, to another the interpretation of tongues. All these are empowered by one and the same Spirit, who apportions to each one individually as he wills." *2 Corinthians 12:4-11 (ESV)*

However, we all need to become much more Christ-like, it is our destiny as Christians; besides, we were created by God with His Divine features, we just weren't given everything yet, and that makes perfect sense to me. Can you only imagine what turmoil and utter chaos we'd have already made of this world when and if we'd been left to our own devices caused by having too much uncontrolled power? Why do I mention such? Because dear friend, this is what Satan has over us, an almost unbridled and uncontrolled power of such

346

Suicide and Christian Beliefs

destructive force that it were not for God Almighty, we already be dead! Yes, to become Christ-like is what we were so commanded to become. We are not commanded to sacrifice our life in vain, or to do something that does not fulfill God's purposes. Such a sinful sacrifice is called a mission incomplete. This is an earthly failure not a heavenly failure. God only wants us to succeed, and suicide is not a success to the Lord, ever! It is a horrible demonstration of human failure and rejection of His love for us and such behavior gets no membership in His Divine family. Your suicide ticket is invalid at this stop! *The Message* says it best, in ***Colossians 1:15.*** ***"We look at this Son and see God's original purpose in everything created."*** His Word also tells us that, ***"As the Spirit of the Lord works within us, we become more and more like Him and reflect His glory even more." 2 Corinthians 3:18 (NIV)***

OUR JOB IS TO BECOME CHRIST-LIKE BY OBEYING GOD'S COMMANDS AND MEETING HIS EXPECTATIONS.

Suicide and Christian Beliefs

It is said in many Christian churches, by many Christians and caring pastors, that we must think and act like our Savior did. The Apostle Paul also tells us that in the **Book of Romans**. By thinking and acting more like Christ we become better and better human beings that fulfill all of the Lord's purposes, especially winning souls over to God. You cannot do that if you are busy killing yourself. If you really want to do away with your life so badly, then join some missionary group ministering in some dangerous foreign country where you could quite possibly be killed for preaching the Gospel of Jesus Christ to the locals – especially if they are Muslims or Hindus. Their country will increase your chances of being executed. Yes, that opportunity in those places is extremely good! Hey! At least you will go down in flames for the Lord. You could be a Messianic Messerschmitt! That may be a crass statement and very blunt, but it was on my mind – so there it is! I hope God has a sense of humor!

THESE ARE DEAD MISSIONARIES IN RWANDA.

Suicide and Christian Beliefs

However, why not become more like Jesus? *"Have this attitude in yourselves which was also in Christ Jesus. . ." Philippians 2:5 (NASB)* and let's look at this scripture even more closely in the translation of the English Standard Version which further states, *"Do nothing from rivalry or conceit, but in humility count others more significant than yourselves. Let each of you look not only to his own interests, but also to the interests of others. Have this mind among yourselves, which is yours in Christ Jesus." Philippians 2:3-5 (ESV)* This is an attitude of caring and humility. It gets you outside of yourself and into the environment of your friend and neighbor. Look to others and not yourself, please! You'll be much better off and your chances of doing something wicked to yourself will not exist – you won't have any appreciable time left for such utter nonsense.

If you mature in the Lord, you can become more like Him and less able to even think about suicide or anything just as bad. It is the attitude and the behaving of a Christ-like Christian that will pave the path to God, and not to Hell. *". . .we shall become nature people, reaching to the very height of Christ's full stature." Ephesians 4:13 (GN)*

We are here for many special purposes in order to fulfill God's powerful and magnificent plan. See my book, *The Plan*, We know because Jesus told us, that we are His friends and not His servants. He has the angels for those assignments, but God wants to use us to perform in ways that are beyond our present comprehension. We are valuable to Him and He wants us to do His Will, but we have to be prepared to do that. We cannot be part of that Holy Plan if we commit suicide. That is a weakness which will cause many to suffer eternal damnation and the everlasting separation from God forever. I cannot state this too much. I hope you have it ingrained in your mind by now. We have to be cleansed and ready to do God's Will here first, before we can continue on a grander scale in Heaven or elsewhere. *"If you keep yourself pure, you will be a special utensil for honorable use. Your life will be clean, and you will be ready for the Master to use you for every good work."* *2 Timothy 2:21 (NLT)* Never forget that *"The Lord has made everything for His purposes."* *Proverbs 16:4 (NLT)* and most important of all, never forget this net verse. *"His plans endure forever; His purposes last eternally."* *Psalm 33:11 (GN)*

We still have a whole Millennium and to go through before we ever get a glimpse of the New Jerusalem and the most beautiful and spectacular home that we will ever know. It will be a home so far outside of our ability to fathom that our imagination can only glean, from bits of Scripture, just what the New Jerusalem will be like.

A CONCEPT OF THE NEW JERUSALEM.

"Then I saw a new heaven and a new earth, for the old heaven and the old earth had disappeared. And the sea was also gone. And I saw the holy city, the New Jerusalem, coming down from God out of heaven like a bride beautifully dressed for her husband. I heard a loud shout from the throne, saying, "Look, God's home is now among his people! He will live with them, and they will be his people. God himself will be with them. He will wipe every tear from their eyes, and there will be no more death or sorrow or crying or pain. All these things are gone forever." And the one sitting on the throne said, "Look, I am making everything

Suicide and Christian Beliefs

new!" And then he said to me, "Write this down, for what I tell you is trustworthy and true." And he also said, "It is finished! I am the Alpha and the Omega—the Beginning and the End. To all who are thirsty I will give freely from the springs of the water of life. All who are victorious will inherit all these blessings, and I will be their God, and they will be my children." "But cowards, unbelievers, the corrupt, murderers, the immoral, those who practice witchcraft, idol worshipers, and all liars— their fate is in the fiery lake of burning sulfur. This is the second death." Then one of the seven angels who held the seven bowls containing the seven last plagues came and said to me, "Come with me! I will show you the bride, the wife of the Lamb." So he took me in the Spirit to a great, high mountain, and he showed me the holy city, Jerusalem, descending out of heaven from God. It shone with the glory of God and sparkled like a precious stone—like jasper as clear as crystal. The city wall was broad and high, with twelve gates guarded by twelve angels. And the names of the twelve tribes of Israel were written on the gates. There were three gates on each side—east, north, south, and west. The wall of the city had twelve foundation stones, and on them were written the names of the twelve apostles of the Lamb. The angel who talked to me held in his hand a gold measuring stick to measure the city, its gates, and its wall. When he measured it, he found it was a square, as wide as it was long. In fact, its length and width and height were each 1,400 miles. Then he measured the walls and found them to be 216 feet thick (according to the human standard used by the angel). The wall was made of jasper, and the city was pure gold, as clear as glass. The wall of the city was built on foundation stones inlaid with twelve precious stones: the first was jasper, the second sapphire, the third agate, the fourth emerald, the fifth onyx, the sixth carnelian, the seventh chrysolite, the eighth beryl, the ninth topaz, the tenth chrysoprase, the eleventh jacinth, the twelfth amethyst. The twelve gates were made of pearls—each gate from a single pearl! And the main street was pure gold, as clear as glass. I saw no temple in the city, for the Lord God Almighty and the Lamb are its temple. And the city has no need of sun or moon, for the glory of God illuminates the city, and the Lamb is its light. The nations will walk in its light, and the kings of the world will enter the city in all their glory. Its gates will never be closed at the end of day because there is no night there. And all the nations will bring their glory and honor into the city. Nothing evil will be allowed to enter, nor anyone who practices shameful idolatry and dishonesty—but only those whose names are written in the Lamb's Book of Life" Revelation 21:1-27 (NLT)

Suicide and Christian Beliefs

A PICTURE OF THE NEW JERUSALEM COMING TO EARTH.

You must see that God has a plan for you which is in effect right here on this earth. And He has many purposes for you, like worshiping him, being disciples for Him, being in constant fellowship with Him, and communicating with Him through our prayers so we may establish a closer relationship with Him. We all have special ministries in which we should serve God. I believe through our various ministries we can find our ultimate earthly purpose. It's called a mission and when we find our mission we must focus on fulfilling it. You'll know what that task is when you are called to it.

Suicide and Christian Beliefs

Several years ago, I wrote a book titled, *Organizational Effectiveness: The Strategic Planning Process*. This book was an outcropping of my personal and group work while on active military service. As I wrote this book, I put it in the correct order in which organizational effectiveness should be practiced. The subject of "mission" was right up front, followed close by "purposes" and "objectives". But not until I read the Word of the Lord, through new eyes and a new perspective, as concerns His mission and purpose/s, did I really get excited. If only we could all know the Lord better and fulfill His purpose/s, for us, with that same excitement and focus I experienced. Unfortunately, many people miss that mark and meander through a religious maze of mediocrity and second-rate direction, following only the tenets, dogma and doctrines of their own religious faith. Therefore, it is very easy to get lost in the unimportant facets of church legalism. A person suffering depression and anguishing, about taking their precious own life, usually doesn't have a clue as to what I am writing about. So, this is for the healthy-minded among us.

That is sad, because many people have not received from their faith and religious training, those tools which are necessary to function as God wants us to. Those folks without God's knowledge are even worse off. So, how can we reach a person before they take their own life? The basics have to start in our own society. We must love and respect the Being of God. We must all begin to honor Him as He so deserves. Every man and woman knowing God must fulfill their missions; they must ultimately reach out to another human being and bring him or her to the Lord, or return them to the Lord, if they have wandered. We must save as many people as we can. If folks get the fundamental training of Christianity, and not some watered down version, we can set the stage for healthy minds and strong inner spirits. We can literally prevent folks from thinking about suicide. Granted, it sounds fairly basic, but most things that work well are very basic; therefore, we will not reach everyone. However, you should know this thinking and realize that we can make others aware of God's wonderful grace and His awesome majesty and mercy. The Apostle Paul told us, *"I run straight to the goal with purpose in every step."* *1 Corinthians 9:26 (NLT)*

CHRISTIAN CLASSROOM GETTING BIBLICAL INSTRUCTION.

Suicide and Christian Beliefs

Our biggest battle is with the satanic surroundings of our world and their deadly influences over our youth. From video games to disgusting rap music with profane and evil lyrics, the intent of satanic influence is in control. Such demonic control leads directly to controlling the minds of weaker human beings, immature and inexperienced in real life, and those that are lost among the fantasies that exist inside their own minds. There are literally thousands of people, especially among our youth that don't know the difference between Godly things and hellish things. This line of ignorance runs and cuts deeply into our society and culture.

So, here is a mission for some strong-hearted and strong-willed Christians to tackle and defeat. Try entering the gang and drug cultures. These are environments totally engulfed in satanic activities; it is pitiful to witness the degradation of the human spirit to stoop so low as to condone living as Satan's puppet. Yes, his strings are around their neck!

Suicide and Christian Beliefs

People living such lives must cause our Mighty God many tears and a huge heartache. This is an American subculture, the kind of environment, atmosphere and perverted milieu that brings God to the point where He demands our repentance as a nation and as a people. We actually commit our own national suicide by putting up with such behavior and blasphemy while not doing more to change things back to the country that loved and needed God. Are we on our own road to national suicide? You tell me!

CONFESSION AND REPENTANCE GET YOU MERCY AND LOVE FROM GOD. REMEMBER: YOU'RE ALREADY FORGIVEN, SO NOW LIVE UP TO YOUR GIFT OF LIFE – DO SOMETHING FOR GOD! WHAT A NOVEL IDEA!

If we can reach out to those we see or learn about that are afflicted with guilt, shame, worry, excessive anxiety, depressive disorders that are especially obvious to the most casual observer, and those with apparent overwhelming pressure and stress, and be able to tell these people about the Lord, such will be a good start, a good beginning. It is imperative that we teach others or show others how to come to

Suicide and Christian Beliefs

know Jesus Christ. *"It's in Christ that we find out who we are and what we are living for."* *Ephesians 1:11 (The Message)* The Lord promises us in His Holy Word that *"Fear of the Lord is the beginning of wisdom. Knowledge of the Holy one results in understanding."* *Proverbs 9:10 (NLT)* Sooo, a good mission for someone that cares and loves people with suicidal problems, would be to devote a study and a ministry towards helping prevent unnecessary suicides. It would be difficult, but God didn't promise easy. It could be your turn to monitor the Suicide Watch of your community. Think about it!

Scripture puts the picture of suicide in perspective. *"The hope of the righteous brings joy, but the expectation of the wicked will perish. The way of the LORD is a stronghold to the blameless, but destruction to evildoers."* Proverbs

Suicide and Christian Beliefs

10:28-29 (ESV) The word "wicked" refers to those individuals falling outside of the Lord's canopy of protection. They are not necessarily evil or wicked in the sense that they commit horrible crimes, but they are wicked in the sense that they have rejected God. The Lord considers them to be wicked and they shall pay the awful price of eventual eternal damnation and separation from God.

Behaving this way and thinking is such an evil manner is a personal choice. Suicide victims may or may not have thought it out before they took their life, but one thing is for certain, and don't fool yourself into thinking otherwise; they have chosen a one way track to perdition. Once they commit the final act, all the prayers of others are not going to send them anywhere but to where they already are. They are where they are and that is in oblivion and darkness. Their body lies in a cold damp grave, of which they are not aware of, sleeping in soul rest and awaiting a resurrection and judgment.

GUESS WHO'S GOING IN THE HOLE? HMMMM?

Suicide and Christian Beliefs

I told you this book would not be easy to read and digest. It is not my mission or purpose to stroke you and make you feel good; however, it is my objective to get you thinking and moving closer to God. That is the objective of every human being who has come to know the Lord Almighty.

At this point, if you don't know God, Your Heavenly Father and have not had a close and personal relationship with Him, I ask you to open your heart and mind to Jesus Christ, He is the answer. If you are or have been considering suicide, I hope you will change your mind – that is why I wrote this book and have been as graphic as I dare, within the framework of decent and good acceptable taste. Those that have already taken their life cannot benefit, but you can! You must! Seek the Lord!

FIND GOD, THE GOD I KNOW AND LOVE, AND TRUST! HE IS MERCIFUL AND FILLED WITH GRACE. DO IT TODAY, BECAUSE TOMORROW MAY NEVER COME AND TOO LATE, IS TOO LATE.

Chapter Eight

God Answers Our Prayers and Meets Our Needs

We are told in *Matthew 6:8 (NLT)* that *". . .your Father knows exactly what you need even before you ask him!"* This is the truth, but who is it meant for? It can be meant for a potential suicide thinking individual, if he or she has come to know God and if they have accepted Jesus Christ as their personal Savior. Why is this important for such an individual? The vehicle of prayer is their life line to Jesus Christ, but they have to approach the throne of Our Living God in a state of holiness, as God is holy, and Christ is holy. Jesus paid the price on the Roman cross for our sins, and He opened the door for our acceptance of His propitious sacrifice for our transgressions. However, we have to accept that gift. If we don't accept that gift, our prayers will not be heard. Why? Most easily put, because sin separates us from God. We cannot go Him on our knees without going to Him in humility and in submission, and those who haven't ever accepted Christ's anointing sacrifice won't pray in that manner. Without Christ's accepted sacrifice a person goes to Him with pride, in ignorance and misunderstanding. This is not what God wants to have coming to Him.

DO YOU GO TO GOD WITH EMPTY HANDS, OR HAVE YOU ACTUALLY PRAYED TO HIM IN THE SPIRIT WITH A LIFE LINE TO HIS THRONE? THIS MEANS, ARE YOU SAVED, OR YOU ARE SIMPLY HOPEFUL. BECAUSE IF YOU'RE HOPEFUL IN THIS PARTICULAR PERSONAL DISPOSITION, HAVING EMPTY HANDS MEANS NO CONNECTION WITH THE LORD, THEN YOU ARE HOPELESS!

God is holy and righteous and one must approach His throne in prayer already covered by the blood of Jesus Christ. This is why and how we go to the Lord in prayer. *"Nothing in all creation is hidden from God. Everything is naked and exposed before his eyes, and he is the one to whom we are accountable. So then, since we have a great High Priest who has entered heaven, Jesus the Son of*

Suicide and Christian Beliefs

God, let us hold firmly to what we believe. This High Priest of ours understands our weaknesses, for he faced all of the same testings we do, yet he did not sin. So let us come boldly to the throne of our gracious God. There we will receive his mercy, and we will find grace to help us when we need it most." Hebrews 4:13-16 (NLT) Ask yourself, what is your personal basis for petitioning God? Are you saved by His anointed sacrifice and His forgiveness? Are you a full-fledged member of the God Club and do you abide by His rules, or are you trying to penetrate the walls of His Kingdom without proper preparation? What do you bring to His Table? Why do you think you have direct access to the Lord without having taken His Gift of Life? Can a sinful person approach our Holy God? What does scripture say about this issue?

ARE YOU PART OF THE GOD CLUB...THE KINGDOM?

Suicide and Christian Beliefs

"Oh, what joy for those whose disobedience is forgiven, whose sin is put out of sight. Yes, what joy for those whose record the LORD has cleared of guilt, whose lives are lived in complete honesty! When I refused to confess my sin, my body wasted away, and I groaned all day long. Day and night your hand of discipline was heavy on me. My strength evaporated like water in the summer heat. Finally, I confessed all my sins to you and stopped trying to hide my guilt. I said to myself, "I will confess my rebellion to the LORD." And you forgave me! All my guilt is gone. Therefore, let all the godly pray to you while there is still time, that they may not drown in the floodwaters of judgment. For you are my hiding place; you protect me from trouble. You surround me with songs of victory." Psalm 32:1-7 (NLT)

KING DAVID SINGING A NEW PSALM!

Suicide and Christian Beliefs

You see, if you reject Jesus Christ, you are not pardoned by God – there is no basis for Him giving you a pardon. You never bothered to explore His gift to you and you may have simply turned your back on it. That's very bad news for you, if you did. If you just never received God's gift of salvation, then you and only you know why that is so. Therefore, don't expect God to hear your prayers, they will be in vain without Christ as your intercessor and Savior. Christ is the only way to God! *"I am the way, and the truth, and the life. No one comes to the Father except through me." John 14:6 (ESV)* **Point made:** you must go through Christ to get to the Father. So Christ will act as your intercessor and the Lord's power of the Holy Spirit will transmit your needs to God. But, you must have Christ as your Savior – He is your ticket to victory and eternal life, nobody or nothing else can be a substitute for Him.

When you know God and have accepted His Son, you will feel this way and understand what the values of the gift is that you've received. *"O LORD, you have searched me and known me! You know when I sit down and when I rise up; you discern my thoughts from afar. You search out my path and my lying down and are acquainted with all my ways. Even before a word is on my tongue, behold, O LORD, you know it altogether. You hem me in,*

behind and before, and lay your hand upon me."
Psalm 139:1-5 (ESV) As David did, he always went
to God in submission and humility, but he also went
to the Lord in prayer with joyfulness, confidence
and very boldly because David knew that God was
with him one hundred percent. Do exactly what
King David always did, and the Disciples of Christ
faithfully did. You will transform your prayer life
by simply acknowledging God and all of His holy
attributes. Do this seriously on your knees with
your head bowed.

IS THIS HOW YOU PRAY? IT SHOULD BE!

Remember: there is no forgiveness without the
blood of Christ and if you don't have it, then you're
wasting your time trying to contact God for His

help. One must go to the throne of the Lord, that throne of mercy and grace, openly and committed to Jesus Christ, as a child of God. When we are on our knees before God, this humbles us and takes our pride away while in His holy presence. This act of ours recognizes God's holiness and righteousness. Consider reading my book, *Recognizing His Presence and Knowing His Perspective* for more information about God's personality and His desired communion with us. When you reject Jesus there is no hope for you – none at all. However, when you accept Jesus into your heart and soul, you receive God's grace, mercy and love. All of your needs will not only be addressed, they will be heard and met by the Lord.

 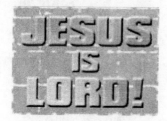

Keep in mind that God had to come to earth in the form of man and lived His life as a perfect human being so He could present Himself as the perfect human sacrifice for the sins and transgressions of all men, for all times. He did this in the form and body of Himself, a man called Jesus Christ. Therefore, read this carefully and understand. ***"Since the***

children have flesh and blood, he too shared in their humanity so that by his death he might destroy him who holds the power of death—that is, the devil— and free those who all their lives were held in slavery by their fear of death. For surely it is not angels he helps, but Abraham's descendants. For this reason he had to be made like his brothers in every way, in order that he might become a merciful and faithful high priest in service to God, and that he might make atonement for the sins of *the people. Because he himself suffered when he was tempted, he is able to help those who are being tempted." Hebrews 2:14-18 (NIV)*

It was paramount that Jesus Christ had to be made just like us. He had to be able to sympathize with mankind; He had to know how we felt about things; He had to understand human emotions as a man, not just as God; He had to be tested and tried, tempted and rejected so He could understand how we felt about those emotions as well. Christ had to feel human pain, suffering, agony, sorrow, guilt, loneliness, and guilt as we do. Therefore, Jesus Christ makes us aware of our guilt and He knows how we feel completely one hundred percent of the time. So, Christ has "been there" "done that" and He must feel equal to what we feel and experience. His perfect sacrifice gives us access, direct access to God's throne when we have accepted His Son's

Suicide and Christian Beliefs

sacrifice on the cross and know that His blood has cleansed us completely of our sins.

Anyone considering committing suicide must take the time to think through all that Christ went through for all of us, not just themselves, as such would be prideful and selfish. If you know folks that you suspect of doing themselves harm, especially if suicide might be in their unannounced but fairly obvious or subtle plans, then get with them and go over these biblical truths and find them professional counseling. Don't let them leave you without getting them medical assistance. Take them if you have to, but get them there. *"For we do not have a high priest who is unable to sympathize with our weaknesses, but we have one who has been tempted in every way, just as we are—yet was without sin. Let us then approach the throne of grace with confidence, so that we may receive mercy and find grace to help us in our time of need." Hebrews 4:15-16 (NIV)*

THIS IS THE GOD YOU MUST
KNOW AND LOVE, TRUST
AND HAVE FAITH IN, HONOR
AND WORSHIP WITH PRAISE
AND THANKSGIVING!
ACCEPT HIM TODAY

Chapter Nine
Telltale Signs of Suicide

Although we've already mentioned various signs of potential suicide contemplation and intension in this text, listed in this section is a conglomeration of all of those things which come immediately to mind that are most pertinent to be on the look for. In an article by *googobits.com* is listed some very good information about what to be watching for, so why re-invent the wheel? However, I have added extensively to the list.

It is extremely important that you do not take these observations too lightly and think that this person you are watching will simply outgrow, get over soon, or forget about what is troubling them any time soon. This will probably not happen and when they do take that final step and check out from this life, you'll feel awful, saddened by what they have done, and worst of all – you'll feel the guilt of having been able to prevent their terrible selfish actions. This is called not being responsible.

"There are several factors that put a person at risk of committing suicide. Obviously, there is no guaranteed equation to determine whether a person

Suicide and Christian Beliefs

will end their life. However, accessing risk factors, and recognizing the signs of suicide will alert family and friends to a potential problem.

Warning Signs of Suicide Include:

Depression and other obvious anxiety disorders, i.e. known existing mental illnesses

Anger and extreme irritability and outbursts of hostility and rage

Isolation and separation from others

Insomnia or sleeping too much

Change in eating and health habits

Giving away valued and/or treasured items

Preoccupation with death and/or fatalistic thinking expressed in conversation/s

Suicidal thoughts expressed in recent drawings, writings, songs, or discussions

Substance Abuse: drugs and alcohol

Sudden change in behavior, judgment, personal bearing, and/or performance of normal tasks

Suicide and Christian Beliefs

Radical change in values, personal long held beliefs and/or morals

Outbursts of hateful resentment and/or an overwhelming bitterness, and animosity that are wrathfully directed towards some specific person/s that cannot be contained and won't go away accept by suicide

A change in self-esteem, self-worth, or self-respect stemming from some recent critical event or personal awakening

A family history of suicide and fatalistic thinking and behavior; obsession with family biblical curses that seem impossible to undue or end

Problems with personal sexual identity, i.e., homosexuality, pornography, and other sexual perversions and leanings

Extreme thoughts of criminal behavior that cannot be effectively dealt with by treatment, i.e. thinking death will protect others from what he or she might do to them

A loss of pride from something recently hurtful, a loss self-confidence which has proven embarrassing,

Suicide and Christian Beliefs

Loss of a healthy self-image and a recent blow/s to self-assurance, i.e, a career ending event, or loss of job and/or position

Huge monetary loss and financial disaster effecting livelihood and family

A sense of total worthlessness and feeling unloved and/or unappreciated, especially from being bullied by others and ridiculed about some issue that is deeply hurtful and seems insurmountable, i.e. prank pictures placed on the Internet that especially hurtful and undignified, not meant for the world

READ VERY CAREFULLY AND SLOWLY THE NEXT THREE ITEMS.

Specific Risk Factors Include:

"**Previous Suicide Attempts:** Many who unsuccessfully commit suicide are twice as likely to try again. These individuals generally do not receive medical attention, thus they are very likely to never be able to resolve any of their negative feelings.

"Personal Failure: Perfectionism is a common characteristic of suicide victims. Everything in these individuals life must be perfect. This includes family, work, home, personal tasks, and so forth. When the perfectionist person cannot meet unrealistic standards, they spiral into a depressed state.

"Recent Loss: The death of a loved one or a divorce places many young children and teenagers at risk of suicide. The pain is tremendous, and suicide appears to be the only way to alleviate hurt feelings.

DANGER

Recognizing Signs of Suicide:

"It is often difficult to determine whether a person is on a path toward suicide. Those that have never had thoughts of suicide are likely to underestimate a sufferer's ability to end their life. However, it is vital to remember that suicide victims have extreme feelings of worthlessness and depression. They may feel unloved or alone. Thus, it is more difficult for them to deal with problems or envision a solution to their problems. Even more so, family and friends should pay attention to tell-tale signs of suicide.

"Signs may be subtle or obvious. The key is recognizing them, and offering much needed support. Everyone experiences some degree of depression during their life. In some cases, depression may last for several days or weeks. Of course, not everyone who experiences the "blues" will commit suicide. Individuals who are contemplating suicide may utter expressions such as:

"It will all be over soon."
"I hate living."
"I wish I were dead."
"Everyone would be better without me."
"Nothing matters anymore."

"Many family members and friends make the mistake of not taking these expressions seriously. A common belief is that those that do make such statements are simply seeking attention. Although many suicide victims are secretive about their plans, other victims express subtle hints. All expressions of suicide should be taken seriously. Those who are good with hiding their true feelings may appear happy or jokingly. However, if you were to have a serious one-on-one conversation about their repeated suicidal expressions, that person may be willing to supply you with their true feelings.

"It may help to directly ask a person if they are thinking about suicide, or if they have ever thought about ending their life. If the answer is yes, the listener may ask additional questions and inquire about the reason/s behind suicidal feelings. Have they talked to anyone about their feelings? What can the listener do to help? How do they plan to kill themselves?

"When addressing this issue it is essential for the listener to speak in a serious, but calm manner. If the listener is smiling or laughing, the victim is less likely to provide serious answers. Suicide is no joking matter. If a victim is willing to openly communicate about their feelings, the listener should use this as an opportunity to offer support. Individuals that are in the early stages of contemplating suicide may be encouraged to seek counseling.

Suicide and Christian Beliefs

"If the person does not agree to counseling, the listener could serve as a continual support system offering encouragement, support, and love. Nonetheless, a listener is not a psychiatrist, a psychotherapist, or a clinical psychologist. Therefore, listeners should continually encourage counseling or speak with another trusted adult such as a victim's parent or spouse."

Clinical Thoughts:

When moments of mania are severe, the person that is suffering, a potential suicide victim, may lose touch with reality and begin hallucinating or suffering from delusions. Psychotic symptoms such as feelings of worthlessness and having no human value at all may also occur. All of these symptoms together make it nearly impossible for this person to function normally on both a personal and/or professional level during the course of this phase.

For your personal information, I do feel that this material could be helpful for your knowledge and understanding, because such behaviors are only extension of manias which also could lead to and cause suicide. These noticeable manias are:

Hypomania: is a less severe form of mania, though the person will feel energetic and euphoric. These symptoms do not interfere, however, with an ability to function and loss of reality usually ever occurs. However, those suffering from hypomania still have poor judgment, which results in making bad decisions that can affect their personal and professional life. In most cases, people with hypomania experience a full-blown manic episode which is then followed by an episode of depression, and we know where that could lead to if fully explored to its limits by someone bothered by thoughts of suicide. Just keep this in mind.

OH, LORD! MY MOJO JUST UP AND DIED!

Then there is the **Depressive Episode:** Bipolar depression affects both a person's mood and behavior, just as episodes of mania do. It results in

Suicide and Christian Beliefs

long periods of worry of feeling empty and a loss of interest in pleasurable activities, including sex. Various behavioral changes include feeling overly tired or listless, and finding it difficult to make decisions, concentrating or remembering. Changes in appetite are normal: they will be either an increase or decrease. This will probably result in an increase or decrease in weight. Inexplicable body aches and pains can also occur, along with feelings of worthlessness and guilt. Psychotic symptoms, such as hallucinations and delusions as well as thoughts of suicide, can accompany episodes of depression. Such behavior is also indicative of being somewhat suicidal as well. Watch out for these signs.

I HOPE I DON'T LOOK AS BAD AS I FEEL! WELL, IT IS WHAT IT IS!

Suicide and Christian Beliefs

Combination or Mixed Episodes: A combination or mixed episode is a fusion or blending of either a manic and depressive episode, or a hypomanic and depressive episode. Its most common signs include depression that is coupled up with the agitation, anxiety and insomnia of a manic episode. This combination of symptoms increases a person's risk of committing suicide. It's like a dual wammy! Many persons clinically diagnosed with being bipolar also may fall into this category, but their depression may go for years before it is noticed by a member of their family, or a close friend. Other apparent signs of possible combination episodes are: fast speech patterns, called fast talking, which is not drug induced from amphetamines (uppers) or such; being sad for no obvious reason; not being able to socialize or connect graciously with others; having memory losses; general fatigue; hallucinations; and the lack of an ability to focus one's thoughts.

WHEN'S THE NEXT TRAIN COMING?

Suicide and Christian Beliefs

Some things which should be considered are the various stages of mania for people with bipolar disorder and their possible stages of depression. These stages are rarely the same for any two people and that increases the difficulty in diagnosing their bipolar disorder. Often times, a depression doesn't manifest itself for years and no one realizes that the person they knew was simply going through a long stage of mania. This can lead to a misdiagnosis of clinical depression and personality disorder, and this can be detrimental when the person in question has suicidal tendencies and HASN'T ever revealed them until, perhaps, it is too late. This happens. A misdiagnosis of a person can be lethal if they are suicidal. I've had patients, not many, who never showed any real signs of being suicidal, but were as bipolar as could be. A clinician has to look for the signs and listen closely to the talk and not arbitrarily assign the wrong disorders or its symptoms to their patient.

WHAT'S BIPOLAR MEAN?

Suicide and Christian Beliefs

I consider severe suicidal thoughts to be a medical emergency and I always consistently advise suicidal people to seek help. This is especially true if weapons, drugs, or chemicals are available, or if the suicide patient has provided me with a detailed plan of what they intend to do to themselves. People that are seriously considering suicide should go to the nearest emergency room, or call the emergency services. Severe "suicidal ideation" is a condition that requires immediate emergency medical treatment.

SUICIDAL IDEATION.

If depression is a major factor, then treatment usually leads to the disappearance of suicidal thoughts. There those critics of mainstream views about mental health, and some advocates of the "right to die" argue, that far from being a sign of poor mental health, considering or intending to commit suicide can be rational, and that it is the right of the individual person to decide for themselves whether to continue living or not. That is not the Christian viewpoint, and it never will be. This is a type of thinking that pollutes reasonable and sensible thought which I see it as a mainstream sickness diluted by ignorant non-Christian nihilists.

Anyone who knows a person that they suspect to be suicidal can assist them by taking them aside and asking them directly if they have contemplated committing suicide. Posing such a question does not render a previously non-suicidal person suicidal. Follow-up questions may be, i.e., if the person has made specific arrangements, has set a date, put their personal affairs in order, written any letters of their intent and especially if they sent them out already. That is assuming they did write such a letter. **The person questioning should quickly attempt to be understanding and sympathetic above all else.** A suicidal person will often already feel ashamed or guilty about contemplating suicide so care should be taken not to impair, worsen, or exacerbate their guilt. Tenderness and care is essential, as is your obvious commitment to wanting to help them get immediate treatment and care. An affirmative response to these questions should motivate the immediate seeking of medical attention. If the doctor who normally treats the person is unavailable, contacting the emergency room at the nearest hospital is definitely recommended.

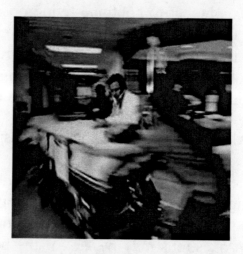

SUICIDE CASE IN AN EMERGENCY ROOM. GET THERE BEFORE THE PERSON HAS ANY CHANCE OF INJURING HIMSELF OR HERSELF!

If at all possible, a suicidal person should go to an emergency room and ask to be admitted to the mental health ward on a voluntary basis. The advantage of voluntarily seeking treatment rather than being involuntarily committed is: involuntary commitment would require intervention by the legal system. In addition, in most jurisdictions, the same process that is followed to be committed must also be followed to be released. However, there are times when involuntary release should not be on the table, this is most true is severe cases of the probability that suicide will take place shortly after release – before this troubled person can be stopped again.

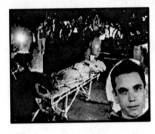

TOO LITTLE, TOO LATE!

PLEASE DON'T TRY THIS – YOU REALLY WON'T LIKE IT AND THE POLICE ESPECIALLY DON'T LIKE IT. YOU SHOULDN'T BE THEIR PROBLEM!

Law enforcement can be involved if the person seems determined to make a suicide attempt. While the police do not always have the authority to stop the suicide attempt itself, in some countries including some jurisdictions in the US, killing oneself is illegal, and deemed a disruption of public order, which could justify police intervention.

Suicide and Christian Beliefs

However, law enforcement does have the authority to have people involuntarily committed to mental health wards. Usually a court order is required, but if an officer feels the person is in immediate danger he or she can order an involuntary commitment without waiting for a court order. Such commitments are for a certain amount of time, such as 72 hours – which is long enough for a doctor to see the person and make an evaluation. After this initial period, there is normally or should be a hearing during which a judge can decide to order the person released or not; or the judge can extend the treatment time further. Afterwards, the court is kept informed of the person's condition and can release the person when they feel the time is right to do so. This is only for your information and enlightenment to any potential legal actions.

YOU DON'T WANT TO FIND YOURSELF HERE IN THIS STATE OF DEPRESSION. FIND TREATMENT IMMEDIATELY!

Suicide and Christian Beliefs

The actual treatment is directed at the underlying causes of suicidal thinking. Clinical depression is the major treatable cause, with alcohol or drug abuse being the next major categories. Other clinical disorders associated with suicidal thinking include bipolar disorder, schizophrenia, borderline personality disorder, gender identity disorder and anorexia nervosa. Suicidal thoughts provoked by crises will generally settle with time and counseling.

For a person with a relatively strong or at least definitive family or community ties, by urgently providing information about whom else would be hurt and the loss that they would feel can sometimes be effective. For a person suffering poor self-esteem, citing valuable and productive aspects of their life can be helpful. Sometimes provoking simple curiosity about the victim's own future can be helpful. If you know this person, then by lighting, igniting, or simply resurrecting some tremendously positive and hidden aspects of a person's life, those that have been forgotten about may now once again shine in their minds. Thus, they see new hope by those suppressed or forgotten memories, and new hope is new life! But don't you forget, and keep this in mind, right up front in your brain, that during the acute phase, the safety of the person is one of the prime factors considered by clinicians, and this can lead to admission in a medical facility's psychiatric ward, and it very well may be unwanted involuntary commitment. Healthy cognitive therapy can reduce repeat suicide attempts by about fifty or more percent and that is a real plus.

A LITTLE CLINICAL HELP MAY GO A LONG WAY!

Various Suicide Prevention Strategies:

- Promoting mental resilience through optimism and connectedness. This can be through various means.
- Education about suicide, including risk factors, warning signs and the availability of help.
- Increasing the proficiency of health and welfare services at responding to people in need. This includes better training for health professionals and employing crisis counseling organizations.
- Reducing domestic violence and substance abuse are long-term strategies to reduce many mental health problems. (See my book *Domestic Violence: Recognizing and Stopping the System of Abusive Behavior*).

Suicide and Christian Beliefs

- Reducing access to convenient means of suicide such as weapons, toxic substances, rope, pills and so forth.
- Reducing the quantity of dosages supplied in packages of non-prescription medicines like aspirin and other similar over the counter medicines.
- Interventions targeted at high-risk groups.

Closing Thoughts:

The subject of suicide and every issue about it seems to increase each year, rather than decrease. And the clinical and religious counseling that can be given does appear to be getting better, of course, depending on who is doing the treatment and how well qualified they are. The material in this book has been carefully selected and edited for the usage of only the best material available today.

As far as the Christian aspects of suicide are concerned, they go beyond the death of such a suicide victim and deal with what comes after the death and where the spirit goes and what is its future state. Any Christian that is interested in learning about such horrible self-inflicted death attempts or how to deal with the actual suicide of a friend, or a family member, should find a plethora of detailed

Suicide and Christian Beliefs

descriptions, ideas, mental pictures, beliefs, and other such material that will get him or her thinking. The principle idea of this book is to introduce to anyone on the street, the concept of what happens with a suicide: before it happens, when it occurs, and afterwards. The finality of suicide is an eternity of separation from our Living God Jehovah and His Son Jesus Christ, and that has been because a suicide victim failed to listen to God's powerful mind as it was spiritually extended by His Holy Spirit for the comfort and peace of the body in which the Spirit of God indwelled. This means that supernatural intervention by God was rejected and not adhered to, so the justice of that decision will be God's when that deceased spirit is brought before the Lord for his or her judgment. That is when the suicide victim will meet the spiritual presence of God, face-to-face.

I do hope this book has been useful to you and that you'll consider keeping it around and handy, as a sort of "what to do if" suicide manual. I also hope you have learned much and that I've given you considerable information to digest and understand. When in doubt about any of this, pray for guidance first, and then seek professional help immediately.

Remember: God loves you and wants you alive, until He doesn't!!! Let Him tell you when that is.

Suicide and Christian Beliefs

1-800-784-2433
National Suicide Hotline

IN CRISIS?
480-784-1500
SUICIDE/CRISIS HOTLINE (MARICOPA COUNTY)
866-205-5229
TOLL-FREE CRISIS HOTLINE (ARIZONA)

REVS
SUICIDE HOTLINE
(212) 592-4133

Addendum

Points of Consideration for Condemnation

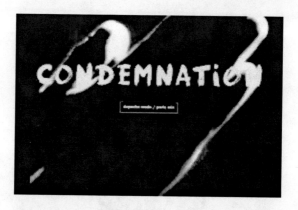

1. All of the suicides mentioned in the *Holy Bible* turned away from God, separating themselves from the Lord and His grace. All except Samson, *Judges 16: 29-30.*

Suicide and Christian Beliefs

    - Saul fell on his sword. *I Samuel 31: 4-5*
Turned away from God. *I Samuel 15:11*
    - Judas hung himself. *Matthew 27:3-5* and
Acts 1:16-25
    - Ahithophel (advisor to King David) hung
himself. *II Samuel 17:23*
    - Zimri (King of Israel) burnt his house
down over himself. *I King 16:18-19*

2. The impenitent always separate themselves from
God's grace. The penitent receive God's mercy and
pardon. Those not trusting or believing in Christ are
not forgiven but condemned. *Romans 5:1, Romans
6:3, Ephesians 2:8-9* and *John 3:18.*

3. Human life is sacred and we should honor God
by valuing His gift. *Genesis 1:27*

4. Our body is a temple to be taken care of and not
destroyed. *I Corinthians 6:19-20*

5. We are all subject to God's final judgment and
for any act of murder. *I John 3:15* and *Matthew
5:21*

6. We are only free of sin at death. *Romans 6:7*

7. We are sinful from birth. *Psalm 51:5*

Suicide and Christian Beliefs

8. The wages of sin is death. *Romans 6:23*

9. There is no hope for the godless because the Lord takes away their life. *Job 27:8*

10. Our life is totally in God's hands, not our own. *Psalm 31:15*

11. Unbelievers are condemned. *Mark 16:16*

Points of Consideration for Salvation

1. All sin is forgiven if we confess. *I John 1:8-9*

2. Jesus Christ died once and for all, for the righteous and the unrighteous. *I Peter 3:18*

3. Our iniquity is fully with Christ. *Isaiah 53:4-6*

Suicide and Christian Beliefs

4. The Lord looks at our heart; man looks at his outward appearance. *I Samuel 16:7*

5. Trust in the Lord and acknowledge Him as God. *Proverbs 3:5-6*

6. Trust in Christ for forgiveness of sin. *John 14:6* and *Acts 4:12*

7. Act in faith and trust in Christ's sacrifice. *John 1:12-13*

8. A slim chance of assurance of salvation. (eternal life by forgiveness) *John 5:24, John 10:27-29* and *John 5:11-13*

9. Christian's cannot be separated from God's love. *Romans 8:37-39*

10. God advocates for us; the blood of Jesus Christ, our Messiah and Redeemer, washes away our sins. God sees His Son's blood as His righteousness and not our unrighteousness. *I John 2:1-3.*

11. Christ's grace, not by keeping the law, is our salvation. *Galatians 2:21, Romans 3:24-28* and *Romans 6:1-3* (Condemns sinning)

Suicide and Christian Beliefs

12. We are saved for and by purity and a holy life. *I Thessalonians 4:10*

13. Since we do not get salvation by what we have done, we cannot lose it by what we haven't done. We are saved by grace through faith, not by works. *Ephesians 2:8-9*

14. Repentance is the final result of the Lord's saving grace and work. Everyone must confess their sins to receive forgiveness and be cleansed from all unrighteousness and iniquity. Without repentance there is no forgiveness from God, nor is there any chance of eternal life/salvation. Unfortunately, suicide victims cannot repent after the fact. See *2 Timothy 2:25*

Suicide and Christian Beliefs

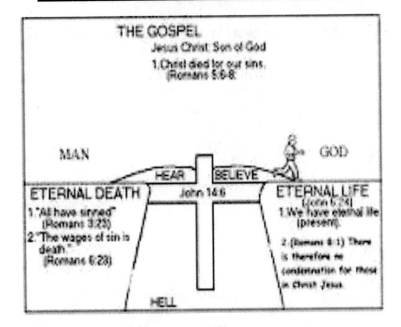

THE GOSPEL
Jesus Christ: Son of God
1. Christ died for our sins.
(Romans 5:6-8)

MAN   GOD

HEAR   BELIEVE

ETERNAL DEATH   John 14:6   ETERNAL LIFE
                                          (John 6:24)
1. "All have sinned"   1. We have eternal life
(Romans 3:23)   (present).
2. "The wages of sin is
death."   2. (Romans 8:1) There
(Romans 6:23)   is therefore no
                                          condemnation for those
                                          in Christ Jesus.

HELL

ALL FINAL HOPE FOR SALVATION RESTS IN THE
MERCIFUL, HOPEFUL, LOVING, AND FORGIVING
ARMS OF JESUS CHRIST THROUGH THE TRULY
WONDERFUL SACRIFICE HE LAID DOWN ON OUR
BEHALF. THE FINAL JUDGMENT OF A LOST SPIRIT
WILL ALSO BE IN THE HANDS OF GOD. HE AND ONLY
HE WILL MAKE THE ULTIMATE RESOLUTION TO THE
DISPOSITION OF A SUICIDE CASE. ALL LIFE WILL BE
JUDGED AFTER DEATH BY THE LORD ALMIGHTY;
HIS WORD IS THE FINAL AUTHORITY. BY CHRIST'S
GRACE THROUGH OUR FAITH WE ARE SAVED.
THANK GOD FOR HIS MIGHTY MIRACLES AND SENSE
OF JUSTICE EVEN WHEN WE SLAP HIM IN THE FACE.
BUT SUICIDE – I REALLY DON'T THINK SO!

Captain of Death, Lieutenant of Life

The shadows cast by a fleeting spirit,
The final signs of a dying soul,
Are buried inside an eternal abyss,
To pay a terminal toll.
The soul it sleeps but will awake,
Again in a different place,
A world of wonder we know not,
Within a phantom space.
The Captain of Death has claimed this spirit,
A victory he has won,
But the Lieutenant of Life knows all too well,
The battle's just begun.

Our God of all we know as love,
The God who'll judge our life,
Is living in His Kingdom home,
Where peace rules over strife.
The soul is lost but not for long,
There's hope with the air,
It seems to call from far away,
A place prepared somewhere.
The Captain of death is stealing forth,
He wants to claim his prize,
But once again,
The Lieutenant of Life will cut him
Down to size.

A vacuum, a void, a colorless plane,
A mysterious land unfolds,
A final resting place named for,
The soul whose life God holds.
The reason for leaving without permission,
Is chief of all concerns,
The hurt it brings upon our God,

Suicide and Christian Beliefs

Within His heart still burns.
The Lieutenant of Life still wars for this sad soul,
So death continues a battleground,
Where flesh is icy cold.

We contemplate the fate of all,
Who take their lives in vain,
For reasons so misunderstood,
They leave a painful stain.
The Lord of Hosts and angelic armies,
Guard against invasion,
Of spirits unclean with demonic goals,
Who cast spells of persuasion.
The Captain of Death who rides his mount,
Draws from his wicked sources,
To fight against the Lieutenant of Life,
And all His heavenly forces.

The Lord is strong,
He looks around and gathers all lost souls,
He then tells again of His great love,
And of His stately goals.
Such souls recount the deeds they've done,
And how they brought such shame,
But God is great, the Lord of Love,
Who forgives them of their blame.
But the Captain of Death will steal the spirit,
Who rejects this God of power,
And the Lieutenant of Life will sadly release,
That lost soul in that hour.
But be of cheer and hopefulness,
And reasons to be glad,
A second chance just may be found,
Beyond all boundaries sad.
The only souls that are condemn4ed,
Are those who deny Christ,
The souls who count their blessings,

Suicide and Christian Beliefs

Lost each time they roll the dice.
The Captain of Death gleans only spirits,
Who do not know the Lord,
But the lieutenant of Life will pull all in,
Who hold on to His cord.

So what is thought and what is truth,
Is still to be determined,
It's not among the rules of life,
Nor found in just one sermon.
It takes a while to find ourselves,
And sometimes we fall short,
That's when our spirit may quit the race,
And life it will abort.
The Captain of Death awaits his tally,
He wants the heads to roll,
But the Lieutenant of Life is in command,
And He will judge each soul.

A soul cries out for fear of death,
While traveling to its station,
They pass by God, by Jesus Christ, their Paradise and
nation.
The land of jewels and wonderful sights,
A place of great elation,
May be for all,
Who come to God with no thought of evasion?
The Captain of Death,
He knows his losses, he angers when he loses,
But the Lieutenant of Life,
Rejoices at all the lost souls that He chooses.

Dahk Knox
Spring, 2001

Suicide and Christian Beliefs

THE ABOVE POEM IS A SIMPLE EULOGY FOR ALL LOST SPIRITS WHO HAVE TAKEN THEIR OWN LIVES AND SEEK A PLACE OF ETERNAL PEACE AND REST. MAY GOD IN ALL HIS INFINITE COMPASSION FORGIVE THEIR CHOICE OF DEATH OVER LIFE AND GRANT THEIR FINAL QUEST. MAY THE LORD OF LIFE BE TENDER IN HIS MERCY BUT SWIFT IN HIS MORAL JUDGMENT.

THIS TICKET IS AVAILABLE FOR YOU AND IT'S FREE FOR THE ASKING.

WHICH FREE TICKET WILL YOU CHOOSE? SELECT VERY CAREFULLY – FOREVER IS A VERY LONG TIME.

Bibliography

- Adam, Juliette. Quote
- Alford, Henry. The Greek Testament
- Calvin, John. Commentaries on the Catholic Epistles
- Cook, James Hunt.
- Dargan, Edwin. The Doctrines of Our Faith
- Delitzsch, Franz. Commentary on the Epistle to the Hebrews
- Denny, James. The Christian Doctrine of Reconciliation
- Edwards, Jonathan. The Works of Jonathan Edwards
- Farrell, Elizabeth. Quote
- Franklin, Benjamin. Quote
- Fry, David. State of Death tapes
- Habermas, Gary. Beyond Death: Exploring the Evidence for Immortality
- Hanegraaff, Hank. Resurrection
- Ingalls, John. Quote
- Josephus, Flavius. The Antiquities of the Jews
- Kreeft, Peter. Everything You Ever Wanted to Know About Heaven
- Luther, Martin. Quote
- MacLaren, Alexander. The True Branches of the True Vine
- Martin, Walter. The Kingdom of the Cults

Suicide and Christian Beliefs

- Moreland, J.P.. Beyond Death: Exploring the Evidence for Immortality
- Nesbitt, William R., Jr. The Illusion of Time: Seeing Scripture Through Science
- Shank, Robert. Life in the Son
- Sproul, R.C. Essential Truths of the Christian Faith
- Wescott, B.F. The Gospel According to St. John

ADDITIONAL RELIGIOUS BOOKS BY DAHK KNOX

Delighting in God's Work ($10.95)

Divine Healing: A Spiritual Medicine ($14.95 & Hardback ($20.95)
Divine Healing: Restoring and Renewal Workbook ($14.95)

Domestic Violence ($12.95)

God's Greatest Gifts ($10.95)

Gypsy Heart, Restless Spirit ($10.95)

HIM ($12.95)

The Jericho Syndrome ($11.99)

The Plan ($19.95)

Political Terms and Definitions for the Layman: Common Islamic Words and Their Meanings ($15.95)

Suicide and Christian Beliefs

Restoring, Refreshing or Renewing What's Missing or Lost ($13.95)

Seasons of Recollection   ($17.95)

Suicide and Scripture   ($15.95)

Who I am in Jesus   ($10.95)

Radical, Fanatical   Islam - Terrorism: Murder for Reward ($9.95) (Pen name: by Hadji Murat)

Eternal Security: Fact or Fiction? ($14.95)

Recognizing His Presence and Knowing His Perspective ($12.95)
The Modern Day Pharisees: The Fleecing of the Flock ($17.95)
Suicide and Christian Beliefs: What's next, mercy or punishment? ($19.95)

About the Author: Dahk Knox has written 104 books and is presently working on two more books at this printing. His books sell in 48 countries and in 25 languages. Although he is a retired Navy commander with 33½ years military service, he continues to practice as a clinical Christian psychologist and psychotherapist, and marriage counselor. He is an ordained minister in two churches: Presbyterian and Pentecostal. His present ministry is Covenant Christian Healing Ministries in East Tennessee. Dr. Knox is also been an active member of the Christian Association of Psychological Studies, for licensed clinical psychologists.

Dr. Knox has two full professorships, one in Psychology and one in Education. He has been a dean for two colleges and a vice-president of academic affairs at another university. He has credentials for running a university, being a superintendent for college districts, and maintains teaching credentials in 21 different disciplines. Dr. Knox has six doctorates, four master degrees and a bachelor's degree. He also speaks and writes in 26 different languages. He is 100% nuts! He speaks his mind openly and is liable to say anything, anyplace, and to anyone. He says it's okay because God still loves him, tolerates him, and has adapted to his style. His name is in the Book of Life, but far down on the page – most likely! But it's there and he has a fax to prove it!

Dat's rat! Ahm'a Southern boy! Y'all heah?

TO ORDER DAHK KNOX BOOKS

CCHM only accepts business or personal checks, money orders, bank drafts, direct wiring, or cash for all orders. Add $3.95 shipping and handling costs for orders of one or two books. The cost for three to five books is $4.95, and quantities over six books should be called in at: (423) 422-4711, or you can order today or any day by email, at: dahkknox@embarqmail.com All orders of ten books or more receive a ten percent discount. All books will be autographed if you request such. Make and mail you're your payments to: CCHM

CCHM Publishing Network
Dr. Jan Knox, CFO
Accounting Department
Belle Arden Run Estate
496 Mountain View Drive
Mosheim, TN 37818-3524

THIS BOOK IS DEDICATED TO THE GREATER HONOR AND GLORY OF GOD!

HE CALLS ME FRIEND! AND I READILY ACCEPT HIS FRIENDSHIP. HE IS MY BEST FRIEND – TRUSTWORTHY AND FAITHFUL FOREVER.